PRAISE FOR *UNLOCK YOUR POTENTIAL*

"As an 'internet guru,' it's tempting to lump Jeff in with the world of 'bro marketers' and hyper-masculine self-help-ers, but I found him to be the total opposite of all of that. His understanding of what it takes to be successful is matched only by his hunger to help others get there too."
—Amberly Lago, bestselling Author, TED Speaker, and Host of the *True Grit and Grace* podcast

"I wish I had read this book before I started my own entrepreneurial journey. The stories are personal, the advice is practical, and the hope is powerful. Well done, Jeff!"
—Jon Acuff, *New York Times* bestselling Author
of *Soundtracks: The Surprising Solution to Overthinking*

"*Unlock Your Potential* is a book not just on how to succeed in the modern world, but on how to create the best version of yourself along the way. It's not easy to be yourself, but Jeff shows you practical ways to succeed at this most important goal."
—Dave Hollis, *New York Times* bestselling Author and Host of the *Rise Together* podcast

"When Jeff told me he wrote a book, I knew it would be incredible because everything he does is incredible. He is an alchemist in the truest sense of the word. By that I mean he understands how to conceive a specific dream, then harness the power of the universe, add in the power of hard work and laser focus, and voila, it manifests for him. This is why I heartily endorse this book."
—Rebecca Zung, Esq., top 1% Attorney, Negotiation Expert,
bestselling Author of *Negotiate Like You M.A.T.T.E.R.*

"Unexpressed possibilities, wealth, happiness, and riches await you as you read, absorb, and use the wisdom, insights, and brilliance in my friend Jeff's life-transforming book."
—Mark Victor Hansen, world's bestselling nonfiction Author,
Cocreator of Chicken Soup for Soul series

"What strikes me most about Jeff is not just his financial success, but his depth of understanding as to why he has been successful. Beneath every story of skill and/or luck is a human mind, and in *Unlock Your Potential* Jeff has written a highly practical guide to harnessing the power within each of us—starting with our mind and extending through our entire life."
—John Assaraf, *New York Times* bestselling Author of
Having It All and Founder of NeuroGym

"By sharing the teachings he's learned throughout the last twenty-five years of his life, Jeff boils down in twenty-eight chapters the most important things we all need to know and apply into every area of our lives to claim our highest potential. If you want to create a long-lasting legacy in a world that's constantly changing, *Unlock Your Potential* is a MUST-READ!"
—Natasha Graziano, *Forbes* #1 Motivational Speaker Under
40, more than 10 million Instagram followers

"Disclaimer: Jeff is a friend. But all bias aside . . . his book is amazing. And his heart is huge. And his work is brilliant and has impacted many, many lives. His new book, *Unlock Your Potential*, is a true guide to reach that potential you already possess and harness it to achieve the life you always wanted. Buy the book. Jeff is a true genius in the business world who does what he says and his achievements with his school ENTRE are phenomenal."
—Sir Marco Robinson, award-winning TV & Film Producer, 2X
Entrepreneur of the Year, Knighted Philanthropist

"Jeff Lerner is as amazing as he is smart. He's a $100 million success story, which usually makes folks keep their secrets to themselves, but he is as passionate as they come about helping others write their own success stories and 'Make Shift Happen,' as I would say."

—Anthony Trucks, former NFL Player and CEO of Identity Shift

"*Unlock Your Potential* combines pragmatic tools and an inspirational story to empower you as you consistently and persistently pursue your potential."

—David Meltzer, Cofounder of Sports 1 Marketing,
bestselling Author, and top business Coach

"Jeff Lerner is a rare breed: an entrepreneur as selfless as he is talented. And while over the last decade his personal success has been fun to watch, what is most inspiring is how many people he takes with him. Now with *Unlock Your Potential*, millions of readers can hop along for the ride—and definitely should!"

—Kale Goodman & Trevor Cowley, Hosts of *Real Business Owners* podcast and Founders of EasierAccounting.com

"I've known Jeff since he was a broke musician just trying to 'figure things out.' To see what he's done, how he's done it, and what he is doing now is inspiring. I didn't even need to read this book to know it was a must-read, but now having read it . . . wow. Do yourself a favor and just read it."

—Aaron Parkinson, Founder of 7 Mile Media

"I hosted Jeff at his first entrepreneurial training event and since I have known him, he has had an insistent passion for learning. In reading *Unlock Your Potential,* I see that passion has evolved into an equally strong passion for teaching and paying forward what he has learned, which he does par excellence."

—Jay Kubassek, Founder of The WAKEUP Co.

Personal Testimonials

"I can honestly say after working with Jeff Lerner and ENTRE, the 3 Ps have helped me grow not only financially but mentally and physically as well. Through this growth I've been able to impact those around me in a positive way. I truly believe that learning the art of implementation is a skill everyone needs to have. Through this knowledge I've been able to run three companies while playing college football."

—CJ Bufkin, Social Media Follower

"Jeff is truly one of the few entrepreneurs in today's world that is passionate about giving back to his audience. I have had the pleasure of following Jeff for two years—he's a modern Tony Robbins/John Maxwell."

—Miko Bacomo, Social Media Follower

"As a young entrepreneur in my late teens/early twenties, turned businessman in my thirties, finding someone to not only listen to but tolerate and accept into my present-day chaos and life is almost unheard of. You offer so much insight across many levels. Thank you for being a positive, reinforcing page to follow and person to see, in the successful mindset that you push forward."

—Chris, Social Media Follower

"Jeff has figured out the key to success, which is finding happiness and helping others."

—Donnie Joseph, Social Media Follower

"Just hearing your messages each day impacts me; makes me want to be better for me. You helped my mental health tremendously! Thanks, Jeff!"

—Chase Mangum, Social Media Follower

"Jeff has made an enormous impact in my life. I feel that even that is an understatement. He was the big brother figure I needed in my life to kick me in the butt, to get me back on track to living the life that I not only wanted, but was proud of. I am in a VASTLY different space, for the better, in every area of my life, than when I first found him online. Thanks, Jeff!"

—Young Min Kim, Social Media Follower

"His inspiration for self-awareness and continued learning is deep rooted and genuine. You can only gain from what he gives. Thanks, Jeff, for the knowledge."

—Thomas Nitting, Social Media Follower

"The level of impact that Jeff Lerner has had in my life over the past two years has been extraordinary and multilayered. From his story to his commitment to his vision, he inspires me daily as I build my business, even while continuing my studies with ENTRE. I have shed decades of self-sabotage and finally given myself permission to be my best possible self, living my purpose. How does it get better than that?"

—Marie Hooper, Customer/Student

"Where do I start? I have ADD and own a cleaning business. Your techniques and methods have helped me create a structured lifestyle for not just myself but also my son. I'm so grateful to have found you and ENTRE when I did. You're truly inspiring and 100 percent real with following your purpose. I find that admirable. Thank you so much for all you do."

—Lesley Dixon, Customer/Student

"If you want to know how to create happiness, build a business on your terms, and discover a secret that traditional educational institutions just don't teach, READ THIS BOOK. The principles Jeff outlines within these pages helped me create a vision for my future that I thought was out of reach. I am now building a coaching business to help other women break through to their best lives, and, more importantly, I am happy and fulfilled! If you want to build a purpose-driven business AND build a life on your terms, you will not find better wisdom than inside, *Unlock Your Potential*. Thank you, Jeff, for showing us what Contribution and Legacy truly look like."

—Melissa Evans, Customer/Student

"I can safely say your teachings have saved so many people without you even knowing. So many (myself included) were let down so many times throughout our lives. Your teachings help us realize that nothing is out of our reach, that the life we dreamed of is in our grasp. All we need to do is reach out, grab it, and claim it as ours. Thank you for creating ENTRE. I don't know where I would be right now without it."

—Abe Alvarez, Customer/Student

"Jeff Lerner has impacted my life by his mission, vision, and values. Because of him, I am able to rewrite my life to have the most impactful outcome. Without him, I would have been OK with being unmotivated and living a normal life. I am so grateful for the opportunity to challenge my beliefs and live an extraordinary life. Eagerly doing hard things well every day!!!"

—Kimberly Scroggins, Customer/Student

"Jeff is awesome! I have rebirthed from an addict and man-child into a productive, enlightened, brand-new entrepreneur, who, with a new vigor, excitement, and love for life and knowledge, will now go and impact humanity in a positive and philanthropic way with a mindset of excellence! Peace and love! Thank you, Sir!"

—Edward Hoar, Customer/Student

I am so glad that I discovered Jeff Lerner and ENTRE! The multitude of classes he offers, the informational and motivational podcasts he creates and hosts, and the vulnerability about his journey and his mistakes have done more for me personally and for starting my own business than I can express. Jeff has already lived what he teaches, and I will always be an attentive pupil of his, because he speaks from experience, not theory. This book will be a permanent part of my library, and I highly recommend it to anyone who wants to grow beyond where they are right now."

—Kevin Haynes, Customer/Student

"Jeff has saved my life. I am a military veteran who served his country faithfully for ten years, and after my service time, I went into a stage of depression where I was lost on the direction of where my life was going. Suffering from PTSD hindered me from performing at my best at any job. Ultimately, I ended up unemployed and worried about how I was going to support my family. Then one day I prayed and I asked GOD for a sign, a word, anything to help me get back on track. Then I saw your video on Facebook explaining the 3 Ps of success and how to maximize their use daily. That was a total game changer. I got your courses and that was the end of that chapter. Thank you so much! Now, I start each day off with a video of yours and then I'm automatically in my 2.0 version. Jeff is truth!"

—Miguel Lopez, Customer/Student

"The impact you've had on my life: when I found ENTRE I stepped out of the 'rut' that I was in and started to see my potential again, started to regain power over my life, and believed that I could once again 'be more.' I am now beginning to grasp my potential and make the most of each day that I have here in this life. So for that—thank you, Jeff Lerner!"

—Katie Shuff Grim, Customer/Student

"I was struggling, personally, with my career, my marriage, and my future. Out of the blue, the universe hands me Jeff Lerner's ad. It's been a climb, but with Jeff and ENTRE, I have become the man, leader, and husband I was always meant to be. Thanks, Jeff."

—Lee Klocke, Customer/Student

"I am so grateful for the vision Jeff Lerner is creating. His vision is changing so many lives for the better, including mine. Jeff is such an inspiration. He has such a great team behind him to continue to grow his vision so that more lives are changed—physically, personally, and professionally. Jeff doesn't just sell you a business: he and his team are there to make sure you succeed at it. It is a pleasure to call Jeff my friend. Thank you for all you do, Jeff; the world is changing, one vision at a time."

—Katie Shuff Grim, Customer/Student

"Meeting Jeff Lerner has been part of a God-answered prayer. He has created a school, ENTRE Institute, that in one short year of being enrolled in it has helped me find my purpose in life, which I am actively fulfilling. He has created a blueprint that I have implemented into my life, which has brought me one more day closer to becoming the best version of myself mentally, physically, personally, and professionally. I will always be eternally grateful to him, his advisors, and coaches."

—Vernon Eubanks, Customer/Student

Unlock Your Potential

Unlock Your Potential

The Ultimate Guide for Creating Your Dream Life in the Modern World

JEFF LERNER

Matt Holt Books
An Imprint of BenBella Books, Inc.
Dallas, TX

Matt Holt is an imprint of BenBella Books, Inc.
10440 N. Central Expressway
Suite 800
Dallas, TX 75231
benbellabooks.com
Send feedback to feedback@benbellabooks.com.

BenBella and *Matt Holt* are federally registered trademarks.

Printed in the United States of America
10 9 8 7 6 5 4 3 2 1

Library of Congress Control Number: 2021062761
ISBN 9781637741740 (hardcover)
ISBN 9781637741757 (electronic)

Copyediting by Ginny Glass
Proofreading by Denise Pangia and Marissa Wold Uhrina
Text design and composition by PerfecType, Nashville, TN
Cover design by Marjanovic Boban
Printed by Lake Book Manufacturing

This book is dedicated to my parents, Ron and Jane Lerner, who showed me that you can work and love with equal intensity; to my wife, Jaqueline, who saw my best qualities before I did and loved them to life; and to my children, Braxton, Jace, Jada, and Stella, who are my best reasons for trying to make this world a better place.

Also two notes of gratitude: to my best friend growing up, Rob, who made it a little less lonely to not fit in, and to my ENTRE cofounder, Adam, who partnered with me to do the greatest work of my life and without whom this book would not exist.

Contents

Introduction

Before you even start reading, I want you to take note of today's date—write it down or make a note in your phone if you have to. This is a day to take note of: a day when a journey begins that, if your mind is open, could jar you awake and send your life down an exciting new path. That may sound grandiose, but I say it with confidence because I've seen this story play out thousands of times. I'm in the "red pill" business—a dealer of truth, the kind it's hard to unhear.

It all begins with this realization: the system that we grew up believing in is broken beyond repair. What originated as "The American Dream" and became the promise of Western-style capitalism around the globe is no longer within reach of the average person, not by a mile, and the obfuscation of that fact by powerful forces, both overt and covert, is destroying the dreams of millions of people. The majority of us are now the proverbial "boiling frogs," with the temperature slowly rising around us such that by the time most of us notice it will be too late to jump out of the water. As for me? I got out. And now I am on a rescue mission, which this book is a part of. I realize this may all sound a bit dramatic and even hysterical, but stick with me. There are no histrionics here. Through this book I will not only defend this position and, I believe, convince you of it, but I will tell you what to do about it. I'm going to get you out of the boiling pot. As they say, when one door closes, another door opens. Opportunities in our new digital economy are booming, born from the collapse of old ways of thinking and doing. They are turning ordinary people into kitchen-table millionaires and creating lifestyles that would have been unimaginable a generation ago. People on the right side of the shift from the old to the new are living lives that combine freedom, personal expression, and financial liberation in ways never before seen in history, while sadly, the vast majority fall deeper into frustration and futility. What these new opportunities are and how to access them are questions we'll discuss throughout this book, along with doing a deep dive into the most important question of all: **Who do you need to become in order to seize these opportunities, beat the odds, and create the seemingly too-good-to-be-true quality of life that's available for those who break out of the old paradigm?** This book will provide answers to these questions and more that you can immediately apply to your life, no matter your age, income level, or background.

This is really three books in one—an autobiography of a high school dropout turned jazz musician turned new-economy millionaire, a how-to/self-help book for *you* to create your own similarly incredible story, and a full-scale manifesto that calls each of us to boldly step into a future that is being rewritten faster than most of us realize. Ultimately, this book is intended to do one thing—help millions of people escape a clearly broken system and achieve their full potential and their best, happiest life. But before we dive in, I need to make sure you realize the seriousness of the situation. When I say the system is broken, I'm talking about from childhood to old age. All of it is broken! It starts with the way we educate our kids in elementary school and continues through college. It picks right up when we get our first job, continues throughout our career, and follows us into retirement.

Almost everyone is stuck in the broken system—and at some point, most people feel it. Whether it's being fed up with a nine-to-five, overwhelmed with college debt, unable to live a life you truly enjoy, or struggling to prepare for retirement, most of us feel at various points in our life that something seems off. That's because it is. Want proof? Look at Hollywood. Why are we so enthralled with movies about life being a simulation, movies like *The Matrix* and *Inception*? Or movies about power and how easily corrupted we are? (cue evil voice) *"One ring to rule them all, one ring to find them, one ring to bring them all, and in the darkness bind them . . ."* It's because these movies resonate with a deep internal sense that something is off, like there's a piece missing from our life puzzle, or even that there's a battle happening somewhere and we are the prize for the winner. And then the credits roll and we go back to our lives. We forget that feeling we had in the darkened theater and lose ourselves in the prosaic. We don't notice the broken system any more than a fish notices water on most days. We've been immersed in it as long as we can remember and during early childhood, when we were the most observant but least discerning we would ever be, the authority figures in our lives presented the system to us as our only option for life. Not only do most of us never question this system, we can't imagine a world without it.

To be clear, I'm not anti-education. After all, I was born a Lerner (which is a Yiddish word for "learner/scholar"), and more than once when I was growing up, my teachers remarked that the name fit. I love learning. I'm grateful for the private school education I received and the hard work my parents put in to pay for it. My problem is not with schooling, or at least not the idea of it; my problem is with the modern educational system. Even if we overlook concerns about the origins of our schools, such as the fact that the current US system emerged in the nineteenth century when Protestants insisted the government take over education because Catholic immigrants, mostly Irish and Italian, were establishing their own schools, there is still great reason to be concerned about current methods and outcomes. Schools today use outdated learning modalities to shove information into kids' brains that they generally don't retain. Many students find school uninteresting and irrelevant because they don't connect what they're learning to what they actually want out of life when they grow up. I remember the same feeling. But like we tell our kids: there isn't another option.

Think about the trajectory that led you to this point right now. After you made your way through high school, you were probably told to go to college, but did you realize that 54 percent of all college graduates are either unemployed or work a job that doesn't require a college degree? That means 54 percent of the $1.7 trillion in student loan debt (roughly $918,000,000,000) is completely unnecessary. Major CEOs have said they couldn't care less if their employees have a college degree, and yet millions of people are unnecessarily accruing debt that takes over twenty years to pay off. And that cripples them because nothing undermines long-term compounding and earning potential more than an early setback, like, for example, six figures of debt at twenty-two years old. I've coached hundreds of people in their thirties and forties who are still far from paying off their student debt. Their social and financial mobility is highly restricted because of their student loans. They often can't borrow money to start a business or invest in a rental property, and they definitely can't take time off to support a spouse's career, or move to pursue better opportunities. And it's getting worse. As of 2020, 50 percent of college graduates still haven't found a job fourteen months after leaving school and half of recent college graduates can't afford to move out of their parents' house by the age of twenty-five.

So am I saying that if you went to college, you wasted your time? It depends. There are really successful people who didn't go to college. There are really successful people who did go to college. There are unsuccessful people who could have benefited if they had gone to college, and there are unsuccessful people who were hurt by college and might have been more successful had they not gone. If someone knows what they want to do with their life, and that career requires going to college, then by all means, they should go to college. The world needs doctors, lawyers, engineers, chemists, and other professionals whose careers require a college education. It would obviously be terrible advice to tell someone who wants to pursue such a career not to go to college. Furthermore, if someone gets a scholarship, or if money isn't an issue, they have much more leeway and could benefit more from college because they won't be burdened by debt upon graduation. But as a purely financial equation, college is a hard economic argument to make for those who don't need a specific degree to pursue a specific predetermined career. Yet most people are told to go anyway, and they do if they can.

What did you do after graduating college? Likely you did what everyone does—you got a job. Now this is where the system really begins to fall apart. I believe that capitalism is the greatest economic system on earth. It's easy to criticize, but I think despite any flaws it might have, what Winston Churchill said about democracy applies to capitalism too, that it is "the worst . . . except for everything else that has been tried." But nowadays most criticisms of capitalism have to do with its application, not its essence. I think in modern parlance there is some confusion between true capitalism and what I call corporatism. People assume that in a capitalist society, the natural next step from college, or whatever level of education is achieved, is to go get a job at a corporation. But there's nothing intrinsic to capitalism that suggests that step. Rather, I would argue that all the best and brightest going to work for the same cluster of companies is counterproductive to true capitalism because it consolidates talent, and thus wealth and power. In a true capitalist system, sure, you might work at someone else's business for a time to learn the industry or trade, but then you would follow the prompting of capitalism to go out and attract capital of your own to start a business. But that's not what's taught in the educational system, so few think to do it or even realize it's a viable option. Did you seriously consider that plan growing up? Probably not. Most people are very confused about what the word *capitalism* really means, and it's become fashionable to use it as a whipping post, a sort of placeholder for a lot of things we all can agree are not ideal—things like corporations exerting undue influence on government, or exploitation of workers, or even geopolitical pillaging and nation-building. But those aren't aspects of capitalism. They are what happens when capitalism gets hijacked by corporatism. It reminds me of the line from the classic movie *The Usual Suspects*: *"The greatest trick the devil ever pulled was convincing the world he didn't exist."* Well, the greatest trick the broken system has pulled has been convincing us that an economic philosophy is the problem rather than people. True capitalism isn't the problem; it's the solution, because it gives people options that right now they aren't being taught.

Case in point: The following conversation happened one day when I was driving my daughter and some of the neighborhood kids to school. This was a group of three girls between the ages of nine and eleven. I asked them, "What do you think is the point of school?"

"To learn," they answered.

"And what's the point of learning?"

"To be smart."

"So, what's the point of being smart?

"To not be dumb."

"Okay. Anything else?"

"To go to college."

"Yes, but that's just more school." I said, "So, what's the point of all that school?" And then they said it.

"To get a job."

There it is! Score one for corporatism!

School convinces kids that the only option for their future is to be employed. It teaches them how to be good employees or, at the very least, deprives them of the idea that they have any other option.

When we arrived at the school, I asked, "How do most of the other kids get here?"

"They take the bus."

"So, how am I able to take you to school?" I asked.

"Because you don't have a job."

"That's right. What do I have?"

"You have a business."

"Yes! I do have a business. A few of them in fact. So, what's the difference between having a job and having a business?"

They didn't have a good answer for that, and again, it's not their fault. When in school, you are told to sit down, be quiet, and trust in the system. Any attempt to drift away from that path is considered risky or unorthodox. As a result, most people graduate high school and college only to grind away year after year, making more money for their employers than they do for themselves, without realizing that there is something better for them out there. Sound familiar?

Jobs and careers are sold on the promise that they will lead to security and fulfillment when they very often do not. For most people, the lives they want and the money they need to fuel those lives cannot be found in traditional jobs, but rather by learning the right skills and applying them in the right industries. In many cases, that involves combining those elements with a mix of risk and exhilaration to become an entrepreneur.

Unfortunately, far too many people never tap into their entrepreneurial spirit because they don't realize that everything they need to succeed is already out there. They're unaware of the opportunities I mentioned earlier that grew out of the collapse of the old American Dream, along with the systems of education, employment, and retirement that were its foundations. Instead, they trade their time for money without ever really being able to get ahead. They can't provide security for their family or leave behind any kind of legacy and are left counting the days until they finally retire at the age of sixty-five. That's when they think they will finally get to relax and live their lives, but is that even true? What is your retirement plan? Do you have one? What does retirement even mean these days?

Did you realize that the modern idea of retirement was invented by Otto von Bismarck in 1883 when he forced everyone over the age of sixty-five to leave the workforce? It was an attempt to create jobs for the unemployed youth and thwart a possible Marxist takeover. The average life expectancy wasn't even forty years old back then. Today it's seventy-eight, and more people are living comfortably into their nineties. The math doesn't work anymore. Conventional wisdom says you need $80,000 a year to live comfortably after retirement (I think you need much more to retire, but we'll get into all of the reasons why later). The average sixty-five-year-old has only $175,000, which isn't even close to being enough to support them if they're going to live for another twenty or thirty years. Yet retirement is the carrot we're dangling in front of people to get them to give up the next forty-five years of their life in a job they don't love. The system has stripped millions of people of the chance to do what they love—the chance to forge their own path through a pursuit that gives them purpose. The old American Dream is history. And if you continue to labor under the illusion that the Dream still exists, it can shatter your hopes of ever realizing yours.

My mission in life is to prevent any more people from failing to achieve their dreams because they are stuck in the broken system. And that starts with the methods laid out in this book, which is a combination of all of the lessons I learned along my own path of escaping the broken system and creating my version of what I call *the New American Dream* (which is a term I coined for the purpose of contrast with *the Old American Dream* but which is not at all limited to just Americans, so we'll just call it *the New Dream* from here on). The New Dream is your dream to live. It is not easy, but it is achievable. All it takes is the courage and commitment to read this book in its entirety and take massive action on what it teaches.

And before we go any further, let me call out what might be an elephant in the room as you read this book. Obviously, everyone wants to make more money, preferably as fast as possible, but this book doesn't have any get-rich-quick schemes. If that's what you're looking for, you might as well stop reading now. What I can promise is that if making money is a goal, the lessons in this book can help you make it faster and more plentifully. I have made so many mistakes and learned from both the successes and failures of so many others, and it's all in this book. If you apply what's in here you will waste no time trying to succeed by playing by the rules of a world that no longer exists. For the longest time, I had the totally wrong idea about money, wealth, and its relationship to happiness. The successful people I met along my journey think about money in a totally different way, a way that's immune to recent changes in society. And even though they all started in different places and faced different sets of challenges, there were everyday habits and behaviors they all shared. It's those habits and behaviors that will become the foundation of your future success, so that's why we're going to start at the beginning and discuss organization, values, goals, mission, vision, character, and other "intangibles" because success and fulfillment aren't about money as much as they are about the person you become. And I know how well this all works because my own life has been a laboratory to test these ideas, and they have exceeded my wildest expectations.

Worry not, this book definitely does explain how to make money. How could it not? My stated goal of helping people escape the broken system and achieve their full potential would be impossible to achieve if people couldn't generate sufficient money and resources to make it happen. The personal and the financial go hand in hand, and getting the financial part of your life in order is a practical prerequisite for creating a life that checks all the boxes of joy and fulfillment. This book will cover accumulating assets, generating wealth, and creating a lasting legacy that will live on for generations, but it also will cover feeling better, performing at a higher level, and having stronger relationships. *It's all connected.*

I've boiled down everything I've learned over twenty-five years into the twenty-eight chapters in this book. They focus on all aspects of life and involve both stories of my own, others that I've learned from, and still more that I've taught. Some lessons will be easy to implement, others much harder, but if taken to heart and properly executed, they will allow you to escape the broken system and set you on the path to achieve the New Dream, just like they have for me and so many other successful people.

PART I

The Rules Have Changed

1

The Evolution
of an Entrepreneur

landed my first and last job at the age of sixteen, working in a law firm supply room, delivering staples and ink cartridge refills to ornery legal secretaries. That lasted three weeks before I got fired. That was all it took for me to know that I wasn't cut out for the typical nine-to-five. I needed to find something else to do with my life, but what?

I knew from middle school guitar lessons that I had some musical talent. And I knew that musicians could travel the world and set their own schedules. The ones who got lucky could even make a lot of money. That all sounded good to me, but I figured that it would be easier to find decent-paying work playing the piano as opposed to the guitar, so, impetuous teen that I was, I dropped out of high school at sixteen and started practicing piano from sunup to sundown.

One year later, I could barely move my hands (there is such a thing as too much practice), but I did start landing a few gigs. A musician friend of mine was connected to the University of Houston music department and helped me arrange an audition. The faculty was not encouraging. I was told that it was biomechanically impossible for someone, particularly a male because of "muscular rigidity," to start playing that late in life and expect to ever perform at a professional level. That was all I needed to hear—it took three years and six auditions, but I eventually earned a full scholarship as the first chair pianist in the jazz department, even convincing them to overlook my lack of a high school diploma. By twenty, I was a working professional playing multiple gigs a week.

For ten years, I was a part-time student earning a degree in jazz piano while working nights and weekends as a pianist in bars, clubs, and at parties. I loved music, and still do, but as a working musician, I discovered pretty quickly that I wanted more for my life. I was a twenty-something playing gigs with forty-, fifty-, and sixty-plus-year-old contemporaries who often didn't seem that happy and were notably broke. And since clearly most of my contemporaries had not cracked the code for abundant living, I decided to start asking my clients.

Many of the private parties I played at were held at the homes of successful business people—even a few billionaires. I started making it a point at every such gig to ask the wealthy hosts about their lives and careers. They were flattered and surprisingly forthright. I honestly couldn't believe the insights I got and the secrets they shared, but there is one piece of advice I received that hit me like a punch to the gut, and I haven't been the same since.

Bob McNair was the billionaire owner of the NFL's Houston Texans. When the Houston Oilers football team left Houston in the '90s to become the Tennessee Titans, it was Bob McNair who brought professional football back to Houston years later by founding the Texans. This made him something of a local hero (Texans do love their football). One year I was hired by Bob to play the annual coaches' dinner for his entire coaching staff and the team captains.

I always made sure to arrive at these types of parties early to set up and maybe even get some face time with the hosts. That evening, Bob approached me with a piece of sheet music and couldn't have been more excited. *"This is the new Texans fight song! I want you to play it tonight!"*

I don't know who he had hired to compose it, but this music wasn't written in any conventional sense that anyone could follow. It was just a few lines and dots scribbled on a page. No time signature. No key signature. Not even a full five-line staff. I didn't know what I was looking at and had nothing else to go on, but Bob said he loved the song and couldn't wait for me to play it.

I had to come through. One of the most successful and influential people in the city of Houston had asked me to do something for him. I could either tell him all the reasons why I couldn't do it, or I could figure something out. I told him it would help if he could sing it for me. I said I wanted to make sure I infused my rendition with an authentic bit of the proud owner's passion, while in reality I was just praying he could carry a tune and I'd be able to decipher what the heck the melody was even supposed to sound like. So, with twenty minutes to spare before the start of the gig, and guests already filing in, he hummed the tune for me. I then went into the back room and put my thousands of hours of ear training to good use and wrote down my best approximation of what Bob had hummed. I made up some chords that seemed to logically fit, and an hour later, I was playing the hell out of some version of the new Houston Texans fight song. To this day, the song they now play at games has almost the exact same chords I made up on the spot at that coaches' dinner!

During a break, Bob came up to me, full of energy. *"You nailed it! Did you hear them all singing? We got those coaches singing like a school choir!"* He was elated. I had made a friend and a mentor, at least for the night. My newfound connection with Mr. McNair meant that when I asked him later that evening about his life and how he became so successful, I didn't get the thirty-second sound bites he gave reporters; I got the extended biography from the man himself. In his appreciation for my musical magic tricks, he took the time to really tell me his story, making sure to share the between-the-lines nuances that you can't get from Wikipedia. He walked me through failure after failure, savoring the details and reliving them with relish. He was proud of not just what he had achieved but of all he had overcome to do so. He reminded me of Ray Kroc, who also had over a dozen failures before founding McDonald's. Then he told me something that I will never forget. He said: *"They tell kids in school that the definition of insanity is doing the same thing over and over and expecting a different result. Supposedly, Einstein said that. Well, I was absent the day they taught that lesson, so I kept trying again and again for decades like an insane person, and that's why I'm a billionaire."*

Emboldened by that advice I committed to starting a successful business. Little did I know how much I would end up needing Bob's sage advice, particularly the part about trying again and again. Here is a list of the entrepreneurial endeavors I undertook in my twenties.

1. **Booking agent:** I had some success booking gigs for myself, so why not do it for other acts? That fell apart after a few months of watching local bands and local nightclub managers try to screw each other over (and me) over. Fail.

2. **Party promoter:** I was confronted by a rival promoter who threatened to have his goons beat me up, but hey, at least I got to meet Wu Tang Clan. Fail.

3. **Sandwich shop owner:** I paid $3,000 for a 13 percent share in a sandwich shop across the street from my apartment. The sandwiches were really good, but I gained twenty pounds, and we only lasted six months. Fail.

4. **MLM:** When the energy industry in Texas was deregulated, I worked with a multilevel marketing company to sell power to Texas residents. I found customers, made money, and got results, but nobody I recruited could do the same. Fail.

5. **House flipper:** Inspired by Robert Kiyosaki's seminal book *Rich Dad. Poor Dad* (a great book even if poorly acted upon by me), I bought single-family homes with no money down, teamed up with a local contractor, and maxed out my credit card with cash advances to flip them, but I was always robbing Peter to pay Paul when things went wrong. In 2006, I lost three houses to foreclosures and couldn't even get a car loan for the next seven years. Fail. Though I did retain a few properties that in the long run made this still a win (more on real estate investing later).

6. **Loan officer:** After the previous debacle, I thought loan officers had the easiest go of it in the real estate business, so I got certified and tried to drum up business from my friends. The industry proved to be more competitive than I thought, and my reputation had been shot with my friends after my MLM disaster. Fail.

7. **Campus coupon marketer:** I partnered up with a bartender friend of mine named Matt who was wired similarly to me to start a web-based business to allow college students to subscribe to a site to download coupons from local businesses. It turns out that unless you're a credit

card company or a student loan company, college students are not a great target customer. They hardly have money to spend in the first place or if they do it is their parents' money and they aren't too worried about being frugal with it. Fail.

8. **Campus text message marketer:** After the last failure, Matt and I tried to create a system that would allow college students to fetch coupons from cell phones via text message (for example, text "Pizza" to 555999). It was an invaluable experience, raising angel money and creating technology, but it never turned a profit. Fail.

9. **Real estate marketer:** Matt and I figured, if college towns weren't ready for our genius technology, we'd repurpose it for the real estate market. Now, instead of downloading coupons, potential buyers or renters could request property info by sending a text message. We landed two of the ten largest real estate companies in the country, but all they wanted was for us to sell our service to their agents and give them part of the money, so we spent our time trying to teach real estate agents how to use text messaging in the pre-smartphone world of 2004. This is possibly my most painful entrepreneurial memory—all the hours spent teaching old ladies how to text on their flip phones. Imagine spending thirty minutes explaining to a sixty-two-year-old realtor that in order to text the letter C she needs to press the number two on the keypad three times on her tiny flip phone while her nails keep sliding off the buttons. Then she needs to wait a full second before pressing the same button once more before moving down to press the number eight. Now you can congratulate her for having spelled "cat." And now you get to explain to her what a short code is and why the phone number only has six digits. And repeat. The idea was good, but we were way too early. Fail.

10. **Mobile marketing agency owner:** As text messaging became more popular, we decided to become an agency to sell the technology to brands and provide services for how to use it. We still hadn't made a dime, but we were hustlers, and it paid off when we landed ClearChannel Outdoor, the largest outdoor media company in the world at the time (think billboards, bus stops, taxi cab signs, etc.), but when some driver in California got into a fatal car accident while texting, they pulled the plug on the program. Fail.

There were more—those were just the big ones. I was always getting into something because I was insatiably fueled by the idea that getting a real job was the only true failure. In my twenties, I probably earned close to $500,000 as a musician, but easily spent half of it failing at businesses.

Today, when people ask me how I kept going, I tell them it was because of that conversation with Bob McNair. It changed my life and gave me permission (in my own mind) to keep going even when things seemed hopeless. Still, it was a painful period. For an entire decade, I was undercapitalized, underequipped, and underskilled trying to copy these billionaires. Things only got worse, and in 2007, my final failure almost did me in.

11. **Restaurant franchise owner:** After spending long days on the road promoting our latest venture, Matt and I often found ourselves in Midwestern college towns grabbing quick meals at a popular franchise restaurant called the Pita Pit. There seemed to be a Pita Pit in every college town we went to, and it was always a favorite with the college students. In 2006, we decided to open our own Pita Pit franchises in Houston. Two years later, the restaurants were closed, and as the personal guarantor my name was on the hook for $495,000 in various debts. Fail.

That was the start of rock bottom. Shortly after that, my marriage fell apart, I was evicted from my apartment, and I had developed arthritis in my wrist, which made it impossible to support myself with regular piano gigs. I was twenty-nine years old, $495,000 in debt, too injured to work, and forced to move into my estranged wife's parents' house so I didn't end up homeless, but in true Bob McNair spirit, I still didn't give up.

For the next couple of weeks, I scoured the internet, desperately searching for ways to make money and turn my life around. That's when I stumbled upon the burgeoning new economy online and a group of successful entrepreneurs I could learn from. I enrolled in a class on affiliate marketing and paid $2,000 using the only credit card I had that still worked. For the next couple of months, I spent over twelve hours every day on my laptop in the small spare bedroom at my soon-to-be ex-wife's parents' house, leaving only to shoot cringeworthy marketing videos in the backyard. It was frustrating at times, but I also possessed just the right blend of desperation, vulnerability, drive, discipline, and fearlessness to keep going. As a jazz musician, it was my job to make up solos on the fly, so I was comfortable living on this improvisational edge.

Then, finally, it happened. As I started to develop the skills necessary for the modern digital economy, business started to get better. After a few months, energized because I could see it working, I cranked my efforts up even further. In month six, it all clicked and in May 2009, I generated $40,000 in commissions in a single month. The next month, $70,000. By spring of 2010 I had paid off all $495,000 of my debt in roughly eighteen months, and I never looked back. Over a five-year span, I would generate close to $10 million in commissions as an affiliate marketer.

In 2013, after some changes in the Google algorithm that would have required a nearly complete overhaul of my affiliate business, I switched directions and created a digital agency to help businesses grow their revenue. That business would go on to do about $30 million in sales over a five-year period and land twice on the Inc. 5000 list, published by *Inc.* magazine—a list of the fastest-growing private companies in the United States. In 2012, I had also gotten remarried and begun the process of adopting my new wife's three children before adding a fourth of our own. Thanks to the fateful decision in 2008 to risk $2,000 on an online course, I had completely transformed my life and generated about $55 million over the course of a decade.

I had fully experienced the power of online self-education and knew that at some point it would be my turn to pay it forward, but I wasn't sure how. Then, in September 2018, I had an opportunity to sell my digital agency, which I took. Doing so gave me the space to take stock of my priorities and consider my next move. As you'll hear it wasn't a perfectly smooth transition, but the transformation that had occurred over the previous ten years from broke and nearly homeless musician to multiple eight-figure entrepreneur had produced not only a dramatic improvement in my quality of life but also a sense that I had something valuable to share. All around I saw so many people struggling, unfulfilled, and feeling stuck, even though they were doing what they thought they were supposed to be doing. That's what's always struck me about the broken system. It's not just that people feel stuck, it's that that they don't understand how they got there. What are people supposed to do when the only plan they were told about turns out to be a bad plan? And here I was, some bum musician turned internet entrepreneur pondering retirement at thirty-nine. I knew I had to do something. That something became ENTRE.

THE ONE-MILLION-DOLLAR CHALLENGE

In September 2018, I was about to speak at a marketing conference in Coronado, California, when I decided at the last minute to scrap my original presentation. Instead, I marched onstage and declared to the audience that I was starting over. I explained that with only an iPhone and a selfie stick that I had bought for $150 on Amazon, I was going to make $1 million by posting videos on social media just to prove that I could and that anyone else could too. I explained how I was going to do it, invited anyone who wanted to to join me, and even started a Facebook group where I would explain my every move and answer questions.

I was a pretty good marketer, and my agency had done really well, but I had never done anything like this before. I had no presence or experience on platforms like YouTube or Instagram. I was not an influencer and even that word seemed somewhere between vain and absurd. I had never gotten into making online videos because I didn't want to look awful, be humiliated, and have to read negative comments. I had a YouTube channel I had started when I was in affiliate marketing, but I had only every posted a few screen capture tutorial videos and in a decade had accumulated a whopping 228 subscribers, mostly agency clients. But that didn't matter to me. I had no idea what I was doing, and that was the point. I was going to show the world what was possible for someone who had the drive, the right information, and was starting from scratch. This was an experiment to prove something for "the little guy" and I had this vague notion that it wasn't so much a business or marketing test but rather an incipient crusade. I decided I wasn't going to do anything that anyone couldn't do even starting with nothing (other than using a phone and a selfie stick).

So, why post videos on social media as a beginner with no following and no real business idea? Because that's the fastest way to get feedback on new ideas in real time and find out quickly if those ideas have a shot at working. Twenty or thirty years ago, you might have had a great idea for a product or business, but you had absolutely no way of knowing if anybody wanted to hand over their money and buy what you were selling. You'd have to create ads and sales materials and then spend thousands of dollars distributing those ads. You'd have to devote time to sending out mailers, cold calling, or trying to convince a store to carry your product that didn't exist yet. Of course, that could work, and sometimes it did for a few, but you had to be really good, and a bit lucky, because you didn't have any credibility yet.

The other challenge with the old model was that it was mostly a one-way creation process. You might think you knew what people wanted, but you couldn't know for sure without asking them, which was expensive and time consuming in the days of focus groups and canvasing neighborhoods with clipboards. The beauty of social media is that it gives you the opportunity to get feedback quickly from large numbers of people. You can ask your audience what their problems are, what they want, and what they think of your proposed solution, and you get your answer instantly. And it will certainly be honest. Have you ever seen the YouTube comments section? It's ruthless. Keyboard warriors are a brutal bunch and for better or worse, they will tell you exactly what they think. And all this feedback is available completely for free. Even if it's not always the kindest, getting feedback on my ideas from actual potential customers seemed a lot better recipe for success than assuming I could correctly guess what people wanted.

Here's how what I did can work for anyone. Let's say you have twenty different ideas you want to test—product ideas, inventions, book ideas, lessons you've learned that you want to share, jokes you want to try out, a song you wrote, it can be anything. Whatever the ideas are, you can create a video or series of videos around each topic and post them to YouTube, Facebook, Instagram, or any other platform (I started with Facebook then quickly expanded to YouTube). Don't try to pitch or sell anything. Just try to offer up something of value, share your idea, and invite feedback. Voila! You know which of your ideas were good and which weren't.

In my case, I was developing my ideas for a new type of education company right out in the open, and I was using both direct, personal feedback and consumption metrics like click rate, watch time, and like-to-share ratio to gauge when I was getting warmer and when I was getting colder.

Whatever you're trying to do, if you put enough volume out, you'll notice that some videos will start to get more traction, and usually, one or a few will go on to get significantly more traction. It might be slow at first, and it was for me too. My first videos got two views, then ten views, then twenty views, but I kept going. That's the key: keep going. The funny thing is that it often won't be the videos you expect that get traction, but you follow the data. Whatever content gets the most attention, that's what you produce more of, and that's the audience you target. Over time you get a sense of what the audience wants, and especially what they'd be willing to pay for. Once you know what they want, that's the product you create. Initially, you don't have to worry about selling it. You already sold your audience on you by showing up consistently and providing value over time. Compare that to the old model of launching a product or business and think about how many steps and hurdles you can skip. You can build your own brand and engage your audience so quickly and for so little money that social media has basically become the gold rush of this century— and just like a gold rush most people stop digging too soon.

Like I said, I started with a Facebook page and quickly added YouTube. For the next year I focused obsessively on growing those two platforms. I didn't even add Instagram until I'd already been at it for a year or so. I did whatever I could to grow my channels. I reached out to all of my contacts, and even had my kids get their friends to subscribe. I was just trying to get critical mass so that the broader market would take me seriously. The first idea I ran with was called School of Awesome, basically a school that teaches you how to have an awesome life. It was broad enough that multiple products could fit under the umbrella and it left me lots of room to be creative. Some videos were sixty seconds, some were two minutes, and some were longer. This went on for about ten months.

In June 2019, nine months after I had issued myself the challenge from the stage in Coronado, I took a two-week vacation in Newport Beach and (ironically) Coronado, California, where it had all begun. It was a big, expensive vacation with my family and a bunch of my kids' friends—fifteen people total. It was supposed to be a relaxing getaway to break up the hard work I'd been doing, but circumstances had changed. I was getting screwed in the sale of my agency (note: when you sell a business, get paid up front, not over time), plus a couple of significant real estate deals fell through. I wasn't broke, but I was nervous and not nearly in the place I had thought I would be. I had a lot of anxiety about taking such a big, extravagant vacation, but I was committed to giving my family the experience they were excited about so I kept a poker face. I figured that either my social media experiment would work, and things would be fine, or it would be our last family vacation for a while. Either way, I might as well enjoy it. On the first day of the trip, my wife, Jaqueline, sensing my anxiety, said to me, *"Unless we want to spend another $25,000 on this vacation by taking fifteen people out to eat three times a day, why don't we go to the grocery store and stock up?"*

We drove to a nearby Ralphs, and while loading up the shopping cart with enough snacks to feed a small army, I had a moment of frustration. Grocery shopping on vacation to save money was rubbing me the wrong way; it was time to monetize the work I'd been doing. I was producing content and getting great feedback, but up to that point, I hadn't generated any income because I hadn't created any product or service to actually sell. It was time to turn on the faucet and prove what I had set out to achieve. I had received enough feedback to know that what I needed to do was create my first course for my "awesome school" and find a gentle but effective way to start marketing that course to those who had been digesting the content.

My big "blue ocean" idea had finally emerged. What if I could take the personal-development industry (Tony Robbins, Brian Tracy, Tim Ferriss, etc.), and combine it with the digital marketing education industry (Russell Brunson/ClickFunnels, Tai Lopez, DigitalMarketer.com, etc.), blend it with the "hustle and grind" mentorship approach of folks like Grant Cardone or Andy Frisella, fold in some Robert Kiyosaki–style financial literacy, and wrap it in a big Oprah-esque blanket of love and positive psychology? Basically, the idea was to create a complete self-education platform that would cover all the stuff school doesn't and teach people what it takes to be successful in all areas of life. I had done a ton of research and didn't feel anyone had hit the mark on anything close to what I was envisioning.

I was still in the grocery store when I phoned my soon-to-be business partner Adam Whiting to convince him to come on board and help me see this vision through. After an hour, Jaqueline was growing understandably agitated because I'd spent the entire shopping trip lagging behind her on the phone, while she did the actual shopping for our summer vacation. I put Adam on hold and told her, *"I'm sorry, but this call is the beginning of the rest of our lives. When I get off, we can check out, go back to the beach house, and I'll be fully present, but I won't enjoy this vacation unless I know the plan. And this call is to figure out the plan."*

I continued following behind her while she checked out, loaded the car, and drove back to the beach house. It was a terrible moment as a husband, but for the next two hours, Adam and I laid out the vision for ENTRE (and decided to sunset the name School of Awesome). Two weeks later, after we returned home from vacation, I rented a suite at the Wynn Hotel in Las Vegas for a week to shoot and edit the videos for our first course—the ENTRE Blueprint. That was more money I was nervous to spend, but I needed a nice backdrop for the course and a quiet, comfortable place to live and work until it was done. That course went on to become the bestselling business education course on the internet and launched ENTRE. The method worked. I had used social media video marketing to build a relationship with an audience that didn't know who I was, find out what they wanted, and launch what would become a massive business on a shoestring budget—a process that virtually anyone else could have afforded to do too, if they knew what I knew.

Not only did I achieve my goal, but also I documented the whole process, so I could now show my students a step-by-step guide for how to build a thriving business online using only a selfie stick and a phone. I had proven once again in my life that you can achieve what looks almost miraculous to the outside observer if you harness your entrepreneurial spirit.

THE BENEFITS OF ENTREPRENEURIALISM

I believe the world needs entrepreneurs, not just for economic reasons, but because the philosophy and ethos of being entrepreneurial is the antidote to the broken system. This philosophy is what allowed me to escape that system, and today, I've dedicated my life to helping others do the same thing. That's what ENTRE is all about. ENTRE is a platform that provides online training courses, coaching, live events, professional services, networking, personal development, online business software, a life development app, and much more, all for helping people succeed and achieve their version of the New Dream in the modern world. ENTRE is not only about how to become financially successful, though that's the foundation and what draws a lot of people to it initially; it's about becoming the best version of yourself.

One of the first times I really felt successful was when I was reflecting on my life and realizing that the reason I was so happy was not because of money. I had taken back control and created an intentional life of my own design. As we often say in ENTRE, I was living by choice and not by chance. I realized people don't need money, at least not in the way they think they do. Money is not what produces or defines success. Real success comes as a natural consequence of becoming the type of person that can attract resources, people, energy, or whatever else we need to achieve our goals. This step of *becoming* is what so many people skip over (I know because I avoided it for the longest time), and it's the reason why so many people fail.

Our company is called ENTRE, not because we believe that everyone should become an entrepreneur, but because we believe everyone should become more entrepreneurial. There is a difference, and it traces back to one of the purported origins of the word. In one origin story of the word it originated as a combination of a connotation of the French word *entre* (which literally means "between" but which apparently also implies "swimming out to sea") with another French word *prendre* ("to grasp" or "to take") into a word that roughly meant undertaker or daring adventurer. In that sense think of an entrepreneur as someone who sees something that people need but is out of reach and who is willing to swim out to sea, braving choppy waters, and bring it back to shore for the benefit of those who were scared to go in the water themselves. Entrepreneurship has not always been a cool or sexy thing with magazines named after it, and it definitely wasn't always about money.

The word *entrepreneur* has a labyrinthine etymology and I've found several other supposed origins for it that are equally inventive. At one time, an entrepreneur was supposedly someone who produced light opera and musical theater in France. That story goes that this person's vocation was to go into the bowels of Paris (think the movie *Moulin Rouge*), find an artist or musician with a vision that deserved to be brought to life, and then convince the wealthy elites on the outskirts of town to back the idea and make it happen. That was no easy feat considering musical theater was, and still is, an investment that rarely pans out financially. The point was that entrepreneurs attract capital to things of beauty and vision that move humanity forward.

The most common etymology I found is from the French economist Jean-Baptiste Say who used the term in the early nineteenth century to mean those participants in the economy who divert capital from less efficient means to more efficient means, often implying those who see things others don't. In all these instances we see the same theme: entrepreneurship has a historical association with being a little "out there," or taking on what looks like risk to those who understand less than the entrepreneur. It's always been connected to a sort of wisdom or prescience that calls some of us to defy the status quo.

Certainly that is apt for people like Elon Musk and Steve Jobs, but in the last few decades the term has taken a beating from overuse and become somewhat of a pop culture term implying some loose combination of business owner, fundraiser, innovator, and celebrity. The word has simultaneously become more esoteric and more banal, and the world is now so saturated with people putting the word *entrepreneur* in their Instagram bios that to my ears at least its essence has been lost. Like Patrick Dempsey's great protagonist of the '80s movie *Can't Buy Me Love*, the word *entrepreneur* has lost what made it special because it got popular, and for very deep social and economic reasons it's really important we reclaim it. Entrepreneurs aren't meant to be popular or cool, they're meant to be boldly and eccentrically themselves, not trying to impress anyone, and in so doing they play not only a critical economic function but also help shape culture. They bring more than resources back to the people on the shore; they remind the shore dwellers that humans were created not to fit in, but to stand out.

If being an entrepreneur is what some people do, then being entrepreneurial is the way the best of those people are. It is a central tenet of this book that the way people are is much more important than what people do; as such I am not suggesting that everyone must become an entrepreneur, per se, but rather that if we all become more entrepreneurial we individually have our best shots at escaping the broken system and collectively our best chance at fixing it. At ENTRE, our definition of entrepreneurialism is a convergence of three qualities—being a dreamer, a learner, and a hard worker. We teach people to take an improvisational, values-first approach to life. It's about breaking out of the box and approaching life differently than most do precisely because you don't want the life that most have. I firmly believe that everyone can benefit from becoming more entrepreneurial and opting into total personal responsibility for creating the life they want.

The first video I uploaded after that event in Coronado was an eleven-minute rant titled "Let's Get Extreme." In it I insisted the world didn't need to "chill" or "mellow out," but to the contrary we as individuals needed to get more fired up about the values that really matter. One thousand videos later, I'm still preaching the same message, and over the course of a few years, ENTRE has grown from an unknown thirty-nine-year-old dad in Utah shooting videos on his phone to a disruptive global company with over two hundred thousand paid students that is at the time of this writing the fastest-growing education platform in the world, at least as far as I know. What started out as an experiment to prove something for "the little guy" has evolved into a groundbreaking platform where anyone can go to learn and grow, personally and professionally, and make over their whole life.

ENTRE, this book, my entire belief set, heck, my entire life at this point, all depend on a singular notion—that anyone can create the life of their dreams, their New Dream, so to speak, *if* they have the right elements in place and that the noblest calling imaginable, which I have devoted the second chapter of my life to, is helping people accomplish it.

2

Becoming Wealthy Is Easier Than Ever

Can anyone really become wealthy?

People ask me that question all the time. Since attending my first live business training event in March 2009 (which you'll hear more about) I have probably attended, spoke at, or otherwise participated in one hundred such events, so I am very often around people seeking some sort of personal and/or professional change in their lives. Based on the questions I get asked there is a pervasive anxiety that massive success isn't achievable for most people, like you must belong to some secret society or exclusive club. It seems whenever a subject related to success is being discussed, particularly anything related to making money by means other than a traditional job, there's a little voice many of us seem to have in our heads that wonders, *Is this really possible for me?*

Well, over 1,700 new millionaires are created every single day in the United States alone and over four thousand more around the world. Most of those are everyday men and women who weren't born with an advantage and didn't go to the so-called right school, and a large percentage of them are being created through means other than traditional jobs, almost all of them if we consider only the multimillionaires. I know for sure that not one of those billionaires I played piano for was born with a silver spoon in his or her mouth. In fact, from what I could tell of the half dozen billionaires I played for, and the dozens of hundred-plus millionaires, the majority of them grew up poor or lower middle class.

My wealthiest clients taught me so many lessons and each had their own slant on success, but if there was a unifying theme among them all it was that if you really want to be successful and create a dream life, start a business. My high-end client list, those who could casually afford a couple hundred dollars an hour for a piano player, were uniformly people who had founded their own companies. It makes sense; if you don't have assets, you aren't building wealth, and for most people who don't have millions to start with, building a business is their best shot at developing assets.

For many people I believe the best place to do that today is on the internet because you can build what I call "digital real estate." That means online assets that function similar to traditional real estate investments by generating income for you now (short term), while also creating real, underlying value and cash flow that can grow over time (long term).

Digital and physical real estate are strikingly similar, but the main difference is that digital real estate assets can be developed for pennies on the dollar compared to physical real estate. With a twelve-dollar domain, a good sales funnel, a strategy for getting traffic (of which there is one to fit any budget), and a lot of blood, sweat, and tears, you can create a million-dollar business based on the one condition that is the core concept of this book—that *you* have *become* a person who is inevitably and unstoppably destined for success. Obviously, that's a big condition and it's why I was insistent that ENTRE would emphasize personal development right alongside business education. Just because there are more opportunities than ever to become successful in the modern world doesn't mean that it's easy. If anything, because the barrier to entry online is lower, the opposite is true.

Most people are terrible at making money, at least in amounts needed to fundamentally change their quality-of-life, and with good reason. Anything that so many people are competing to do is going to be hard, which is why you need to be willing to do what most of your competition isn't, namely be willing to grow. If we were to rephrase the opening question of this chapter to read, *"Can anyone become wealthy without taking risk and being willing to stretch way beyond their natural comfort zone?"* the answer would be a big fat *no*! Effort, attitude, and changeability are the X factors, and if you aren't willing to grow, even when painful, you might as well not even try to make more money.

Here's a test to see if you have the right attitude. Let's say you bump into a super successful billionaire, and you two hit it off. He then invites you on his private jet, so you can take off and go wherever you want. I don't know many people who'd turn down that offer. Now, let's imagine that he says you can go, but you have to split the cost of the pilot, fuel, staff, and all of the fees for the trip, which comes out to about $25,000. Now the offer isn't as appealing. It's understandable that maybe you can't afford to go on that trip, but the test is in how you would respond.

Do you part ways and never speak again, or do you say something like, *"I can't split the cost—I literally don't have the money—but what would it cost for thirty minutes of your time? I want you to teach me what I need to know so that ten years from now, I can repay you with a trip on my own jet."* When you meet someone who has outlier results at anything you're interested in, you should be drawn to that person like a magnet. You want to soak up what they know and learn what is possible, just like I did at my piano gigs.

Far too many people I know have the opposite reaction, including many of my fellow musicians at those same gigs. They look at those who are successful with cynicism and judgment. Be it insecurity or shame, they put up walls to protect themselves. If you're one of those people, you have to get out of that mindset and start looking at money and success differently, because the real competition is with yourself, not anyone else. Notice I'm not saying you *might want to* get out of that mindset; I'm saying you *have to*, assuming you're a good person that is. Here's why.

CONSIDER IT YOUR OBLIGATION
TO MAKE A LOT OF MONEY

How does society view those who hunger for money? People tend to think of Gordon Gekko from the movie *Wall Street*, crooks like Bernie Madoff, or drug kingpins from the latest Netflix series—all people only looking out for themselves. Yes, there are plenty of horrible people out there who fit the classic stereotype and have no qualms about cutting some legal or ethical corners to make a lot of money. Hollywood loves to play on these stereotypes (while ironically embodying a lot of them), but does everyone who wants to make a lot of money fit into that category? Of course not. In my experience of meeting many hundreds of extraordinarily wealthy people the vast majority are role model worthy and use their resources to make a positive impact and help large numbers of people. Still, in our society today the desire for money is often labeled as "greed" and looked at as a negative attribute. I'm here to tell you that way of thinking only hurts the person who thinks it.

In my opinion, we should be passionately obsessed with making a lot of money. If it's generated in an aboveboard way, the money we have earned is the scoreboard of the value we have created in the world, so it should be a source of pride. It seems obvious to me and always has—if you're a good person, you have a moral responsibility to make a lot of money. Every dollar belongs to someone or is controlled by someone, so why leave it to those people who are only looking out for themselves to control it all? Why play into the stereotype? The people who need to be obsessed and passionate about making money are the good people of the world. If you want to do amazing things that improve the world, money is much better in your hands, and under your control, than anyone else's. You have to believe that!

People get so hung up on money being either "good" or "bad," but that's the wrong way to think about it. Money is just a tool. If you have to nail something to the wall, do you use a hammer, or do you use your fist? Do you answer that question by considering the inherent morality of a hammer versus a fist? No, you just use the hammer because it's the tool that allows you to efficiently get the job done. That's the good and proper use of a hammer. Hammers can also be used to kill people, which we would generally consider a bad use of the tool, but even then, what if you were defending your family from an attacker? Now our use of the hammer would be good again.

You get my point. Money is a tool, and tools aren't good or bad. Circumstances and intentions determine the moral nature of using any tool. The fact is, if you want to change the world for the better, you will probably need money and lots of it. Money equals power and influence. The people with the money are the ones who control the resources and the governments. We need to build up the war chests of the good people in the world, so let's get negative associations we might have around the desire to make money out of our heads. I encourage you to take a positive view of money, and especially of those who have successfully acquired a lot of it. It's okay to desire a lot of money, and it's okay to want to emulate those who have acquired much of it. Being open, rational, and willing to learn from those who have achieved what you desire dramatically increases your chances of fulfilling that desire, whatever it is. There are so many opportunities to make money in the modern economy and live the life you want to live. This book will point you to many of the best of them.

And believe me, if me and many of the most successful people I know are right about where the world is headed, you're going to need a lot more money than you may be thinking.

3

A Million Dollars
Isn't Nearly Enough

Millionaire is a term people throw around a lot, but what does it actually mean to be a millionaire today?

I'm sure you realize that just earning a million dollars in income does not make you a millionaire. The term *millionaire* refers to net worth, not income, and that's a huge difference. I had earned a million dollars in income by age thirty, most of it in the previous twelve months), but still had a net worth of $100,000 at most, basically just the equity in a couple rental houses. Nearly every dime I had earned prior to that had gone out as living expenses or been sunk into various failed business ventures (which I now collectively refer to as my "real education"). But I don't think income or net worth is really what most people mean by "millionaire." Generally when people talk about becoming a millionaire, it's more of a qualitative statement about the life they want than a quantitative statement about their finances. It's generally a synonym for financial freedom, a state of being where money isn't a stressful part of life and there is no need to trade time for it. Being in this position allows you to take care of your family and the people you love while still doing what you want.

So, by that definition what number actually makes a person a millionaire? Is it one million dollars? Probably not. One million dollars doesn't mean the same today as it did twenty or thirty years ago because one million dollars doesn't go as far as it used to. Depending on your situation and where you live, a one-million-dollar net worth probably won't even support a good quality of life long term, if you don't keep working for income.

Don't believe me? Let's do some basic math. The basic financial planning formula used by most financial advisors says that you should have twelve times the highest level of income you achieved in your career in liquid, investable savings in order to be able to retire and maintain your standard of living. Let's say that you peaked at $100,000 a year. That would mean you need $1.2 million to retire, not counting equity in your home, that is. If you made $50,000, then you need $600,000. Personally, I think twelve is too low of a multiple but the financial planners have letters after their name and I don't, so sure, let's use their numbers. But before you start doing your own calculations, there are a couple things you'll want to consider.

1. The value of a dollar today will not be what a dollar is worth when you retire. On average, prices double every twenty years, a trend that is accelerating.
2. People are living longer, and by the time you retire, life expectancy could be higher. This is one of several reasons I personally think twelve is too low of a multiplier.

So, if you make $100,000 a year and are twenty years away from retirement, $1.2 million suddenly becomes $2.4 million because everything is going to be at least twice as expensive. If you end up living longer than average, that number could be as high as $4 million or more. How close are you to that figure? Very few are close enough.

Don't forget that we're not only talking about you and potentially your spouse. Do you have kids? If so, you know how fast money can go. I have four kids—two that drive (so far). Our car insurance rates are through the roof. They all have the option to go to college, which I'll be paying for if they choose it. As I said above, I'm not against college, I just think it should be a conscientious decision based on necessity for a predetermined career outcome, not just something kids do out of societal inertia or to have some mythical "college experience" where they "find themselves." My daughter currently wants to be a nurse, so obviously college would be necessary for her and I'm glad to be able to pay for it so she doesn't end up in six figures of debt or more by her mid-twenties.

And what about health care? At any given time, I'm either self-employed or employed by a business I own, so one way or another, I pay for my own health care. Could you pay for yours? Will you be able to when the government can't (more on that later)? Inability to pay for one's own health care is one of the biggest traps that keeps people stuck inside the broken system. Are you taking care of your parents? What if one of them gets sick, and you have to pay for their hospital bills or treatment? What if someone else in your family has a medical issue that insurance won't cover fully? Do you want to be in a situation where you have to choose between taking care of your children financially or taking care of another loved one medically? I've lived this situation twice and thankfully was not forced to choose. I assisted my mother-in-law with cancer treatment that was not covered by insurance because it involved experimental gene therapy that the insurance company wouldn't pay for. It was a six-figure experiment that sadly didn't work but that I would do again if asked. I also assisted my father-in-law during his battle with cancer. He had health insurance that covered his sadly unsuccessful treatment, but no way to support himself during his last year on earth. So I paid his bills. It was that or watch the home my wife grew up in get foreclosed. These are the kind of choices that most financial advisors aren't factoring into their twelve-times calculation. What if one of your kids or grandkids gets addicted and needs rehab? At the time of this writing, out of the approximately twenty-one million addicts in the United States, only two million can afford to get help. And what about vacations or bucket list items you want to accomplish? All of this adds up. Life can be full of large, unexpected expenses—some looming, some in the distant future, some by choice, some by necessity, some for fun, and some for love. Yet the vast majority of people's strategy for dealing with the unforeseen is to just hope it never comes. Personally, I'd rather be prepared for the worst.

The biggest problem in our perception of money and how much of it we need is avoidance of uncomfortable facts. It's common for people who have as much as $500,000 in the bank to think they are fine when, in reality, they are not close to fine. How many times have you heard someone say, "Once I can make six figures a year, I'll be good"? The truth is that a hundred grand a year won't get you that far, especially if you're providing for a family. At that level there are still numerous compromises and "best of bad options" choices required just to get by, and not just when it comes to luxuries. We live in a world today where most of us will have to make major quality-of-life sacrifices until we earn at least a couple hundred grand a year, probably much more than that if you live in a major city.

Financial restrictions drastically limit our possibilities in this world, but in a broken system that denies us knowledge of options to increase income it seems futile to look at this reality. So we bury our heads in the sand. Or we blow our paycheck on lottery tickets. Or we read Reddit threads on what penny stock to buy. Instinctively we know that when it comes to money, every one of us has a number that, if reached, would immediately remove the governing limits from our lives. Most of us just don't know how to reach it without a few more lifetimes to work and save. Granted, everyone's number is different based on where they live, what their expenses are, the size of their family, who they're responsible for, and the quality of life they hope to maintain, but what isn't different for most people is that they are far from their number and have no real, viable plan. So, here's my controversial and, for most, unpleasant, conclusion. If you want to have an awesome life, you need $10 million, or more depending on when you're reading this. At the time of this writing I am declaring: *$10 million is the new $1 million.* The way most people use the word *millionaire* I think correlates to a $10 million net worth at bare minimum. At that net worth, you will likely be financially insulated from crisis, so if you get sick, sued, or your house burns down, money won't be a crippling issue. At $10 million, you start to achieve financial security (for now anyway—we'll talk more about inflation and other economic factors a little later).

I know from beta-reader feedback on this book that saying a $10 million net worth is the minimum threshold for financial security is a provocative claim, one that angers many people. But math isn't about feelings (more about that later too). I've seen compelling arguments that push for amounts as high as $50 million or even $100 million. Consider that in 2016, when billionaire Peter Thiel was asked why he paid for Hulk Hogan's legal defense in a defamation case, he remarked *"If you're a single-digit millionaire like Hulk Hogan, you have no effective access to our legal system. It costs too much."* The comment was met with mockery and indignation by much of the media, but no one ever seriously claimed he was incorrect. I realize statements like that can trigger some people while sounding ridiculous to others, but we have to be on guard against our own cognitive bias, and make sure we aren't dismissing things that are true just because they are outside the conventional narrative. There is a tendency among humans to be overly focused on small issues we can easily understand while distancing ourselves from more complex issues that are harder to grasp. It's called Parkinson's Law of Triviality. In this context it might appear as someone complaining that the price of beef rose 9.3 percent in the last twelve months (true at the time of this writing) while ignoring what should be a much bigger concern that the money they need to retire likely increased by hundreds of thousands of dollars in the last twelve months. As a society we've been using the term *millionaire* to mean a wealthy person since 1786 (Thomas Jefferson coined the term), but surely we can agree that what was fabulously wealthy over two hundred years ago is not so impressive anymore.

You can ask around, but you'll be hard-pressed to find anybody in the mainstream financial services industry who will tell you this because they know $10 million is a daunting figure for most people. It may be unpopular to say such a thing out loud, but that doesn't mean it's not accurate. Ignoring it or being willfully ignorant will hurt much more in the end, which is a big reason why I wrote this book. And why should you trust me over a financial advisor (after all they do have those letters after their name)? Because I have no dog in the fight of your personal finances. I'm not trying to get paid for managing your money!

Consider that the median income in the United States in 2020 was about $62,000, while the median retirement savings was about $50,000. If you make $62,000 a year and have only managed to save $50,000 for retirement, do you really think most financial advisors are going to look you in the eye and tell you that you need $5 million, or even $10 million, to retire comfortably? They're not going to advise you against their own self-interest, and if most people heard that they'd feel helpless and start looking for another financial advisor. Be it financial advisors, teachers, the media, or the government, none of them have a vested interest in telling you the truth and would probably suffer for doing so if they did. Goodness knows I get hate all the time for it! Nobody wants to shed any light on what a raw deal the mainstream approach to making a living really is. All of those people telling you that you'll be fine once you get a degree and a job have not done the math, because unless that job pays you around $500,000 a year and puts you on a path to reaching a $10 million net worth, you're probably setting yourself up for a struggle down the line.

I have family members who retired with a million dollars in the bank, and they walk around like they're broke. And honestly, they are. If you break down a million dollars into passive income, that amounts to maybe $4,000 a month if it's invested safely—$1,100 of which goes to the average US mortgage payment—and then there are capital gains taxes and a slew of other expenses, so after all of that, there isn't much left. It's hard to live on $4,000 a month even without unplanned expenses popping up.

BUT JEFF, ISN'T THERE MORE TO LIFE THAN MONEY?

Yes! This book is not trying to convince you that money is all that matters or that it will solve all your problems. Having an amazing life is about much more than just making money. The point is to look better, feel better, perform better, speak better, relate better, communicate better, and have better relationships. It's a holistic transformation. There are so many different levers you can pull to improve your life. You can lose fat, build muscle, improve your marriage, go to therapy, take a vacation with your family, spend more time with your kids, or do any number of things to become an overall happier person. That stuff all works, but in my experience, far and away, the biggest lever you can pull is the financial one, because building assets and generating a high income provides the foundation or at least the lubrication for most of the other changes you are constantly telling yourself you could or should make. Money is what makes so many other things in your life possible and can insulate you from many of the problems that can reduce your quality of life and destroy relationships.

What's the source of most marital troubles and the number one cause of divorce? Even most kids know the answer to that. It's money! When you fix your money problems, you will naturally reduce friction with your spouse. And if that doesn't happen, you can afford a good therapist. Money may not solve all of your problems, but it is a tool that can help you avoid or fix so many of them. It will free up your time to address other challenges, allow you to travel and enjoy the other luxuries it can provide, empower you to help and care for people in a way you never could without it, and is a prerequisite for escaping the broken system, which is the whole darn point of this book! In fact, the broken system depends on people not having enough money! That's why I want to open people's minds and change the conversations we have about money. Not because I'm focused on money; like we said before money is just a tool. I'm focused on helping people achieve security, fulfillment, enrichment, and being able to help others, but to achieve these things, we need money.

And we need to stop telling ourselves we're okay without enough of it. We aren't. I realize we tell ourselves this because we don't think we have a choice and life would get pretty discouraging if we constantly felt we weren't okay because of something we didn't think we could change, but two wrongs don't make a right. It's not our fault that we were misled by the broken system over how much money we need and our ability to earn it, but that doesn't excuse lying to ourselves that growing old without sufficient financial cushion will be okay. And the fact that our friends and neighbors are telling themselves the same lie doesn't make it okay either, however much comfort we might derive from the commiseration. Always remember that just as misery loves company, so does financial unpreparedness. The hard truth is that while only a small percentage of people will be comfortable in the final quarter of their lives, almost all people will spend the last quarter of their lives with an awareness that something went off course and at some point they were misled about money. They will realize that they weren't told how the game really works and, as a result, never put themselves in a position to succeed. Tragically, by the time this awareness dawns for most people it seems too late to do anything about it. Usually that's not true, but it definitely gets harder the longer we wait. As we age, our energy wanes as do our physical and mental capabilities. And as we become less capable, and life gets harder in so many ways, the idea that we can still change the course of our life seems more improbable, even as we become more clear that we should. It's horrible and sad, so I completely understand why people don't want to be the messenger to millions that their ending isn't going to be a happy one unless they do something drastic. Hopefully they don't shoot the messenger.

Unfortunately, I know not everyone *will* reach the $10 million mark (or whatever the right number ends up being for each person), but I firmly believe two things: I believe that most people *can* achieve financial freedom *if* they follow the ideas prescribed in this book, and I also believe that doing what this book teaches now is most people's best shot at realizing the New Dream we discussed in the introduction. And regardless of whether or not you reach true financial freedom, I can guarantee you will be in much better financial shape if you follow what's in this book than if you don't.

Everyone starts from a different place, faces a different set of challenges, and has a different likelihood of hitting any specific target, but in the internet age, anyone who is of sound mind with a few years of vitality left in them can make millions of dollars if they learn how the new economy works. And yes I know that sounds like hype, but it's true. That's how much the world has changed and it's why I'm constantly talking about things like "new economy business" and digital real estate. It's not that I have some abiding passion for the internet or technology—personally, I find a lot of it to be kind of dystopian and weird. I would much rather meet a friend IRL (which means "in real life"—an abbreviation the necessity for which only proves my point) than in any chat room or metaverse cafe, but I want people to be happy and have the best shot at life transformation, and this is the world we live in, like it or not. For most people, rapidly increasing income is not going to be just an analog process. If the average person could generate amazing income and achieve their best quality-of-life life by weaving baskets, I would be an advocate for basket weaving. In fact, I'd probably prefer that over staring at computers all day, but I have not yet found a better way for the average person to rapidly generate income and build assets than with digital real estate. Every person trying to get from A to B financially needs some sort of "income vehicle," and when all such vehicles are compared it is the ones that have a digital backbone that offer unparalleled leverage, scalability, flexibility, automation, and overall quality of life for the owner. That's why I'm so passionate about online business and recommend it for most people.

The clock is ticking. None of us are getting any younger. It's time to get started. Learn the skills of the new digital economy. Get that training. Bring that idea to fruition. Make something. Create something. Build something. You have to start thinking of money the same way you do your health. It's not enough to have some of it. You have to keep working for more of it because what you have is constantly losing its value. Health and money have that in common, that if you don't take care of each of them, life will eventually make you pay the price. And the longer you wait, the higher the price will be when you pay it. Don't wait. Take action now—and start by answering one all-important question.

PART II

Laying the Foundation

4

What's the Point?

How many times have you heard someone ask, "What's the point of it all?" That question is usually asked in a moment of defeat, expressed as a sign of hopelessness. And when hope is abandoned, it usually reflects a lack of purpose.

In one of the most popular TED Talks of all time, author and motivational speaker Simon Sinek talks about his book *Start with Why*. Sinek explains how most people and businesses know **what** they're doing and **how** they do it, but very few actually know **why** they do it, their **purpose**. From modern psychology all the way back to the ancient Greeks, there have been countless insights into the importance of purpose and how it's a basic human need right up there with food, clothing, and shelter. The most famous behavioral model in psychology, Maslow's hierarchy of needs, teaches us that self-actualization is the final need of human beings once lower-level needs are met. The Oxford English Dictionary defines self-actualization as "the realization or fulfillment of one's talents and potentialities." Said another way, self-actualization is realizing and fulfilling the purpose for which you were created. That is the highest need of every human.

This isn't new to anyone. We all know that we need purpose; certainly no one thinks that a pointless existence is a compliment, but why do we struggle to find our purpose? For one, it's easy to be distracted from the search by a society that entices us with materialistic or superficial goals. These things can be fun, but we won't find true fulfillment in merely pursuing financial gain or social status. Money isn't the answer. Granted, I talk a lot about making money, but this can't be what drives you. If it is, you might become wealthy, but you will never become truly successful, and you certainly won't have a fulfilling life. I've been an entrepreneur for over twenty-five years, which is over half my life, and have been what most people would consider to be financially successful for about half of that, but it's only been in the last few years that I have found my purpose and, with it, true happiness.

Mark Twain said, *"The two most important days of your life are the day you are born and the day you find out why."* Having now found out why I was born and discovered my purpose I can see that true happiness would have been impossible until that second important day arrived.

And having now helped thousands of other people adjust the direction of their lives and move closer toward their purpose, I can report that in almost every case we usually haven't nailed our life's purpose until it includes other people. It's through other people that we develop true connectedness and meaning. Personally, I didn't find fulfillment until I had people to go to bat for. The more I view my work as going to bat for other people, and the more other people I go to bat for with my work, the more fulfilled I become and the more secure in my purpose. Incidentally, what I just said about *finding more other people to go to bat for* speaks to something I've recently become convinced of: taking care of your family, however great, is not a big enough purpose. I hear people all the time say they do what they do "for their family," they make sacrifices "for their family," they'd do anything "for their family." That's great, but it's not unique and it's not a higher purpose, that's just biological self-preservation. The world needs more than just billions of people doing what they do "for their family." The world needs people doing what they do for each other!

Hear me out on this. Family is a structure that evolved biologically and sociologically to perpetuate and develop the self, not to enslave the self. How many people lead lives of quiet desperation in the name of "breadwinning" or "feeding their family"? It is my belief that a truly fulfilling purpose must do three things.

1. It must honor our own unique greatness.
2. It must benefit humanity in some way.
3. It must be responsible to the people who depend on us.

The third item alone is not a purpose in and of itself, and plenty of history's lesser moments consisted of families, tribes, and clans doing horrible things in the name of their family.

And deep down, we know this, even if we try to cover it with bromides about family and why we do what we do. My vantage point as founder of ENTRE gives me a revealing perspective and I'll tell you straight up, family is not why people pursue their dreams. It would be funny if it wasn't sad, how often I see people strike out to pursue their entrepreneurial dreams "for their family," and then when they abandon their quest they do so, once again, "for their family," because they didn't have their family enrolled in the idea in the first place. It would have been more honest to say they wanted to pursue their dream "for fulfillment," or "for purpose," or "to avoid regret," and then use their family as extra fuel to not give up and make it work. I think sometimes those of us with families feel guilty for having a purpose beyond our family, but if it were wrong, we wouldn't be wired that way. I'm not saying that biological self-preservation isn't noble, but I am saying it's not enough for most people to achieve their purpose. I was a committed husband who "did everything for my family," but it wasn't until I discovered my passion for helping other people who I wasn't related to find their purpose and achieve success that everything in life clicked and I truly discovered why I was put on this planet.

Today, I am finally crystal clear on the point of it all, and it has made me better at every aspect of my life, including as a father and a husband. Once you clarify your purpose, not only will it help you meet your obligations, but it will help you enroll those around you in supporting that purpose. The skill of "enrollment" is one of the most essential skills for a leader, business owner, parent, spouse, and entrepreneur because you need to get others on board with what you're trying to accomplish. And since your purpose is yours alone, and won't necessarily inspire others, something else is needed, something that can align with others' purposes. You need a mission.

DO YOU HAVE A MISSION STATEMENT FOR THE WORK YOU DO IN THE WORLD?

I've coached hundreds of people, and I always ask them this question. Only once did a person ever have an answer that was theirs alone rather than the company they worked for. Most people don't think about crafting a mission statement beyond the mission statement of their employer. This is unfortunate. In my experience, the best employee isn't the one who slavishly adheres to their company's mission statement, it's the one whose personal mission also aligns with their company's mission. And that would be a lot easier to determine if everyone actually had their own mission statement for what they do in the world.

So let's talk about writing a mission statement for just ourselves—a singular statement that answers the question "What do I work toward in this world?" You can't win a battle if you don't know what you're fighting to achieve. If you don't have a mission, how can you succeed? For me, getting clear on my mission changed everything.

My personal mission statement is simple:

Demonstrating daily that we were created to pursue excellence and act with courage.

Meanwhile, ENTRE's (current) mission statement is this:

Enrolling 1 million active users to drive physical, personal, and professional growth through the ENTRE platform.

My life works so well because my "job" as the founder and public face of ENTRE is about helping people grow in all areas of life and create the lives they were destined for, which is perfectly aligned with my personal mission of "demonstrating daily that we were created to pursue excellence and act with courage." In fact, if you were to write a role description for the face of ENTRE it would basically be my personal mission statement. That's the type of congruence that allows you to do your best work—when your personal mission statement is perfectly aligned with your professional vocation. Every other one of my businesses has its own mission statement that is always congruent with my personal one; otherwise, the business wouldn't work for me and I wouldn't work for it. Being clear on what your personal mission is and making sure the work you do aligns with it is the key to feeling fulfilled in your work.

Many businesses have mission statements, but they use them merely for optics or, worse, as an implement of discipline when an employee needs a reprimand. I look at mission statements as an operational tool. These statements are filters. Anytime I'm asked a question or presented with a choice pertaining to a professional opportunity, I map it against the closest relevant mission statement—does this opportunity, client, invitation, product, or idea align with my mission or the mission of the relevant business? If so, I'm interested and will dig deeper. If not, I don't have the time for anything that's off mission. Nobody has the time to fully think everything through on the spot, so the mission statement becomes the ultimate heuristic for deciding whether to commit other resources to exploring an idea or cutting your losses. It allows you to take many of the decisions you're faced with and break them down to first principles. If you're anything like me this will have a far-reaching impact on your life—not just in business, but in your personal life as well. Many decisions you might have previously wasted time in making get very fast and easy, and also much of the daily fray of life just starts to seem less important. Living from a place of mission makes everything that isn't on mission trivial, and that in and of itself saves a ton of time and energy! Think how much time I save and how many mediocre ideas I dodge by rejecting anything from my daily life that isn't demonstrating that we were created to pursue excellence and act with courage.

So, how do you come up with your own mission statement? Start with these three tips.

Tip #1: The Rule of Sixteen

I learned this from a friend of mine in Hollywood. In film school, students are taught to have a pitch ready in case they ever find themselves in an elevator with a producer or studio executive. That might be the only shot they get, so they'd better be ready and not get tongue-tied. The trick is to keep the pitch tight—*sixteen words* or less. That's short enough so you can remember it under pressure, and so even a *sixteen-year-old* can grasp the concept. You don't have much time in that elevator, so you want to be able to have a conversation about it in *sixteen seconds*. You want to do the exact same thing with your mission statement—a statement that is sixteen words or less that can be understood by a sixteen-year-old and discussed clearly in sixteen seconds.

Tip #2: Start with a Gerund

Yes, we're going back to English class. Don't roll your eyes. I promise to make this quick and painless. A gerund is a word that is derived from a verb but functions as a noun. Think of a verb that you put an "ing" at the end of. Running, pushing, inspiring, leading, or in my personal case, demonstrating, or in ENTRE's case, enrolling. This makes the action the subject of your sentence. When you start your mission statement with a gerund, you start with action and pack it with power out of the gate—you "verb" your "noun," so to speak. You can see this with "Demonstrating daily that we were created to pursue excellence and act with courage." Every day I wake up, and it's not enough just to tell myself that courage and excellence are priorities. By the time I'm even thinking it I already need to be demonstrating it actively. Even lying in bed after my alarm goes off becomes hypocritical with a mission statement like that.

Tip #3: Make It All Encompassing

Although simple (Tip #1), your mission statement is not small. On the contrary, it needs to be big enough to cover everything you do in your life. You have to find that perfect blend of being broad enough to govern everything you do, but specific enough to instruct every action you take. This nuance is one of the hardest parts to get right, but it's worth taking the time to do so. A mission statement done well is a "small hinge" that swings all the huge doors in your life.

If it doesn't meet all three of these criteria, your mission statement won't serve its purpose as a quick and effective filter for all decision-making, and if it can't be that filter, it just ends up being what most company mission statements are: words that sound nice but lack impact and don't get obsessively applied. Take your time creating it. That's why I spent four hours rewriting mine, all thirteen words of it. I wrestled over every word until I got it just right. And when you get yours right, you'll know it because it clicks.

PUT YOUR MISSION OUT INTO THE WORLD

I'm nonnegotiable about this. It doesn't matter if it's personal or business: a mission statement needs to live and breathe. You have to share it. That means putting it in your email signature or on your company website or personal blog (or in your book). Let friends read it. Throw the daily decisions you face against it and see if it can sustain the weight and serve its purpose as the ultimate filter for every decision in your life. If you've done it right, with a little practice it will naturally assume that role in your life. It will create guidance for how you serve others and what you expect from the people around you.

If it's not right, go back to the drawing board. It might take a few hours to hone your statement, but the emotional energy you'll save in the long run will make it well worth your time. It's not easy. You have to earn clarity about what your mission is in this world. Clarity is power.

Speaking of clarity, let's talk about . . .

5

Seeing Into Your Future

I have been fortunate to get to know a gentleman named Dr. Alex Mehr. You may know who he is. He's a fairly well-known entrepreneur and a business partner of the very well-known entrepreneur Tai Lopez. I interviewed Alex on my podcast on September 21, 2020, almost two years to the day after I posted my "Let's Get Extreme" video, and he told me his story. Alex grew up in Iran and knew from the age of five that he wanted to become a NASA scientist. When he was twenty, he set out to make that dream a reality, but it first required getting to the United States, no small feat when starting out in Iran. There was no US embassy in Iran, so he would first have to travel to Turkey, but there were no flights between the two countries, so Alex and his friend set out on foot. Not only did he cross the Turkey–Iran border on foot, make it to an embassy, then to the United States, and then on to becoming a NASA scientist, but he also became a successful entrepreneur and owner of numerous businesses, one of which sold for $300 million.

Alex told me that everything noteworthy in your life happens three times. The first time, it happens in your mind. The second time, it happens in your life, and the third time, it happens in your perception of reality. However, before anything can happen, you first have to convince yourself that that thing is possible, and once you see what you are capable of achieving, it changes the way you look at life. No matter what you're trying to do, it all starts in your head with a clear vision. This is a modern restatement of what Napoleon Hill said in *Think and Grow Rich*: "Whatever your mind can conceive and believe, it can achieve."

I can personally attest to the power of visualization. I was sixteen when I first started to learn how to play the piano. I was very late to the game. So late that many people told me that I would never be able to become a professional because "you have to start playing when you are young" to develop the proper biomechanics. Fortunately, I always had a rebellious streak. If you told me no, I would prove to you that I could do it, so that's what I did. Plus, I had no desire to work a day job, so in my mind, I didn't have a choice.

Mike Lowe was the local teacher I hired to help get me ready to audition for music school at the University of Houston. Mike admitted that I was way behind. I was too old, and my musculoskeletal system too rigid as a postpubescent male to catch up quickly in terms of technique, but that didn't mean I couldn't work on other things to give myself an edge. He taught me that there was more to playing the piano than world-class virtuoso technique. The technique would come over time through repetition, but what mattered more, he said, was to experience the instrument as a communication device, a conduit for the language of music, because that is what makes a musician a true professional. And that, he said, could never be achieved through technique alone, so we got to work through other methods while my technique slowly caught up. We got to work through visualization—building a world in my mind where I played the piano, and still do to this day, better than I ever will in this world.

My visualizations went deep. I'd feel the creak of the bench I was sitting on, see the keys in my mind, even feel a tickle of dust in my nose if the soundboard hadn't been dusted in a while. I focused on learning to play the piano like I was a blind person—with sight and even the instrument itself optional. I practiced in my mind away from the piano just as much if not more than on the physical instrument. And it worked. In a couple of years I did what the college music faculty had told me I'd never be able to do. I got a full scholarship for jazz piano, became a professional musician by age twenty, got hired to play some really good gigs, and was one of the better working piano players in Houston. I did what they had told me was impossible, but more significantly, I learned a technique that would have a major impact on my life. Ten years later, $495,000 in debt, I'd utilize this same habit of visualization when sitting at a different keyboard, a computer keyboard, trying to succeed as an internet entrepreneur.

This isn't anything new. Elite athletes such as Michael Phelps, Cristiano Ronaldo, and Conor McGregor have all spoken publicly about the power of visualization. Michael Jordan talks about playing entire basketball games on "the hardwood of the mind." These athletes watch each race, play, or fight unfold in their heads. They see the obstacles and picture themselves not just overcoming them, but they go into even more detail to feel their heartbeats and take notice of the settings around them. They experience it all beforehand so that when it comes time to do it for real, they've been there before. Like Alex said, everything notable happens three times, and by the time other people know about it the first two times have come and gone.

LIVING THE DREAM

Visualization is a form of practice, and even if you aren't an athlete or trying to become a professional musician, you want to do the same thing. Why? Because if you don't clearly see where you're going or why you want to get there, it is harder to commit to the process deeply enough to achieve your dreams. And if you have no idea what you want your life to look like, you have no idea if the things you're doing are getting you where you want to go.

Being productive is not easy. The results may be appealing, but the daily grind to get those results can take its toll. That's why it requires a different level of discipline and focus. If you don't have a reason, and you don't know where you're going and why, there is very little stopping you from slipping back into old habits and doing everything you used to do that wasn't generating your desired results. If you want those results, you have to do things differently.

Mindset and mission are important, but no matter how focused your head is on your goal, your chance of success is minimal if your heart isn't in it as well. When I used to do one-on-one coaching with entrepreneurs, I would often talk about "heartset" as an essential counterpart to mindset. In simple terms, I describe the right mindset as a willingness to do what something takes, while heartset is a deep conviction that something should be done and is in alignment with our created purpose. Heartset is every bit as important as mindset because our heads aren't always in charge, nor should they be. Sometimes our heads follow our hearts, and other times our hearts follow our heads. If you don't have both in alignment, you'll probably be off course a good amount of the time. This is why vision is so important, and our heartset is ultimately the feeling we have about our vision of the world we are working toward.

To develop the right heartset, we have to paint a vivid picture, so take the time to lay out what it is that you truly want. Start by asking yourself one simple question:

> If money wasn't an issue, and your job was not in the equation, what would your perfect life look like?

That means you're financially secure enough to go anywhere in the world with anyone you want. There is no boss. You answer only to yourself. What would you do? Some people might call this daydreaming, but what I like to do is a little different. This practice is much more intentional and goes into much more detail. It's called *dreamscaping*. That's a term my business partner Adam taught me, and I love it. It reminds me of landscaping, but we're shaping and refining every detail of a dream to get it exactly the way we want it.

Try breaking the process down into a series of categories. Before you do this, disengage from your current situation—skepticism, self-doubt, and all—and take the leash off your imagination. Remember that nobody is going to see this but you, so take your time and be as honest and detailed as possible.

Your Dream Day

From the moment you wake up to the moment you go to bed, visualize what your perfect dream day would look like. Write it down.

- What would you do?
- Where would you go?
- Who would you see?
- What kind of food would you eat?

Get specific, right down to what you see, taste, smell, and hear.

Your Physical Body

- What about your physical appearance would you like to improve? Maybe six-pack abs, upper-body strength, bigger biceps, or a tighter butt. It's different for everyone, but picture your body at its physical peak and think about what you would need to achieve it. No shame or judgment allowed!
- What would help you along the way? Go beyond exercise if you think that's what it takes. Would it require liposuction, hair transplants, breast augmentation, mole removals, braces, teeth whitening?
- This is not meant to be negative, so don't be afraid to indulge yourself mentally if that's what you want. Would you enjoy a luxury spa session? How often would you go?

Remember: money and time are not factors. If you had the freedom to get your body in the exact condition you want it, what would you do?

Your Relationships

- Who are the most important people in your life? Make a list of everyone—spouse, children, relatives, friends, business partners—and now write up how those relationships could be improved. What would you like those relationships to be like?
- Next, go beyond the people in your immediate circle, and even the people you know, to include the people you want to be associated with, either personally or professionally—business tycoons, famous actors, professional athletes. If given a choice, who would you rub shoulders and spend your time with?

Your "Income Vehicle"

- What type of income vehicle would you like to have? Is it a business? A freelance career? A traditional job? Just remember this dreamscape has financial freedom as a precondition, so it would need to be an income vehicle with the potential to create that.

- How would this income vehicle operate? Would you have a fancy office with many employees, or would you work from home and do everything online?
- Would you travel the world? Would you lead seminars and speak to hundreds of people? Maybe you'd like to run everything from an exotic beach in another country? Write it all down.

Your Lifestyle

- What does your home look like? Do you have more than one? It's okay if you do. This is your dream, so you can do whatever you want. There are no wrong answers.
- Where would you live? Do you want a beach house, ski cabin, or a lake house?
- Do you have any staff working at your home to take care of the cleaning and landscaping? What about a personal chef or a fitness trainer?
- What types of clothes would you wear?
- What types of vehicles would you drive?
- What about toys? Boats, bikes, planes, guns, video games, and so on?
- What about hobbies? Do you want to play an instrument, learn to fly a plane, sail, collect comic books, or maybe compete in some kind of motorcycle or road race?

Your Experiences

- What are the top ten places you would like to visit?
- What would you do there? Take cooking classes in France? Paint in Italy? Sample beer in Ireland? Climb Everest? Hike the Appalachian Trail? Maybe a cross-country motorcycle trip?

Your Legacy

- What do you want to leave as a legacy for your family and future generations? Life insurance, real estate, stocks, businesses, and so on?
- What causes would you like to support? Church, homeless shelters, animal shelters, cancer research, women's health, disaster relief, mental health, and the like?

Don't rush this list. Take your time and get specific. Provide every detail and sensory perception. When you're done, look back over this list and notice how you feel about this exercise. You might find yourself feeling indulgent, selfish, or materialistic, but those feelings are valuable insights for you to realize that something in you is resisting the achievement of your own dreams. Use any such feelings to push yourself deeper into the exercise. Some of the things that give you the most joy and fulfillment might be the less obvious things that aren't expensive and that you can start doing immediately. Maybe you want to hire someone to help clean the house or the yard once a week. That won't cost a lot of money and might easily fit in your budget.

This process of dreamscaping is much different than daydreaming because it's not random. You're breaking down what you want into the most minute detail possible, so you notice everything going on around you. You're intentionally living your life in your mind as if you've already lived it. More significantly, you're becoming more aware of how you feel about the different elements of your dream (your heartset) so you know what to focus on going forward.

This exercise tunes a part of your brain called the reticular activating system (RAS) that determines what you notice consciously versus what passes by unnoticed. By feeding your minutely detailed dream into your conscious mind, you calibrate your RAS to be on the lookout for opportunities and clues that move you closer to your dream as you move through your daily life. In turn, this makes you more productive because you naturally start to prioritize doing the "right" things (those things that move you in the direction of your goals) because you are now more likely to notice those things to do. The RAS is the actual neuroscience behind Napoleon Hill and Alex Mehr's statements, and for that matter, much of what has been written on visualization across thousands of pieces of spiritual, religious, and metaphysical literature.

In practical terms it's really simple: develop a finely detailed dreamscape of your ideal life and then every day obsessively ask yourself if what you're doing is moving you closer to creating that ideal life. Discipline yourself to do at least one thing every day that gets you a little closer to living that perfect day than any previous day before. In ENTRE, we teach a daily living template called The ENTRE Day, where every day requires a "deposit" into each of the three main "bank accounts" of life—physical, personal, and professional. We call those the 3 Ps and we will discuss them later in more detail. I promise you that this sort of self-analysis will never stop paying dividends. It never gets old or goes out of style. I still do this today, and I will do it forever.

Here's the secret: no one ever achieves their perfect day. I'm never all the way there, nor will you ever be. I know there are things today that I could have done better, and that's okay, but I feel like I'm getting closer than I have in the past, and that's all that matters. It doesn't have to be perfect, but you want to continually inch closer. It can be difficult to make progress if your goals are broad and seem like they are out of your control. Dreamscaping is how you keep this concept from being too broad or fluffy by breaking the dream down into such specific elements they are always definite and actionable. Once you've done your dreamscape work, you can work toward achieving micro-wins on a daily basis. No win is too small to celebrate and the compounding of them is what drives progress.

One final thought: don't dismiss dreamscaping as just another "motivational exercise." Even though it can certainly do wonders for your motivation by clarifying the prize you are after, this is tactical training that if applied rewires the brain and changes what you notice in the world. It will help you condition the muscle of keeping your thoughts and intentions focused on the work you want to do and the life you want to create and shift your RAS from being a defense mechanism that resists change to an ally in creating your best life. Dreamscaping is a highly effective process that has made a huge difference in my life and in the lives of countless people I have worked with.

6

Getting the Right Help

I n one of the most famous "tough love" mentorship movies ever made, *The Karate Kid*, Mr. Miyagi takes "Daniel-San" under his wing, builds him up, and turns him into a champion, out of a spirit of benevolence and paying forward hard-earned life lessons. It's a heartwarming story about fatherhood, respect, and redemption. As a kid I loved it, as an adult . . . it seems totally far-fetched. This is not how real life works. There are not people sitting around waiting for a good cause to take on.

In today's world, you can't go out there expecting some benefactor to coach you to success just because they are a good person and want to help. That's more like charity, and expecting to find someone who will take a charitable interest in using their time and other resources to better your life is setting yourself up for disappointment. No offense but there are better charities they can donate their time to. It's not that successful people don't want to help or give back, it's that the people who have the most to teach you are typically the ones who have the most going on and the least time to spare. The things they have to do to sustain the life they live and have whatever impact they are having in the world are what attracted you to them in the first place.

The other reality is that there just aren't that many of those people out there. An unfortunate byproduct of the broken system is that there are many more unsuccessful people than successful people in this world. Consider my experience when I was an affiliate marketer. For the first three years that I did affiliate marketing full time, my name appeared consistently in one of the top three spots on the gross commissions leaderboard in a community of forty thousand affiliate marketing students. I would get dozens of messages a day from people wanting help. If I had even attempted to respond to each of them personally, I would have had no time left to do the work and no longer have been the person who people wanted help from in the first place. It was quite the conundrum, and ultimately, a lot of messages went unanswered. I'm sure there are people to this day who think I am a jerk for not responding to them.

So, if *Karate Kid*–style mentorship isn't realistic, what is? The dictionary definition of a mentor is a person experienced in a particular field or business who shares the benefits of that experience with a younger person who is up and coming. But I think that definition needs updating for the digital age. Given the way information is dispersed on the internet, I believe mentorship has evolved to mean finding someone you can work with directly or indirectly to improve your life, skills, or knowledge. They can be younger, older, someone you know, a stranger, an expert, or someone who's just learning. The idea is that the relationship is any that inspires you to grow and be better and where the other person has your genuine best interests at heart.

If you want to find direct mentorship, you have to make yourself the obvious choice to the direct mentor for their standards. Of all the mentorship opportunities available to them, are *you* where they are likely to have the most positive impact—not just *on* you, but *on* the world *through* you? It's a high standard, but there are steps you can take to attract those at the top of their field.

#1. Educate Yourself

What industry or area are you trying to develop yourself in? It may sound simple, but you'd be surprised by how many people begin their search for a mentor without even knowing what they want to do; they're just searching generically for someone to help them succeed. What skills would you like to acquire or grow? Maybe you don't know exactly yet, but write it down. The act of writing it down will help you focus your thoughts.

- **Books:** Read as many books as you can on the subject matter and profession you want to be in. One of the great things about this world is that if you are a smart person who succeeds, at some point, someone says, "You should write a book!" A lot of them do, and once they've written a book, they've provided you a portal into their brain. If you want to know how that person thinks, how they achieved their success, read their book. That is a version of being mentored, and it's taking place in a controlled environment, so you can reread the book, take notes, and even have discussions with others to see what they think.

- **Podcasts:** A lot of people who write great books also have podcasts out there that can serve the same exact purpose, only in serialized audio format.

- **YouTube:** Many of those same successful people also have a YouTube channel. It really depends on the nature of their content, but there are a lot of inspiring YouTubers who have a passion for mentoring others, so they pass along their knowledge in videos.

- **Live Conferences:** These are great resources, and some can even be life-changing experiences. Not only can you find content from a possible mentor, but also you can make friends with people who are on a similar journey as you. They can act as support, reinforcement, and encouragement for you and you for them.

- **Webinars:** If you're not familiar, picture a seminar happening over the internet, usually with a combination of people talking on screen and explaining with slides, often with a live chat component where a lot of the best interaction and Q&A happens. As with anything, there are good ones and bad ones. The bad ones will try to sell you something. The good ones will also try to sell you something, but will first offer a ton of value if you listen and learn. I can say as an absolute fact I have learned more skills that helped me succeed in the world from watching webinars that were trying to sell me something than I got from the years of traditional school I'd already paid for.

- **Online Courses:** Nothing has had a bigger impact on my life educationally than online courses, many that I bought through webinars.

In the world today, it makes so much more sense to learn at our own pace from people you know have been successful at what they're teaching and who have created course content in a way that's personal and free from a larger institutional agenda, unlike, say, a college course. Online courses usually have a more casual feel than other types of courses and you often get to know the instructor personally in a way that's very different from how college professors are taught to show up in their classes. There's a freedom and openness that tends to happen when instruction is virtual, independent, and prerecorded. I know this because I've created a lot of these courses and have also taught live in lecture halls, and the former has a completely different energy that's much more approachable. This creates an important secondary benefit I've observed with online courses. Often the students are as impacted, if not more, by their connection to the instructor than by the subject matter of the course. The main goal of education is inspiring confidence and self-direction, and I have heard people remark countless times that online courses helped them see themselves being successful with the material far more than traditional school ever did. In traditional school you know that nine times out of ten your instructor is not a real-world practitioner of the material they are teaching, whereas you would likely never take an online course from someone who had not been first successful doing what they were teaching.

#2. Surround Yourself with the Right People

The key is to get a feel for the world you're looking to operate in. That clarity is a great stepping-stone to figuring out what's good for you and how you will fit into the landscape. You want to think of mentorship like dating in that you have to be fishing in the right pond. If you're dating someone who doesn't have the same values and you aren't on the same page, the success of that relationship is limited. Start by looking closer at your own inner circle.

In all my experience training and observing people, many times the variable that leads to success is changing the people you hang out with to better match your own goals. Look at the three to five people you spend the most time with. What's their average level of success? If it's not at least as successful as you, you have a significant problem. Your surroundings, or the people you interact with, reflect back to you what you're comfortable accepting in your own life. So, if you're surrounded by people who are at a station you don't aspire to, you're telling yourself that you are comfortable where you are. If that sounds like you, you immediately want to change your environment and get yourself uncomfortable, because discomfort is where growth happens. You want to flip a switch and strive to be around people who are at a level you aspire to be at yourself.

#3. Know Your Goals

Where do you want to be in a year? What about ten years from now? Try to be as complete and specific as possible. If you have a strong mission statement, this should be a no-brainer. Too many people don't know where they're going, or they have a vague goal, like trying to be happy. That's not a bad thing, but I'd recommend picking a more specific target you can actually aim for. This is why we were so detailed in our dreamscaping exercise.

Take a hard look at yourself to figure out what you're looking for in a mentor. Too many people have a vague idea about mentorship, so even if they found good mentorship, they couldn't declare what they wanted from it. Some people have a traditional idea of mentorship in that they want ideas, insight, and direction, while others are just looking for inspiration and energy. If you're looking for the latter, call it what it is (more like coaching or even cheerleading), because it might change who you need to be around. If you're looking for someone to believe in you and encourage your efforts, you might find that from a family member or an educator.

Remember that just because a person is successful doesn't mean they will make a great one-on-one mentor. There are some brilliant people out there with amazing minds who just don't have the energy or the mentor mentality. With some people, you can read their books and learn everything they have to give. When considering a mentor, success and accomplishments are just two of the many variables.

#4. Offer Value for Value

The best way to stand out to a potential direct mentor is to impress them with your attitude and offer whatever you can in return for whatever you're asking for. You want to show up with a ton of energy, be of service, and bring value to the table however you can. Even if you don't think you have value to offer, muster whatever you can—they'll be impressed you aren't there asking for something for nothing. I can think of numerous times where this attitude got me in the door before any merit kept me in the room. Whether it was raising money from "angels" to build a text messaging platform, convincing the dean at University of Houston to allow a high school dropout into her university, or asking a famous inventor to produce a musical I wrote (a story you'll hear later), I always made sure that whoever I was approaching knew I was scrappy, hardworking, driven, and willing to add value for them in any possible way. I would be upfront about whatever I had to offer in exchange for whatever I was asking and let them know I was committed to leaving the exchange with a new friend if nothing else. These were successful people who didn't need or want anything from me, but they very much appreciated that I valued their time and wanted to give value back.

This sets up my favorite way to mentor people—through the process of working together. One of ENTRE's team members started working with me when he was still in college. I needed help editing the videos I had started putting out, and he was looking for part-time work. That was four years ago, and now he is a valuable full-time team member who has a budding career and has been promoted twice in the previous year. He recently sent me this note:

> Hey Jeff, just wanted to send you a little appreciation message. I'm really glad I have you in my corner and you have pushed me up the chain to where I am now. I feel like all of the learning I have been doing for the past few years is finally coming into play. I definitely wouldn't be where I am today without your help. I know we are more disconnected from each other in processes nowadays (naturally), but I know we both remember the beginnings.

The beginnings he is referring to was the first year we worked together when I actively mentored him. I did it because it felt good to do, and I had the opportunity to do it without sacrificing my own goals since he had valuable skills that aligned with my mission. Working together, with his skills supporting my objectives, created an environment for me to mentor him. That's often how one-to-one mentorship happens, so you can help yourself get into proximity with any person you want to learn from if you develop skills that are valuable to them (remember my story with Bob McNair as another example).

What's your skill set? What can you offer in exchange for mentorship? Are you good with computers? Can you design websites? Can you write? Can you sell? Sometimes all you have to be willing to do is run errands. If you don't feel like you have anything to exchange for the type of mentorship that can move you forward, that's on you, not the world. All of the indirect mentorship models I mentioned above (books, podcasts, YouTube channels, webinars, online courses) are also great ways to learn specific high-value skills. It's on you to develop skills and create value so you have more to offer in exchange for the guidance you want. Go back to the drawing board. Do what it takes to create value so you can offer value. Teach yourself how to do something, and make that the asset you can use to open doors.

#5. Call Out the Elephant in the Room

Not only are there fewer potential mentors out there than there are those looking for mentors, but as I've said those who you can learn the most from usually have the least time to give you. Successful people are busy. People who accrue wealth and assets constantly think about the relationship between time and money. Success is hard work, and between the time it takes to develop the skills for it, build the network for it, do the work of it, and rest and recover from it, time gets whittled down fast. When you talk to someone who is successful and who you know you can learn a lot from, they will likely be cordial at first, but be assured their internal clock is ticking. They know the value of their time, and they can't spend it all on you. As I'm writing this, I'm still smarting from an encounter last night at the front desk of a hotel where someone attending one of my own events tried to pin me down to do tech support on their computer. After about five seconds my internal alarm bells were blaring. I started to feel flushed and fidgety, and immediately began searching for a graceful exit. I'm sure it was the opposite response the person had hoped to elicit from me, but to be blunt that's what the wrong approach produces. Of course, I'm not that way with my kids or friends, and I derive so much joy from helping people, but the imbalance between those who are perceived to have the answers and those who are trying to get them forces a game to be played between those parties when a direct time swap is in question. And to play that game well you never want to be the one asking for something for nothing.

Like it or not, that's the reality of our world. For anything people strongly desire to have there will inevitably be more have-nots than haves. We can't choose to live in a different reality, so we need to find a way to thrive in this one. We must accept that the time of people who have what we want is more valuable than our time, and we can't take that personally. That's the elephant in the room. Instead of pretending it doesn't exist, call it out and get to the point. Ask them directly. For example, try saying, "I know your time is immensely valuable and you have many demands on it. Is there anything I can do or trade for X minutes of your time?"

The simple fact that you offered something in return and addressed the elephant in the room is likely to engage that person. The energy will change, and they will be more receptive, even if all you get is, "I have two minutes. Hit me with it." That's probably more than they give most people, and whatever you got, you got because you came off respectful and appreciative of whatever time they had to give you.

#6. Think Plural

Where does it say to have just one mentor? That's fairytale mentorship. The truth is that you'll likely have many mentors along the way, and they will come in all shapes and sizes. Incorporate everything you learn, and constantly look for ways to expand your circle and your network. There are a lot of resources out there, but here are three that will help you connect with and learn from like-minded people.

- **Facebook groups (or other social media groups, like Telegram or Discord groups):** These are free but can be extremely valuable. Getting started can be as simple as making a post and asking a question. See what happens in the comments and reach out to the person with the most informed answer. That can blossom into a mentor relationship or even just a collaboration. When you ask good questions, people reply, and great relationships can be formed. I've watched this happen in our ENTRE Facebook groups.

- **Membership programs:** Think of these like private Facebook groups. Typically, one or two figureheads lead the group, but all the members participate and contribute. The good ones typically have a recurring cost (monthly or yearly), so you know that everyone in the group is serious because everyone is investing money to be there. In ENTRE's small group coaching program, the pods that form are immensely valuable to everyone, and often collaborations and joint ventures emerge from like-minded people investing to be in proximity and sharing common interests in entrepreneurship, personal growth, and professional skills development.

- **Masterminds:** These programs can be more expensive than other types of membership programs, but they are invaluable. Masterminds are often hosted by one mentor and have a small, focused group of people who participate. Everyone in the mastermind contributes so you can get value from the entire group. Some of these programs are ongoing so they don't have to end. I've belonged to multiple, I lead one myself, and I definitely would not be where I am without them.

However you do it, it's essential to have a group of people you can get feedback and advice from. In ENTRE, we have a concept called the 3 Legs of Action, of which *environment* is one. *Environment* is a broad word but when it comes to proactively managing environment, most of that work is about people—which ones to draw closer to, which ones to distance from, and strategies for how to do both. No matter how steeled we think we are in our convictions we are energetically and psychologically vulnerable beings and will naturally absorb the attitudes, goals, and values of the people around us. You want to proactively seek people to be around that make you better when that happens. You can do that through one or more of the above methods, and just like dating, don't be afraid to play the field. It might take some trial and error before you find your place. There were periods of my life when I didn't have a direct personal mentor, but I had authors, speakers, and content creators to help me learn and grow.

One small note on these types of peer groups: in my experience, the quality of the group and the growth that occurs in it will usually correlate to how much people invest to be there. It's perfectly reasonable to start inside free groups, especially if you lack experience or are still deciding your own level of interest in whatever subject a group is organized around, but at whatever point you want to accelerate your growth in an area, it may mean investing to be a part of a higher-caliber group.

#7. Take Action

Mentors do what they do to impact others. They want to pay it forward and make a difference. I can say from experience it is highly disheartening when people receive advice and then never take action. If I am learning from the experience of someone else who gave blood, sweat, and tears to have that experience, I owe it to them to transfer the lessons from their experience into my own by taking action. If not, I not only wasted their time but potentially I cost someone else an opportunity because that mentor may be less likely to mentor another because I took no action. Failure to take action on knowledge is one of the world's great scourges that atrophies human potential and keeps the broken system chugging along.

Let's dig in to this for a moment. Oftentimes, when people don't take action, it's not necessarily out of laziness, fear, or other negative qualities. Sometimes a beginner at something gets so enthralled by the sensation of learning they spend all their time educating themselves and none of it applying what they're learning. That is pseudo-progress and I recommend an opposite approach, where the majority of our time and energy goes into action, whatever stage we're at, and our learning time fits into the cracks between our actions. If you find yourself spending much more time learning than taking action, look for ways to flip that.

My life changed in March 2009. I had discovered internet marketing a few months prior and started what would become my first really successful business, but I was frustrated, still struggling to get traction. In hindsight, it's obvious I just needed to stick with it and trust the process, but at the time, I was questioning myself and feeling very alone. Fortunately, I had done enough personal development to know that was probably a sign I needed to shake up my environment, get around other people, and find some new mentors. I attended a live training event in Lake Tahoe that cost $2,000 and was three days long, time and money I couldn't really spare but I knew I needed to invest. That's when everything changed. At that event I learned tactics and strategies and all sorts of great information related to the business I was trying to build, but more important was that the information had come directly from people who were successfully doing what I was trying to do. I gained a newfound confidence that came from being around real people I had much in common with who were getting results. There were even a few people I met whom I would later pester enough with offers of value and service that they took an interest in mentoring me. Shortly after, I started making decent money, was able to hire a coach, join my first mastermind, and a little over a year later, had paid off that $495,000 in debt.

One of my mentors from that time, a gentleman named John, drilled the importance of one simple practice into my head. It's so easy and often overlooked, yet it can instantly alter your mood, and profoundly change your experience of life and the results you get. John had been a manager at a Home Depot store when he had found internet marketing, started earning his previous annual salary each month, and completely shifted the direction of his life. I haven't talked to John in years but I can still hear him saying, "You don't get what you want, you get what you're grateful for." John was six-foot-seven with hands like a bear. I did what he said without much questioning, and following his advice gave me that much more to be grateful for.

7

The Subtle Art of Gratitude

I don't know if there is a more misunderstood but powerful tool you can implement in your life than gratitude. Gratitude is not just some new age cliché. Learning how to harness the benefits of gratitude is like releasing an energizing chemical in your body, the ripple effects of which can completely change the trajectory of your life.

In his book *365 Thank Yous*, John Kralik describes how he used gratitude to change his life at a time when he was at rock bottom. His law firm was failing, he was going through a divorce, he was losing touch with his children, he was overweight, and all the goals he'd set out to achieve when he was younger felt completely out of his reach. He then noticed how reading a simple thank you note from his ex-girlfriend altered something inside him. With nothing to lose, he decided to do something similar, but on a much larger scale. Every day, for an entire year, he would write someone a heartfelt thank you note. That meant he had to find 365 people in his life to reach out to, so he dug deep to track down people from his past. This wasn't like sending an email; he hand-wrote every single note. He made it a daily ritual, and slowly, it turned his life around, physically, personally, and professionally. The things that were broken in his life started to come back together.

When you make gratitude a daily practice, I can attest that you will experience this kind of power. But why do so many people find it hard to implement it, subconsciously ignore it, or flat out reject it?

WE ARE HARDWIRED TO BE UNGRATEFUL

Gratitude is something that's really easy to talk about, but it's significantly harder to make it a mental practice because our brains have a natural inclination to focus on negative things. As human beings, we tend to be cynical and pessimistic because anthropologically that is what has worked to keep us alive. As a species we have survived by assuming things are worse than they might actually be and living defensively. In an era when not getting killed or eaten was our primary concern that was good strategy, but it was hardly a formula for living in gratitude. In modern times it's essential to shed this tendency. Tony Robbins says it this way, that *"one of the key traits of successful people is their ability to see things only as good or bad as they are, but not worse!"*

There are two authors whose writings have illuminated this concept for me greatly and helped me overcome my own cynical tendencies.

#1. Hans Rosling

A Swedish physician and professor, Rosling wrote an excellent best-selling book titled *Factfulness: Ten Reasons We're Wrong about the World—and Why Things Are Better Than You Think*, in which he lays out the following ten human instincts that change the way we think about and interact with the world. I recommend taking the time to think of an example of how each of these shows up in your life.

- **Gap instinct:** We divide everything in two and assume there is a massive difference between the two extremes.
- **Negativity instinct:** This is our tendency to see the bad instead of the good or the glass as being half empty.
- **Straight-line instinct:** It's easy to assume that trends follow straight lines from A to B when every single trend curves.
- **Fear instinct:** We pay more attention to things that scare us.
- **Size instinct:** We have a tendency to misjudge proportion.

- **Generalization instinct:** We automatically categorize things, but that can be misleading because it's often done incorrectly.
- **Destiny instinct:** This is the assumption that things have and always will be the same for some immutable reasons.
- **Single-perspective instinct:** It's easy for us to look at things only from our perspective without considering other ways to do things.
- **Blame instinct:** We naturally look for scapegoats or a way to assume that others are the reason for our problems.
- **Urgency instinct:** Everyone is in a rush, so when we see a problem, we try to solve it immediately.

This is all pretty logical when we consider how we've evolved as a species. Take the emotion of fear, for example. For most of our history it wasn't just physical threats that could kill us. We also had to worry that if we didn't follow the social mores of our tribe, they might cast us out into the wilderness to die alone. Thankfully, in the modern world we are at low risk of being eaten or even dying from isolation, but our biological systems haven't adapted to modern times so we still react the same way even when the threat levels aren't nearly as high. And we can't count on evolution to eradicate our negativity bias, for while cynicism isn't much of a recipe for fulfillment, it will likely always contribute to biological survival. Take that time, for example, when I was dating my ex-wife and her parents told her she shouldn't marry me because I was an artist and would likely never amount to much. They were negative, they were biased, and though part of me wants to dismiss them as cynical curmudgeons, statistically, they were probably right. Their biological self-preservation instinct was trying to protect their offspring from choosing a weak mate. It was good advice from a survival standpoint that I cannot begrudge them (though I am proud to have proved them wrong).

The goal with these "cognitive distortions," as they are known in psychology, is not to dismiss them entirely but to develop a heightened awareness of them so we can refine them over time to align with our goals as opposed to our fears. It's natural and unavoidable to jump to conclusions—our subconscious minds will always work faster than our conscious minds—but ideally, we develop an internal mechanism for evaluating conclusions before acting on them. We'll never do away with instinct, and by its nature instinct will always be an anachronism and slightly out of place in the present, but I do believe we can train and modernize our biases. In fact, at a high level, that's what this entire book is about—retraining our affinity bias for a system that no longer serves most of us.

#2. Martin Seligman

Martin Seligman is a psychologist and author who since the 1990s has been a leading innovator and promoter in the field known as positive psychology, which is now a formal subdiscipline of psychology with its own certifications and practitioners. One of the most useful elements of his theories that I reference often is "the 3 Ps of Pessimism," also sometimes referred to as "the 3 Ps of Learned Helplessness." These are three errors in perception that influence the stories we tell ourselves and make things seem much worse than they are. Understanding them can make it much easier to be on guard against the negative effects of our own biases.

- **Permanence:** This is an error of time. We assume that because one or more things are bad right now, they will remain that way indefinitely.
- **Pervasiveness:** This is an error of size. We believe that if there is something in our life that's negative, it applies to all aspects of our life.
- **Personalization:** This is an error in assigning responsibility. We tend to think we are more to blame and responsible for fixing negative things that happen than we actually are.

Both of these authors helped me understand how, when left to its own devices, my subconscious will always resist gratitude and, therefore, a practice of gratitude will, much like a practice of fitness, always require work. Even as gratitude becomes conditioned, it will likely never become automatic. Biologically, it will always be easier and safer in the short term to be ungrateful, but unlocking our full potential demands that we transcend short-term survival instinct and play a longer game, one in which gratitude is essential.

START RIGHT NOW!

Before you move onto the next chapter, I want you to put the book down and take an immediate action of gratitude. Write a letter. Pick up the phone. Pay someone a visit. Whatever it is, make it heartfelt. Tell someone how you feel.

Identify those people in your life who you are the most grateful for and let them know it. For me, it's my wife and children first. I am constantly obsessing about making sure they know how much I appreciate them. I leave notes and messages they can wake up to in the morning, I intentionally buy them gifts when it isn't a holiday or birthday, and I try to make sure there are fresh flowers on my kitchen counter at all times so every time my wife walks in she is reminded how grateful I am for her.

If this is uncomfortable for you, dig deep to figure out why. What is it about unbounded expressions of appreciation that makes you uncomfortable? Don't judge yourself; just sit impartially on your own shoulder and watch yourself be you, taking notes. Studies show that gratitude has both genetic and neurological components and is harder for some than others, but, again, just like fitness, that is no excuse to not work at it every day. If you are willing to take the risk of practicing gratitude consistently and without expectation of reciprocation, you will be greatly rewarded. One article posted at PositivePsychology.com reported twenty-eight scientifically supported benefits of a regular gratitude practice across five different areas of life—emotional, social, personality, career, and health. Again, don't gloss over this section or dismiss it without actually doing it. Try out gratitude for a few days. See how you feel. Watch how it changes your posture, breathing, motivation, and drive.

And as gratitude becomes more natural and frequent for you, hold on tight. That is just the warm-up; now you're ready for "the shift." The shift is what happens once you start sliding down the slippery slope of positive growth this book is trying to engender for you. Gratitude is just the first step, a catalyst for becoming outward-focused and unburdening ourselves from the beliefs and patterns that keep our potential locked up. It is a series of changes that looks different for every person, but in hindsight will be a defined phase of our life when awareness was awakened and potential was unlocked. Life after the shift is fundamentally different than life before it. In the next section I'll document many components of the shift that I believe are common to all who go through it.

PART III

The Shift

8

Be, Do, Have—Revisited

I f you've watched any motivational videos or read self-improvement books, you've most likely heard of the phrase "be, do, have." I first heard it from Jim Rohn, and it was popularly recycled by Stephen Covey (author of *The 7 Habits of Highly Effective People*—a must-read, in my opinion). It is one of the core concepts in the modern personal-development world.

Simply put, "be, do, have" turns the way most people think ("have, do, be") on its head. Most people think that if they can just *have* the rewards of success, then they will *do* the things that successful people do, and they will then *be* successful, when in fact, it works the opposite. Take, for example, the person who thinks that if they *had* a fitter body, they would *do* more physical activities and *be* more social and outgoing. It's tempting to think this way, but you can easily see how it leads to stagnation and hopelessness. If flipped, however, a person might start *being* more social and outgoing, join a sports league or boot camp to *do* something physical, which will ultimately result in them *having* a fitter body.

This holds true across all major areas of life, personal and professional, and it doesn't matter where we're starting from. If we're broke, that doesn't mean we're broken, and we are never so far down that we are out. But we have to put things in the right order and start by *being* the person who *does* the things, so we can *have* the results. It never works the other way around.

There's another idea that's a close cousin of "be, do, have," and that is the power of thinking bigger (nod to another great book, *The Magic of Thinking Big* by David Schwartz). When we feel low, that's when thinking big matters the most. It might sound counterintuitive, but when it comes to what's possible for our life, we want to think at a level that seems unreasonably big for two reasons: nobody will dream bigger for us than we will dream for ourselves, and big dreams inspire us in ways that small dreams do not. They increase the likelihood we will take the level of action required to achieve anything worthwhile. It's counterintuitive, but the bigger the dream, the more likely we will achieve it because it's more likely to inspire us to do the work. To even imagine ourselves achieving a big dream, we have to change how we see ourselves (which catalyzes the *be* part of the equation).

One of the books that impacted me the most along my journey was *The 10X Rule* by Grant Cardone. In it, he proposes a radical idea that I have found to be profoundly useful when combined with be, do, have. Whatever you want—be it a problem to solve or a goal to achieve—multiply it by ten and then start being the person that solves *that* problem or hits *that* goal. For example, if you make $60,000 a year and your goal is to make $75,000, you could try being like a person that makes $75,000 a year, but that's probably not that different from being like a person who makes $60,000 a year. But if you start being like a person who makes $750,000 a year, you'll think, feel, and behave quite differently. A person who makes $750,000 a year speaks differently, walks differently, dresses differently, and has vastly different expectations of themselves and others than a person making $60,000 a year. So, *be* that person, the 10X person, and eventually you'll likely not only make that extra $15,000 but much more than that as your new behaviors convert into new results and a new impression of your value to the world around you. The added benefit of this approach is that it will divide the people around you too. Having coached hundreds of people through "be, do, have" transformation, I can report that there are likely two kinds of people in your environment, those who fully support your potential and those who tacitly long for you to stay who and where you are. Nothing flushes out your silent detractors like embracing the "be, do, have" mindset and showing up 10X for a few weeks.

This is exactly how I approached ENTRE in the beginning, and it had exactly the effect I'm reporting. I was a thirty-nine-year-old dad in a small town in southern Utah with no social media influence who wanted to help millions of people transform their lives and disrupt the educational system—a pretty big goal to start with, much less when multiplied times 10. So I had to ask myself, who would I need to be to pull this off and what would ten times the required level of effort look like? The answer involved adopting a set of behaviors very unusual for someone in my station. To many, it probably appeared like a midlife crisis when I went from being a quiet business owner, husband, and dad to an outspoken content creator who posts daily evangelism about a "broken system" and people "unlocking their potential." It seems natural now that a successful business has grown around it, but at first, I could feel varying degrees of skepticism from those around me. Even some who I knew agreed with me ideologically seemed very put off by my suddenly being so vocal and demonstrative. One person, someone who I was sure would be a big supporter, showed his true colors by suggesting that maybe I should "tone it down" so people didn't think I had "gone a little crazy."

Ah, there was that word . . . the most confusing word in the language. What is crazy, after all? Galileo was incarcerated as a lunatic and heretic for suggesting the earth was round and revolved around the sun. Steve Jobs, who famously said, "The people who are crazy enough to change the world are the ones who do," was labeled unreasonable and impractical many times in his career. Elon Musk, who perhaps embodies the intersection of 10X and "be, do, have" thinking as much as anyone alive today, was written off by many during the early days of Tesla and considered crazy for investing his $180 million proceeds from his PayPal exit into a gambit to disrupt both the automotive and energy industries, along with a side project to colonize Mars. The list goes on and on. History is full of people who thought bigger than the status quo, acted accordingly, and got dismissed until their accomplishments became too large to ignore. Why? Why are most of us so skeptical of this approach, *even* after we've been exposed to ideas like these and desire to start thinking and being different? There is more than one answer to that question, but one of the answers is a common trap I see, especially in people beginning to make these types of shifts. It's called . . .

THE PERCEPTION-PARALYSIS LOOP

This is the name I've given to a crippling trap that about 90 percent of the people I've consulted or coached run into. This happens when we want to put "be, do, have" into practice, but we don't believe we can because "have, do, be" is so deeply ingrained. We just can't imagine a person *being* before the *doing* is done and the *having* is had. At ENTRE we've helped thousands of students through this conundrum, and as part of our process we try to pinpoint when the resistance to "be, do, have" thinking sets in for most people. I won't claim we've documented the results with scientific rigor, but in talking to our several dozen advisors and coaches there seems to be a strong consensus that for most people the idea that we can steer our lives by how we show up in them starts to diminish around the time we finish high school, college, or whatever ends up being the highest level of formal schooling we attend. What seems to happen is that at that time in our lives we matriculate in our own minds from the *learning* phase of our life to the *doing* phase of our life, and thereafter, we are embarrassed to be seen as not already competent at the things we think we are supposed to be doing. Once our identity shifts from "student" to "adult" we start resisting situations that would result in learning because we don't want to be seen not already knowing things. This is absurd if you think about it (to avoid a learning experience because of embarrassment over not having previously had that learning experience), but nonetheless, as adults we are constantly measured by our competence so it makes sense we would want to hide gaps in our knowledge and avoid doing things we haven't successfully done before. Thus the perception-paralysis loop is when we are paralyzed by our own perception of ourselves as not competent or successful in a certain area, so we avoid doing the things we would need to start doing to become competent and successful in that area. It's a self-defeating loop that is a subset of what is often referred to in entrepreneurial circles as *imposter syndrome*, which is defined as "the persistent inability to believe that one's success is deserved or has been legitimately achieved as a result of one's own efforts or skills."

This is serious stuff and is one of the most inhibiting aspects of being a human being, so lest it come across as too abstract or theoretical, let's look at a hypothetical example of imposter syndrome driven by a perception-paralysis loop. For this example, let's create a character, Diane. Diane has decided to quit her job as a website developer and launch her own marketing agency.

Diane knows she has the technical skills to provide the relevant services but feels deep down that she lacks authority and gets especially nervous about creating promotional or "salesy" content because she doesn't have experience or tangible results from helping her own clients. Logically, Diane knows she won't get the experience or results without producing the content to attract a client, but the fear center in her brain (her amygdala) isn't responding to her logic.

The first step is recognition. Diane must identify the situation as a challenge that needs to be overcome, not a permanent condition. If Diane were my client I would advise doing what Mel Robbins describes in her book *The 5 Second Rule* and deal with the challenge *immediately*, every time, removing hesitation from the equation. Diane is wired just like the rest of us. Within five seconds of her impulse to take action on her new business idea, her internal monologue starts screaming at her about all the reasons why she shouldn't do it. In every such instance, time is of the essence and Diane must train herself to preempt her amygdala's objections by already having taken action within five seconds of the original impulse, before her objections can register. Momentum is a strong counterbalance to insecurity. If we're already in motion when insecurity attacks, it will often bounce off, but if we allow it the chance to strike while we're sitting still, we can end up feeling relieved that we hadn't moved in the first place. And that is the death trap for our potential—when insecurity starts to be experienced as validation for not having taken action.

So practically, what is Diane to do? One common solution I often hear taught in entrepreneurial coaching circles is to approach a potential client and offer to do something for free. In Diane's case she might offer to run some ads, do a website audit, or offer to produce a marketing video—anything that allows her to provide value and prove her abilities. The thinking goes that having done that she will have a case study and might feel more confident in producing content to sell her services. However, as I see it this approach doesn't address the real problem, which is the lack of confidence to sell her services and charge appropriately for her time in the first place. Giving services away does not build the confidence to sell yourself and anyone who thinks they can unlock their potential in this world without selling themselves to it hasn't even left the denial phase. If we want to *be* the person who can sell themselves, we must *do* the thing that person does (sell ourselves) so we can *have* what that person has (money from selling themselves). And this is not as hard as it sounds when we understand a basic fact of human nature.

Most people accept things at face value because it's impractical to live any other way. And this tendency is intensifying as we get more inundated with information. One of the reasons "fake news" is such a rampant issue in our society is because, according to a media survey by Zignal Labs, 86 percent of people do not fact check information, even if it contradicts their existing viewpoint. There is even discussion now in psychology circles of a condition called "technology-augmented autism" to describe how the way information is curated and tailored to the individual consumer causes us to lose our critical faculties. And while this may have horrifying implications for society as a whole, we can use it to our advantage when we understand it. I know firsthand that when you present yourself with authority, know what you're talking about, and keep the conversation focused on what you can do for the person listening, people will tend to find you credible. It may take a few repetitions, but eventually people start to trust what they see, which means you can influence what people trust by what you show them consistently. This phenomenon is how someone with no degree or formal credentials in the education industry gets traction as a thought leader in education and starts one of the most disruptive education companies in the world by just showing up consistently in people's feeds talking credibly about what needs to change. Now, to be clear, I'm not suggesting a "fake it 'til we make it" approach (ick, I've always hated that saying), but I am suggesting we learn to "be it 'til we see it." Of course we should be competent and knowledgeable and use the ability to shape perception for good purposes, but when it comes to being influential you probably don't need as much expertise as you think. From what I've observed, you just need to know a little more than the person you're speaking to about whatever you're speaking about *and be sincerely committed to helping them.*

In that spirit, I would advise Diane to consider an alternative approach to her situation, one that will feel less natural and a bit riskier. I would suggest she own her insecurity and lack of experience, get comfortable with the feeling of vulnerability it produces in her, and approach the market from that place. I would tell her to, without hesitation, pull out her phone, hit record, start speaking, and authentically put herself out there as someone deeply committed to helping her clients and who will more than make up for whatever experience she lacks by going the extra mile to deliver amazing results. I'd advise a pitch like this:

> Unlike veteran agencies that have dozens of clients they spend a few hours a week on, I, Diane, will be entirely invested in your outcome. You will be my first client and the results I get for you will be more than just results for your business, they will be results for my business and proof that going out on my own was the right move. You can be sure I will get results for your business because I am betting my entire career on it. In fact, I am so committed to overdelivering for you as my first client that I am not recording any other ads for my agency until I deliver for you, because my next ad is going to include a testimonial from you about how incredible it was to work with me. Marketing is about two things: competence and care. Hop on the phone with me and my competence will be obvious, but how much a person cares, that's harder to judge. So ask yourself, who cares more, the been-there-done-that marketing agency that adds you to their long list of clients or the brand-new agency owner who views your satisfaction as her entire future livelihood? I'm not gonna BS you and pretend I have hundreds of satisfied customers. The opportunity here is the exact opposite of that—this is a rare opportunity to get 100 percent of the attention of a high-caliber marketing professional whose time and care isn't already divided among a list of clients and whose singular obsession is providing you results you can't help but rave about. Call now for your free initial consultation. Whoever does will be glad they did, and whoever waits will only be able to hire me in the future at a higher price and with less dedicated attention.

Obviously not every prospect would go for that pitch. Some businesses would insist on working with someone with experience. But the right client would go for it, Diane would end up with the client she can learn from and grow with, and the relationship will have kicked off with the unique brand of trust that is created when people appear confident from a place of honest vulnerability.

It really is that simple. When I first had the idea to start ENTRE, I was terrified to start making videos and a lot of the early videos talked openly about how nervous and uncomfortable I was. Typically I would have an idea for something to talk about and then (within five seconds) whip my phone out, hit record, and start by saying something like "Hey, Jeff here, once again wondering what the heck I'm doing and when the butterflies are going to find another stomach to inhabit . . ." But after a while, as people realized that I was so committed to what I was doing that I was willing to weather consistent discomfort to do it, it built trust with the audience and the nerves dissipated. What started as shooting campy videos on my phone grew into a massive business because I pushed through imposter syndrome, refused to get caught in a perception-paralysis loop, and combined 10X thinking with a "be, do, have" approach to *act as if* I was a confident authority who believed he could start a movement that would impact millions of people and disrupt education long before there were any results to support such a "crazy" idea.

When we encounter confidence wrapped inside honest vulnerability it has a gravitational quality that draws us in. We see a person standing in their fear while simultaneously acting in spite of it, and we cheer internally because it connects us vicariously with our own potential for heroism. This in turn has the potential to influence how others see that person and even how that person sees themselves because, as we all know, beliefs are highly contagious. This is a huge life hack because it gives us a simple four-step formula for developing belief in ourselves in areas where we might not already have it.

- **Step 1:** Publicly acknowledge our fears in the area of our insecurity.
- **Step 2:** Take action publicly in spite of said fears.
- **Step 3:** Become trusted by others for having taken action even when they know we were afraid.
- **Step 4:** Learn to trust ourselves as we see others trusting us.

It's a tongue twister of a formula—to build trust in ourselves by doing what we openly do not trust ourselves to do so others will trust us for having done it despite our mistrust of self and thus influence us to be more trusting of self. But it works and the fact that it works reveals one of the great cheat codes of life. Though we are often unable to change how we feel about ourselves with consistent action, we can change how others feel about us, which can, in turn, change how we feel about ourselves.

Cool, right? But what about the person who thinks that all sounds nice but is still too paralyzed to take the required actions to change the course of their life? I know from experience that everyone has a different relationship with fear and for some it is insurmountable no matter what logic is applied to it. So what would I say to that person? Well, I would say that you are who you are, so rather than try to change it, let's make overcoming fear someone else's problem. What if you had a friend you could hand this off to, someone who wasn't afraid who could take the action for you? Yes, that's it, let's make a friend or, more accurately, let's create a friend.

CREATE YOUR SUCCESS CHARACTER

A couple years ago some very successful friends of mine reached out to me for advice about just this issue. They were starting a new division of their business that required them to create social media content and had seen what I had done to start ENTRE. Intellectually they knew it was the right approach, but their damn amygdalae were not cooperating. They knew what they wanted to say and it sounded great when they rehearsed, but as soon as the red recording light on their camera turned on, they froze, everything they'd prepared went out the window, and they retreated into doubts they knew were logically unfounded.

Bear in mind: these are extremely successful friends of mine (a husband and wife) who are smart, attractive, make millions of dollars a year from their business, and are recognized experts in their field. If anyone *should* have felt confident, it was them, a fact they knew and which only exacerbated their frustration. Fortunately, they called the right person, and after a half hour of explaining the Success Character concept to them and walking through a few practice exercises, they were well on their way. To this day, I see their ads and content in my social media feeds all the time and they are naturals now. You'd never know they were nervous wrecks when they started and once called me on the verge of throwing in the towel.

Whether it's watching what we eat, going to the gym, starting a business, shooting videos, or doing anything else that might be out of our comfort zone, conventional wisdom teaches us to "just do it." Power through, right? Just put your head down, work hard, stretch your boundaries, and you will persevere. And that can work for a time and to a point, but eventually we seem to run out of gas whenever we're having to "power through." The problem stems from using our conscious mind (willpower) to try to override our subconscious mind when our subconscious mind is a lot more powerful and we will wear ourselves out trying to wrestle with it. I've heard the idea of our conscious mind trying to control our subconscious be likened to a ninety-pound jockey trying to steer an elephant and I think it's a pretty apt analogy. If we are having panic when the record light comes on, maybe we can force ourselves to muster a good take or two, but eventually our performance will degrade as our reservoir of willpower depletes and we get exhausted. Once again, we find that *fake it 'til we make it* is a fallacy and instead we're going to *be it 'til we see it.*

In my teens and early twenties, I was socially awkward and had trouble communicating with other people. I am naturally an introvert, which was one reason why becoming a musician appealed to me. Music allowed me an outlet to connect with people without having to make actual conversation, and there was a comfort to hiding behind an instrument. I remember often looking out at the audience on piano gigs and feeling relief that they were looking at my hands and not my face. For years I ignored advice that I could get paid more if I would sing because I thought I looked so dumb when I did. Outside of music, I struggled to do many of the things I wanted to and would often sabotage opportunities by showing up late, disorganized, or disheveled. I was always an astute student of success and took copious notes from all the mentors I came across, but year after year, business after business, I kept failing, which only reinforced my deepest insecurities. Even in my late twenties, after years as a working musician who people assumed was a natural performer, I still constantly vacillated between who I wanted to be, the extrovert who would walk up to billionaires and ask them for success tips, and who I deep down knew I was, an awkward kid who shied away from social situations and was really only comfortable when he had a piano to play. The exhaustion of being constantly at odds with myself was bad, but the real torment was a creeping realization that my repeated failures were actually a pattern of self-sabotage to make sure I never ended up in a situation where my true nature as an awkward introvert would be impossible to hide (or hide from). Thankfully, in 2009 at that Lake Tahoe event, I stumbled upon the concept of a Success Character, and not surprisingly my run of success began only a couple months later.

So there I was at that online marketing event I had spent my last $2,000 on when I wandered backstage and found myself standing with a group of some of the best digital marketers in the world. The digital marketing industry hadn't yet matured, and unlike today, the idea of "kitchen-table millionaires" making money living a "laptop lifestyle" sounded impossibly far-fetched to most people. But there were people already doing those things and that's the group who I met at this event. At first, it seemed like they had magical powers (like alchemists who had turned their laptops into ATMs), but the more I observed them, the more I realized that they were just regular people like me, almost eerily regular, if that's a thing. In fact, this particular group sounded like a setup for a joke—you know, haven't you heard the one about the muffler sales-man, the nightclub bouncer, the personal trainer, the mortgage broker, and the amateur bodybuilder? That's the real description of who this group was, or who they had been before they went through their *shifts*.

Whether it had been going broke, falling ill, or finding themselves stuck in a dysfunctional marriage, this was a group of people whose turnaround sto-ries all shared a common antecedent—the discomfort of staying stuck in their old lives had overwhelmed the discomfort of making a change, so they had each done what I was trying to do and reinvented themselves. And just like I would go on to do, they had done so with digital marketing as the vehicle, generating income over the internet and experiencing unique lifestyle perks that go way beyond simply having lot of money and are generally reserved for either online business owners or ultrawealthy investors. This group lived where they wanted, hung out with who they wanted, got to be their own boss, rarely had to do things they didn't want to do, and had plenty of money to do the things they did. Standing next to them I was initially awestruck and, doing what comes naturally when we meet people who have achieved goals we doubt our own ability to achieve, I was focusing on how different they surely were than me and scanning them suspiciously for evidence of those differences. Then a casual observation changed my entire life: at six feet tall, I was taller than each of them. This group of titans that loomed so large in my mind was a group of average height males, while I am a slightly above average height male. This trivial realization humanized them, and in a moment, I real-ized there were no special advantages to be found; the only difference between this group and me was decisions made and actions taken. And to prove it to myself, I was going to make friends with them. But despite my epiphany and the ebbing of fear that should have resulted, my feet were staying planted and my jaw still felt locked.

It was frustrating. Why couldn't I just go right up and talk to them? After all, I had casually talked to billionaires when I played at their houses, and this group didn't contain any billionaires that I knew of. In hindsight I can now see the difference in the situations. At the time I was chatting with billionaires I did not reasonably entertain the idea that I could someday become a billionaire, which made it subconsciously safe to learn from them without jeopardizing my personal status quo. But this group was a genuine threat to my comfort zone. They proved what was possible for me and I could instinctively sense that proximity to this group would debunk excuses, eliminate hiding places, and convict me for my failings to date.

I was torn. I felt myself wanting to walk away but I also knew this was a once-in-a-lifetime opportunity to invite change in my own life by creating new relationships that opened up new possibilities. And besides, I was taller than they were! If I could just figure out how to break the ice. Then it hit me. I had taken acting in college and remembered how freeing it was to be in character. So, quickly in my mind I did a "Stanislavski method" makeover on myself and conjured up a character that was much braver and more socially adept than me. I gave him the best fictional "motivation" and backstory I could come up with on a moment's notice, including an alcoholic father he was ashamed of so he had learned to be light and jovial in his social dealings to mask his pain (admittedly, yes, it's dark, but it worked in a pinch). I even gave him a pseudonym, though I honestly can't remember what it was. Then that person walked up to that group and introduced himself (as Jeff Lerner, so the fake-named character used a fake name that was actually my real name). For twenty minutes or so the conversation flowed naturally, and by the end I was invited to a VIP dinner with that group and others that evening. By night's end I had built the beginnings of relationships that have since led to countless lessons learned, half a dozen businesses started, millions of dollars made, and some of my closest friends.

And that's how I discovered my Success Character. I've gotten smoother about the whole process, and my backstories aren't as oddly specific or morbid, but it still pretty much works the same way. Whenever Jeff Lerner needs to do something he would naturally be scared to do, he just calls up his Success Character, tweaks him for the moment, steps in, does what needs to be done, and then steps back out.

I will admit that at first I harbored some concerns about this approach. I worried that maybe I was "faking it," and I didn't want to be inauthentic or phony. But eventually I realized this approach wasn't about pushing myself to be someone I was not; after all I was the one creating the character so it must be in me already. My Success Character was allowing me to remove psychological blocks that keep me from being my authentic self. When I think back to early childhood, I was not born scared and insecure, and I suspect few, if any of us, were. We get made that way through experiences that we do not choose for ourselves and that are not intrinsic to who we are, but the subconscious, once trained, is very stubborn and does not relinquish its conditioning easily. So we can trick it into lowering its defenses by reducing the required actions for success to lines and blocking in a script played by a character we write for ourselves.

It's kind of like telling a really involved joke. Have you ever gotten really caught up in telling a joke? You're in character, in the moment, controlling the energy of the delivery, bringing the joke protagonist's feelings to life, reading the cues of the listener, and generally being much less self-conscious than usual. Joke telling is one of the times in life most of us become fully ourselves by "not being ourselves." In that situation we're just having fun and letting a less-inhibited part of ourselves lead for a minute. Telling a joke isn't inauthentic or "faking it." Humor just gives us permission to not take ourselves so seriously and removes the heaviness of "being ourselves" that some of us can't seem to get out from under.

Years later, I now know that none of this is new. This idea is commonplace among performers and celebrities. Some go so far as to give their characters different names—for example Beyonce stepping onstage as Sasha Fierce or Marshall Bruce Mathers III becoming Eminem aka Slim Shady. Some will give it a dark twist like Bo Jackson, who used to see himself as Jason (the hockey mask–wearing serial murderer from the Friday the 13th movies) before he walked on a football field. But this is not a technique reserved just for performers and athletes, and while it's been popularized recently by modern proponents like Tim Grover (private trainer to "Black Mamba" Kobe Bryant) and Todd Herman (whose work on the "Alter Ego Effect" I am a huge fan of), it actually connects all the way back to Freud and his concepts of the id, ego, and superego that became the foundation of modern personality theory. If you're not familiar, here's a quick primer. The id is our basic animal instinct, the part of us that wants to eat until we are stuffed, take what isn't ours, have sex with people we shouldn't, and generally disregard all aspects of the social contract that defines human society. On the opposite end of the spectrum is our superego, a refined level of identity that we assemble based on combining those whom we respect the most (our ego ideals) and society and parental expectations. The superego begins forming during our first five years and is both a powerful influence on our personality throughout our life and an expression of our potential. It not only already possesses all the traits we admire in others but has worked out in advance what it would look like to put those traits into practice in our own lives. Unfortunately, instead of enthusiastically inviting this to happen, we spend most of our time arguing with the superego and telling it to stay in the passenger seat of our lives. And who's doing the arguing? The ego, the moderator, the "voice of reason," telling us not to let either the id or the superego get too in charge because life might get unpredictable. Better to settle for the devil we know, right?

It's not a perfect analogy in psychoanalytic terms, but you can get pretty far just thinking of your superego as a prefabricated Success Character, a part waiting to be played or even a suit waiting to be stepped into. It already exists, it's composed of those traits you admire the most, it's everything you want to be, and it's already inside you, waiting to be expressed. The problem is that our ego evolved as a mechanism for protecting our identity, which for most of human history was important because our survival in our tribe or village depended on our role (our identity) in that tribe or village. If the medicine man woke up one day and decided he was going to be the midwife he'd be deemed unfit to be either and probably rejected from the tribe and left to die alone. But for most of us now, "identity" isn't life or death, and as products of a broken system that's designed to shove us into categories, most of us have identities that feel as much like a cage as any sort of real self-expression. And our egos are the guards that keep us in the cage by convincing us the door is locked or that life outside the cage is too dangerous. But the ego is a liar, willing to deceive us to keep us what it perceives as safe, so it has to be thrown off the scent of our own potential. By allowing the superego to express itself as a "character," rather than a replacement identity, we remove the threat to the ego and keep it from interfering. It's a subtle trick that requires practice to make smooth and automatic, but over time the switch into Success Character can become as easy as flipping a light switch. And the more we flip into it and show our ego it is not a threat but rather an asset, the lines start to blur and our ego starts to merge with our Success Character. Eventually, slipping into character becomes as simple as smiling, an easy choice we can make any time that we know changes how we feel and how we appear to others.

I've been the guinea pig on this now for over a decade and I can report that after years of stepping into character on a regular basis, I am not remotely the same person I used to be. Sure, the "old me" is still in there with his social anxiety and lazy tendencies, tempting me to settle in life, be disorganized, act miserable in the morning, stay up too late, procrastinate, and be a taker not a giver, but fortunately, I have practiced being the better version of myself so much now that I've largely forgotten how not to be in character.

Thanks to experiencing years of positive reinforcement that good things happen when I live up to my potential, my ego now fully trusts my Success Character to run my life and has stopped interfering. But I must remain vigilant. This is why I'm such a creature of habit and ritual. Every weekday I wake up at 3:30 a.m. and have a very specific routine. I brush my teeth in the same pattern every day, counting strokes always in the same order (yep, it's pretty nuts), and then I get dressed, take my first vitamins of the day, prepare my coffee in my favorite mug (to be drunk after my workout), and get in the car by 4:00 a.m. It's when I get in the car that I feel *the shift* happen. Like Clark Kent stepping into his phone booth I'm now in character for the rest of the day. By 4:10, I'm at the gym. By 5:25, I'm practicing piano, and by 6:45, I'm back home, picking my oldest daughter up for breakfast and then school. My Success Character is very disciplined, and by 8:00 a.m., I've accomplished more than the old me sometimes used to do in an entire day.

Granted, that character of mine is a little out of his mind by some people's estimations, but I can't argue with his results. He's created a life far beyond what "the real Jeff Lerner" could have ever reasonably expected. There's no way I could have done all this without him, and frankly, it's been pretty fun to be a passenger along for the ride waiting to see what my Success Character is going to do next. I have a life beyond my wildest imaginings today because my Success Character built it for me.

It may sound a little "woo woo," but don't knock it until you try it! Think of your Success Character as a ride-along with a better version of yourself who has been patiently waiting his or her turn and who you're finally letting drive. Instead of pushing yourself and relying on willpower to "be something you're not," let your superego be exactly what it is, and treat the whole experiment as an act so your ego stays out of the way. Do this for one day, and you'll have some fun. Do it for a year, and it will transform your life.

So, now that you know how to access the best version of yourself, let's talk about what that person is worth. Seriously, how much is an hour of your Success Character's time really worth? Here's a hint: far more than you may realize, but you will have to get clear on your worth before you will ever have a chance at earning it. One thing you can bank on is that the world will never pay you more than you believe yourself to be worth.

9

Time Is Money, But How Much?

Once back home from Lake Tahoe, with some new friends and my Success Character starting to call the shots, I did something that stretched me way outside my comfort zone that I never would have done prior to that event. I went on camera and made what at the time was a bold and arguably ridiculous declaration about the value of my time (which I pegged at $1,000 per hour). Then I immediately and without hesitation posted it to YouTube for all the world to see. In came the comments, and as you might expect they were pretty unkind. I admit I did not look the part of someone who was worth $1,000 an hour, and people seemed strangely offended that some guy on the internet was declaring that moving forward that would be his worth in the world. Frankly, considering I was living at my soon-to-be ex-wife's parents' house after having been evicted, I can understand people's incredulity (though I'll never make sense of their vitriol). I still watch that video sometimes (though it is now unpublished on a private link), and looking back I'm glad to have evidence of the pasty, overweight, unkempt version of myself talking his crazy talk and declaring to the world how valuable he intended to become. If anything proves the truth of much of what's in this book, it is that video of my thirty-year-old self, who at that point had failed at nearly a dozen consecutive ventures while succeeding at none, boldly declaring to the world a new hourly value for his time of $1,000 an hour.

At that time, there was no actual way I was going to earn that from anyone, but it still had a powerfully positive effect as I found myself no longer willing to do things that did not compensate me accordingly. And because at that time nothing compensated me accordingly, that basically meant I stopped doing everything I had been doing. This created space I could fill with new activities based entirely on what was most likely to propel me toward a life where I could actually get paid that much for my time. It was a total reset and, holy crap, it worked!

Outside of family, and maybe a few real friends if we're lucky, most of our relationships in the world are transactional, which means there is a value placed on them that correlates to time. Our mom may want to hang out with us all the time, but most people won't beyond a certain point. And the hourly rate at which we're compensated for all time spent working pretty accurately expresses how valuable the world perceives a time-based transaction with us to be. Once the market deems you worth a certain amount, it will pay you that amount over and over. If you want to be worth more, you just have to convince the market of your adjusted worth *in overwhelming fashion*. That's what I started doing, and a big part of the reason it worked is because by refusing to do anything that didn't meet my new standard, I eliminated all evidence to the contrary. People could tell me I wasn't worth that much, but they couldn't prove it because I refused to do anything professionally for any less. Of course, that meant for a time I had no work at all, but there was still something so powerful about allowing space only for activities worth what I had determined the value of my time to be, and eliminating those commitments that didn't align.

Time is the most precious resource we will ever have—the only thing it is impossible to make more of—and yet most of us so freely trade it away for a depreciating asset that is easy to make more of. The first step to getting more done with the time we do have is by deciding what our time will be worth and refusing to let anyone else dictate it ever again. Imagine for just a moment that you valued your own time at $1,000 an hour. How many things that you're currently doing would you stop doing because of what it costs you financially? Your perspective would dramatically shift. Instead of *earning* $20 an hour, for example, you'll experience that as *losing* $980 an hour. Until you make this mental shift, you probably won't ever realize how many things you sign up for or agree to that you wouldn't think of doing if you held your time to a higher standard.

Ultimately, this is just a thought experiment. It isn't even about money as much as it is about priorities. If you look at the time in your day as gold dust in an hourglass depleting by the second, you can't help but approach what you do differently. One of my favorite sayings is "good is the enemy of great," which is the name of a book by Kurt Reece-Peeplez, but which I took from *Good to Great* by Jim Collins. It is such a liberating concept when we realize that so much of what holds us back in life is not bad things that happen to us, but *good* things that we accept as being as good as things get, when they could be better. I don't do it much anymore, but I used to coach online entrepreneurs a lot, and after working one-on-one with hundreds of people, I can say with absolute certainty that for most people it is the *good* stuff that is crowding out their potential for *greatness*. Putting an accurate value on your time is the first step in opening yourself up so you won't be tempted to settle for *good* when you could achieve something *great*.

After making that video, I got fanatical about auditing my life. If something wasn't worth the value of my time, I didn't do it. I started by cutting out every small item I could. I changed my frequency of meals and stopped snacking between them. I started getting up earlier. I stopped having conversations with people about things that didn't move me in the direction of my goals. The fanaticism bled into every single thing I did. There was literally a point where I tried not showering for a few days because it didn't feel like a good use of my time. Fortunately for the world, I did decide that feeling clammy and covered in germs would ultimately cost me more than the time I was saving, so I abandoned that part of the experiment, but you get the idea. I became obsessed with reaching the point where the market valued my time the same way I did.

You don't necessarily have to take it as far as I did, but take it as far as you can. What's most important is that you can change the way you think about the value of your time because that will intrinsically find its way into every single thing you do. And let me state the obvious: this isn't some woo-woo thing where you throw this out to the universe and the universe sends you back money, and it doesn't mean that you're suddenly going to make $1,000 an hour for everything you do. It actually took me a couple years to reach that mark. The point is to change your mindset around your own value so your level of discomfort with your current use of time increases. Remember: nothing will change until the pain of staying the same is greater than the pain of changing. Walking around frustrated every minute of the day because you are being undervalued (for example, feeling *"I'm losing $980 per hour"* rather than *"I'm earning $20 per hour"*) is a good way to ratchet up your frustration (i.e., your pain) and motivate yourself to make a change.

Over a decade after making that outrageous declaration, I can honestly say that, between consulting, speaking gigs, investments, and my businesses, I am paid well over $1,000 an hour for every hour I work. And I can say with absolute conviction that I owe that present reality in large part to my thirty-year-old self who was willing to make such an "unrealistic" declaration and be ridiculed for it. A life less ordinary has to start somewhere, and when you're down and out, it's as good a time as any to become unreasonably optimistic. Optimism, as you're about to discover, is a true superpower and a nonnegotiable component of achieving outlier success.

10

Don't Wish It Were Easier, Wish You Were Better

D*on't wish it were easier; wish you were better.*" Jim Rohn said that. It's possibly my favorite quote of all time, and if you scroll all the way back to my first post on Instagram, it's what you'll find (posted September 25, 2018, when I started the content campaign that grew into ENTRE). This quote reminds us to "embrace the suck" (as the Navy SEALs say) and look at every challenge as an opportunity to grow. As we've discussed, most people don't like being bad at things, but a willingness to be bad at things is a prerequisite for getting better at them. Life takes on a very different feel when we look at every occurrence asking, "How can this help me improve?"

We're all going through stuff. Problems are unavoidable. People disappoint, devices break, technology fails, plans fall through. Wait long enough and someone will be mean to you, probably more than one person and probably more than once. Life doesn't go as we expect. Much of that is out of our control, but the one thing we can control is how we react to those unavoidable problems. The trick is learning to find the good in the bad and reframing *problems* as *challenges* to be overcome. That one semantic swap of "challenges" for "problems" can change your whole life. We naturally look at challenges differently than we do problems. Challenges motivate us. Challenges make us want to strategize. Challenges get us excited. Challenges force us to dig deep and figure out how we can become better to overcome our shortcomings. At the time I'm writing this I am preparing to host a "5-Day Dream Business Challenge" online. Sounds exciting, right? Certainly, it sounds a lot more exciting than a "5-Day Dream Business Problem." No one would sign up for the latter, yet so often in our own lives that's exactly what we do.

The next time you're faced with a problem, here is a process for turning it instead into a conquerable challenge. At the very least this approach will help you get clear on the most important aspect of problem-solving, which is understanding what elements of a situation we can control versus those we cannot, and focusing our energy entirely on the former.

#1. Reframe the Issue

Let's say I have a sales problem, and I find myself getting all worked up over people not buying my widget. The reality is that I can't control the customers and if they don't want to buy something from me, they shouldn't. After all, I wouldn't want to be forced to buy something I didn't want to buy. So by getting upset that people are merely exercising their right to choose in a free market I'm giving power to what is really just evidence of the problem. If people aren't buying, it's for a reason, not personal spite. So if I reframe the issue and challenge myself to figure out what in the situation I can control, I will find the actual problem and my energy will shift as I focus on something I can control.

So what's preventing me from making sales? If it's a lack of experience, I can learn more about influence and persuasion, or I can reread the earlier section on the perception-paralysis loop and follow its recommendations. If it's a lack of conviction, I could find something else to sell, or maybe go have a personal experience with the product I'm selling to see if my conviction increases. If it's time management, now I know what I need to work on. If it's a lack of leads I can ask, "What would my Success Character do?" What isn't productive is to sit there and stew about anything, ever (unless someone is paying me $1,000 an hour to do so). Of course some challenges will take longer to solve than others, but you have to get honest about your strengths and weaknesses and take full responsibility for the challenge and the solution.

A final note on reframing: half of all reframing can usually be accomplished by just saying out loud, "No one else is going to fix this for me."

#2. Build Your Power List

The great thing about the challenges we're speaking of is that you don't have to do this alone. You might not yet know how to overcome a particular challenge, but the chances that there is someone out there who does are good. A big part of overcoming challenges involves building your network, because when you build your network, you exponentially increase the resources you have access to. Remember, every person you add to your network adds hundreds of people to your network. We talked earlier about attending live events, joining Facebook groups, and enlisting masterminds, and the benefit of these actions is that you get to meet like-minded people and build up what I call your Power List.

Your Power List is your network of people who have skills and relationships that you don't and with whom you have a symbiotic relationship, so if you need something, they will share a solution with you if they can. Your potential to accomplish great things in the world has far more to do with your Power List than it does with your own skills. Let's say you meet someone who is great with computers and designing websites. Whenever you encounter a challenge in that area, you can call that person, and if your relationship is symbiotic, the chances are good that they will take your call. But that's a big "if," right? How do you make a professional relationship *symbiotic,* especially with someone who has enough "power" to be on your "Power List"?

The key to building your network is the same as finding a mentor—you must be willing to offer value in return. If you're open to helping others out, they are more likely to help you out. A network works because of reciprocity. If you want to utilize that network's resources, you have to be one of the network's resources. That's how you build relationships and can turn to others when you need help. The larger your Power List, the more potential problem solvers you have at your disposal and the less problems—er, challenges—will discourage you when they arise.

#3. Don't Be Afraid to Make Mistakes

I've seen too many people delay taking action because they were too scared of failing. They feel like they can't act or take that first step until they know for sure how things will play out. That's like saying you don't want to leave the house and go for a drive until you know that all the streetlights are going to be green. That's not realistic. It's never going to happen, so if that's what you're waiting for, you'll be waiting forever. Successful people don't wait, and it's a fallacy to think you can wait until you have all the answers to create certainty in your outcome. Real certainty comes from what you know how to do, not what you think is going to happen. And there is never any certainty without action; the idea of passive certainty is a contradiction in terms. Action is always what gets us unstuck, and certainty is action coupled with confidence and patience.

The beauty of taking action is that you don't have to succeed every time. Life is like hitting a baseball; you can fail more than you succeed and still be great. The best batters in history only got a hit 30 to 35 percent of the time. And did you know that the best poker players in the world only play on average one out of five hands? That means the best they can possibly do is to lose something on 80 percent of the hands they are dealt. Everyone who has done something great has fallen flat on their face and failed many times before achieving success, but that didn't slow them down. If you're hesitant, the trick is not being afraid and realizing that every mistake you make will be a chapter in the book that you will one day write about your life.

The risks most worth taking are not the smallest risks, they are the most asymmetrical risks, where the upside is proportionally much larger than the downside. If a bet has 10-to-1 odds you can lose 80 percent of the time and still double your money. That's how you fail more often than you succeed and still come out ahead. Here's an example. Recently, I had an investment go up 800 percent in three days. About two months prior, a friend called me and told me about a new cryptocurrency coming out. He was someone I trusted, and he told me it was worth throwing some money into and holding for a few months. Now, I do not have a great track record with investing in tradable assets that I don't understand. I am pretty good at building businesses and have a good track record investing in things with stable fundamentals, like real estate and large cap stocks, but get me into cryptocurrency, alt-coins, NFTs, memecoins, penny stocks, options, futures, and the like, and I have a pretty abysmal track record. But I understand these are asymmetrical risks, so when something comes along that seems credible, I'm usually still willing to play.

For two months, my money just sat there, and then out of the blue (yesterday, as of the time I'm writing this), he texted me asking if I'd checked my cryptowallet that day. It was up 800 percent. I had made a million bucks in the previous three days, more than offsetting every dime I'd lost on other gambles in that space. Of course, I wouldn't invest money I couldn't afford to lose in such a thing, but the metaphor goes a lot deeper in life than just investing in digital tokens.

Take lots of shots on asymmetrical risks, because when one hits it can totally change your life. It's similar to the first eleven businesses I started. My twelfth business (affiliate marketing) paid back every dime I'd lost over a decade of failing at the eleven previous businesses, and kicked off a string of wins that I've been riding ever since (including the book deal that produced what you're reading now). Without all those swings, we're not here having this conversation and nobody cares what I have to say. The problem most people have is they try something, fail once or twice, and start listening to the naysayer chorus, with their own ego as the featured soloist, singing, *"Ha ha, I told you so."* By stopping after a failure or two, you virtually guarantee that you will never succeed and you make it so your only chance to do so is to get lucky.

#4. Attitude Is Everything

It's not just what you do that's important when trying to overcome a challenge; it's how you do it that will really make the difference.

When I was in college, I wrote a musical. After the end-of-semester performance, the professor, a Tony Award–winning Broadway producer named Stuart Ostrow, told me and my writing partner that the show was good enough to be produced professionally. I became obsessed with seeing our show on a real stage, so we set an intention to produce it ourselves.

We started applying to theater festivals around the country, and after sending out a hundred applications, it was accepted to a festival in Minneapolis called the Minnesota Fringe Festival. We scraped together about $15,000 between us to produce the show, held auditions, cast local actors (three months of work for a whopping $1,000 was our payscale), bought tickets to Minneapolis for a dozen cast and crew, and got to work. Rehearsals were going according to plan until four weeks before we were supposed to fly to Minneapolis, when one of our lead actors disappeared on us. After a few days we realized he wasn't going to resurface and we had a tough choice to make. It was too late to find a replacement, and we'd already spent most of our money, but we were determined. I had never acted in a real production, nor had I ever sung or danced on stage before. I was a musician, not an actor or dancer, but I was not going to let the dream die. I went to the other male lead in the show and asked him to teach me to act, sing, and dance in four weeks. One of my roommates took over rehearsal piano duties, and I got to work memorizing lines and dance steps; it helped that I had written the music, so I already knew the songs.

I was still memorizing lines as my roommate and I made the twelve-hundred-mile drive from Houston to Minneapolis, hauling a trailer with our props and set (a bunch of Ikea furniture). Over the next two weeks, we put on a dozen or so performances to tiny audiences. Usually, that meant five or six people, with the biggest crowd being fifteen, which still felt empty in the 250-seat theater we were playing. But it didn't matter to me. This was my baby, and I put my heart and soul into each performance. Was I polished? Absolutely not. Was I even good? That's debatable. But I had an amazing attitude. At one show, there was a gentleman in the single-digit audience who was a big patron of the arts and happened to be a prominent entrepreneur and philanthropist (the inventor of the Breathe Right strip, of all things). After watching the performance, he came backstage to congratulate us and started asking me some questions. I told him the story of how we wound up there, and he was impressed with the hustle and determination I had shown. He told me that he'd genuinely enjoyed the show. In fact, he'd like to produce it, for real. Over the next several years, he became a great friend and mentor. We created a larger production in St. Paul, Minnesota, and he ended up backing me on other entrepreneurial ventures that had nothing to do with theater (those text-message-marketing business ideas mainly). To this day, he remains a good friend, and though I don't need his money anymore to invest in my startup ideas, I am forever grateful that he gave me this unforgettable lesson on why attitude is so important.

There were multiple moments during that musical production when I could have quit and no one would have blamed me. I was an introverted and not-terribly-athletic musician who suddenly had to sing and dance in tights and crack jokes to keep the show alive. But I attacked each challenge and kept moving forward with a positive attitude. And because I did, I created opportunities that never would have happened otherwise—I earned a friend and a mentor, I got to see a show I wrote produced on a professional stage, I got to have dinner with Meryl Streep and Kevin Kline (a story for another time but it happened through him), and I had the financial backing to start multiple businesses that led me to where I am today. Most lives come down to just a few fleeting moments that determine their trajectory, which is why it's so important to show up the right way every minute of every day. Every time we show up with a bad attitude or put a bad vibe out into the world, we cut ourselves off from whatever could be great about a situation and potentially blow a once-in-a-lifetime opportunity we'll never know existed. But when we have the right attitude, doors open. If we want to get ahead, we must have a winning attitude and offer value for people whenever possible.

#5. Document the Struggle

At that marketing event in 2009, I asked one of the guys I met backstage what he would do differently if he had the chance. He told me he would "document the struggle." That means when we're starting out or when times are hard, writing it down, shooting a video, or otherwise capturing it for posterity.

The benefit of this is twofold. On the one hand, it's cathartic, and the very act of capturing the struggle is a form of release that can help get us unstuck, out of our head, and out of our own way. In my experience, it is therapeutic to "get it out" onto paper or video so it doesn't feel like I'm keeping it inside. On the other hand, there's an even more practical benefit—we want to capture that moment so that one day we can look back at that moment, see how we persevered, and have material for our personal brand, personal storytelling, or even our first book deal!

Here's another way to think of it: we want to encounter challenges. Yes, we do. Think about any good story; it's not all good times—if it was, nobody would care. We need ups and downs, and we need problems challenges, or else we can't appreciate our wins, and we can't inspire anybody else. Challenges come with tension, stress, conflict, and other dramatic components of a good story, so we must learn to see them for what they are, which is proof that we're alive and living the range of human experience. No one in history has ever succeeded without difficulty, and in a world where so much could be improved, it is our job to write a good story and be the hero. And we can't be the hero of our story without obstacles. Documenting our struggle helps contextualize our moments of greatest strain for what they are, the moments that will ultimately define us. Will we be dragged down or persevere? Will we succumb or overcome? And once we get through to the other side, think about how much better our story will be and how many people it will be able to inspire.

There's another subtle reason to document our struggle. Whenever we document our struggle and reframe our life as a narrative arc in a story, we are subconsciously telling ourselves that we will overcome whatever we're facing because we wouldn't be bothering to document it if the story wasn't going to have a happy ending. By making our struggles plot points in a great story, and documenting them as a biographer or investigative journalist would if they were writing that story, we condition ourselves to be the heroic protagonist and to stay true to the plot and theme of our story (i.e., our mission statement, vision, core values, beliefs, etc.). This in turn helps us re-center and persevere as we refocus on our mission and get reminded that our struggles are worth it as part of our larger cause. As we adhere to our mission our life becomes more worthwhile and our pain threshold increases because we know that nothing worthwhile is easy.

You're probably noticing a common theme to some of these strategies. Whether it's creating your Success Character, documenting your own struggle, or arriving at a fixed value for your time, there is an aspect of self-objectification to success. This ability to step outside of ourselves and consider ourselves rationally and without emotion is an essential element of personal mastery (remember the concept of being an impartial observer in our own life, credit to Buddhism). One of the nice things about doing this type of work consistently is how it impacts our self-communication. By objectifying ourselves and creating a space between our *experience* of ourselves and our *perception* of ourselves, our inner monologue becomes more of a dialogue, like two passengers in a car talking to each other. Our lesser self (ego, id, child persona, etc.) still gets a voice, but because it is not the driver, ultimately our Success Character/superego gets the final word and decision. In this way, we do not suppress or dishonor any part of ourselves, but we reduce the likelihood that our lesser self will throw a tantrum and hurt us because we allowed it to be heard while also keeping it out of the driver's seat. Which brings us to the next critical element of success—communication.

11

The Science of Attractive Communication

G o to any bar after 10:00 p.m., and you'll find plenty of people with big ideas. If you sit down and indulge them, you'll hear an array of grand plans. Some of them might even sound good and have potential, but most people never see their ideas through because the difficulty of implementing them seems far more real than the potential payoff for having done so. But what if the work of implementing was less? If so, then the potential payoff would be more enticing to go after. And how do we make work less? Well, we've been taught since we were kids that "more hands make lighter work." We have to learn to get other people on board with our ideas to make our ideas more achievable.

More often than not, the difference between having support versus being forced to go it alone comes down to our communication. And by communication, I don't mean rah-rah leadership speeches. I'm talking about everyday interactions that build rapport, trust, and confidence in what we're trying to do. Over the course of our life, our communication becomes either the glue that holds our efforts together or the solvent that destroys them.

COLLABORATIVE COMMUNICATION

Think of all the ways we communicate today. There's face-to-face communication, phone calls, text messages, email, Zoom, direct messaging, and of course the horror show that is social media comments' sections. No matter the method or mode, communication is the key to delivering our message so people understand what we're saying and why we're saying it.

Psychologist and author Marshall Rosenberg wrote a book called *Nonviolent Communication*, which lays out a philosophy for communication that I've found quite effective. Nonviolent communication is defined as "an approach to communication based on principles of nonviolence. It is not a technique to end disagreements, but rather a method designed to increase empathy and improve the quality of life of those who utilize the method and the people around them."

Studying nonviolent communication has changed my life; however, I have found that many people resist the idea that their communication has shades of being "violent," so I often use Rosenberg's softer alternative term "collaborative communication." Call it what you want, but the basis of this communication style is about increasing the connection and trust with the person you're conversing with, so you can work together to avoid conflict while achieving goals.

The basic idea is that as human beings, we all have the capacity for compassion and empathy, which is a natural way to resolve differences peacefully while creating connections and meeting other people's needs. It sounds simple, but this is much easier said than done because so many of us don't acknowledge our own feelings, are clumsy in dealing with the feelings of others, or both. Many of our misunderstandings, and the reasons why conversations leave us feeling frustrated and distraught, come down to poor communication that doesn't consider what the other person is feeling or where they might be coming from.

So many of the comments we casually say every day might seem innocuous on the surface but are really creating unnecessary tension and conflict. "You never listen to me!" How many times have you said something like that? Probably many. And of course in a strong relationship that single statement will not be its undoing, at least not right away, but it is still a poisonous seed planted. Aside from being a technically self-contradictory statement, it's an extreme judgment that the other person can't help but hear as a criticism and, at least internally, feel the need to defend. How are they supposed to react? That statement set the other person up to be defensive or potentially offensive. That statement also falls short in that it doesn't offer a solution or provide an avenue to improve the problem—if anything, this form of communication impedes the problem-solving process by driving a deeper wedge between the parties.

Here's another example that really challenges a lot of people. Have you ever told your child, "Good job"? Although unintentional, that would be considered a technical case of violent communication because it assumes a power dynamic that places you in the position of judge to determine the quality of the job your child did. Said another way, if you claim for yourself the authority to deem their job "good," then you are also claiming the authority to deem their job "bad," and if they grant you that authority, they give you not just the power to build them up but also the power to tear them down. And we should never give anyone that power, nor take it from anyone else. Collaborative or nonviolent communication operates on a level plane of power and orients all parties' self-worth to their own internal values. A substitute for "good job" would be "I loved seeing how hard you worked on that." See that? Now you're only evaluating yourself, while still passing along a positive sentiment and validating how they feel instead of telling them how to feel.

Rosenberg's is a sophisticated approach to mastering communication that felt awkward at first, but having practiced it for years now and using it to, among other things, dramatically improve my marriage, I have found it invaluable for creating alignment and enrollment with teams, friends, and loved ones. The best leadership is servant leadership, but it's hard to be a servant leader when your language constantly suggests you are the master in the relationship.

Of course, we can master all the great communication techniques we want, but the real challenge will come when others are not so conscientious. Fortunately, Rosenberg's framework helps us modulate our reactions to people. Before we react to someone, we can go through Rosenberg's four-step process.

#1. Observe

Here we stop and take in what's going on. We listen to what's being said, while also assessing body language and any other nonverbal elements, so we can accurately gauge the situation for what it really is. We are trying to figure out what the other person is needing in the situation.

#2. Acknowledge Our Feelings

There's a difference between what we think and what we feel. We often get caught up in what we think and the need to voice our opinion about a situation and miss the wisdom of our feelings. Plato said, "Opinion is the wilderness between knowledge and ignorance." I agree, and believe the value of opinions is for testing them, but a conflict is no place to do that. Feelings, on the other hand, give us clues about how to successfully navigate a conflict.

#3. Discover Our Needs

As Stephen Covey said, "Seek first to understand, then to be understood." Having observed first what the other person seems to need, it is now time to ask the same of ourselves. And our feelings are our best clue. What outcome would resolve any negative feelings?

#4. Make a Request

This is your chance to get what you need, but you'll rarely get what you don't ask for. And asking works better than you might think. In 1977, a research team at Harvard led by psychologist Ellen Langer conducted a study on human behavior that came to some conclusions that might make you rethink how you communicate in the future. They had someone approach a person standing in line at a library copy machine and ask to cut ahead of them in line one of three ways.

1. Without giving a reason.
2. By saying, "Because I'm in a rush."
3. By saying, "Because I have to make copies."

In reality, none of those express a very good reason, or even any new information, but after studying the data, they learned that the first (lack of a) reason was 60 percent effective, the second reason was 94 percent effective, and the third reason was 93 percent. What's the difference? The difference is providing a reason and the use of the word *because*. It doesn't even matter if you're giving a good reason; you appeal to people significantly more just by explaining why you're making a request.

At its core communication is about sharing. The word literally comes from the Latin *communicare*, which means to share, and sharing is a magical act in that when we share something we are using division to create connection. Using "the shared" to unify "the sharers" is the point of sharing and, by extension, communicating. Once again, this is right there in the etymology. The word *share* has its origin in two seemingly contradictory German words: *scheren*, meaning to divide (think to shear), and also *schar*, meaning troop, multiple parties bonded together. Sharing divides in order to unify and proper (i.e., nonviolent) communication that is free of power imbalances or judgment does the same thing. This is why the "make a request" trick works so well, however silly the request may be. When Ellen Langer's experimental subjects *shared* their request, they invited the temporary formation of a tiny "troop," united in that moment by the need to make a copy.

SLOW DOWN

Remember this moment because it's probably going to be the only time that I advise you to slow down. Most people go slow when they should be going fast. But when it comes to communication, that dynamic is flipped, and so many people are rushing when they should be slowing down.

We all want to wake up in the morning and have every encounter, personal or professional, be smooth and easy, but that's rarely ever the case. Conflict lurks around every corner, but whether we steamroll headfirst into that conflict or effectively navigate our way through a potential issue without hostilities often hinges on how quickly we are trying to get the process over with.

The piano is such an excellent metaphor for communication because you need your two hands to work independently while also working in harmony. Look at any piano, and it seems so simple. Eighty-eight black and white keys all laid out in perfect order. It should be easy to play, yet there are so many millions of combinations and possibilities that just being able to play a basic piece like "Für Elise" takes years of practice to get each hand to do its part. When done right, it seems effortless, but rarely do we see the work that goes on behind the scenes to reach that level.

When I used to teach kids to play the piano, it was often difficult for them to get their hands to work in coordinated but independent fashion. They'd play the piece fine with either hand by itself, but as soon as it was time to put the hands together that's when they'd get frustrated and start rushing to get it over with. Of course, that would backfire, set them back, and undo progress. Increasing speed and improving coordination cannot happen simultaneously. Whether it's two hands playing polyrhythms on a piano or two people collaborating on a project at work, improved coordination comes from slowing down.

"Slow is smooth, and smooth is fast." That's a Navy SEAL saying that pretty much sums it up when it comes to communication. Precise and effective communication is an essential part of leadership, including self-leadership, and miscommunication is never worth the risk. However big our hurry, it is always worth slowing down to avoid miscommunication, and when communicating we ought to carefully track what we have made explicit versus what we are just assuming the other party knows. In my experience it helps to approach every conversation as if its merit lies only in what happens next. Seriously, what value is there in having a grand old time yukking it up with so-and-so about such-and-such if what happens next isn't positive or productive? Keeping an *"I'm responsible for whatever comes next"* mindset ensures we do not make assumptions or rush conversations.

OUR COMMUNICATION ABILITIES ARE HOMEGROWN

Good (and bad) communication typically starts at home and we will rarely be better communicators outside the home than inside it, regardless of what we tell ourselves. If we can't communicate well with our spouse, children, siblings, parents, and close friends, we are naïve to think that communication is going to go well outside our inner circle.

When my wife and I first got together, we were committed to creating excellent communication because we each came from relationships that broke down from a lack of it. She also had kids, who I have since adopted, so the stakes were high not to do any damage. So within months of dating, we hired a therapist and started taking classes on parenting and relationships. And we took the work home with us, practicing nonviolent communication to the point where over a decade later our therapist says we did more of "the homework" than any couple he's ever worked with. It was awkward and uncomfortable but paid exponential dividends.

Through practicing nonviolent communication, we learned that just because the other person isn't acting the way we want them to in the moment doesn't mean they are wrong. We learned to communicate opinions as opinions ("I don't like that movie.") and feelings as feelings ("I feel sad when . . .") rather than opinions as facts ("That movie sucks.") and feelings as judgments ("You make me sad." or "That is mean."). We learned to express ourselves in ways that didn't diminish whatever the other might think or feel and didn't necessitate turning disappointment into conflict.

People ask us now how we get along so well and often tag pictures of us online with the hashtag #relationshipgoals, but what doesn't show in a picture is the thousands of hours of painstaking work practicing communicating slowly and deliberately, often to the point of ridiculousness. True story: we once took an hour-long detour on the way home from a parenting class and drove around our neighborhood having a practice discussion around what we wanted for dinner. It was silly, and there was a lot of laughter, but years later we are a testament to the value of the work. We drove around saying things to each other like, *"In this moment I acknowledge an anxious feeling in my arms and stomach and am choosing to interpret that feeling as historical shame that rears up at times when I express my needs or wants around food. Your preference for Italian over my preference for Mexican was the activating event, but I see clearly that any feelings I am having source from past experiences and have nothing to do with you. Thank you for expressing your desire for Italian food as a personal preference, rather than a value judgment or opinion laced with subjective truth. By doing so you helped create a space where I can feel shame without associated fear that might tempt me to retreat from our connection."* It was like learning a new language and, of course, we both felt ridiculous and could hardly keep a straight face much of the time. But supporting each other in this awkward process of sanitizing our communication style created a deep connection and a foundation for lifelong trust.

As adults, we often don't allow ourselves and each other the space to be clumsy. We just want to come off as polished all the time, but we end up constantly trying to pass off polished imperfection instead of slowing things down to get them right. Taking the time to think about and process what is being said on both sides, and to properly interpret the feelings and needs behind it, leads ultimately to faster and more effective communication, even though it will feel much slower at first. I can also report that once you experience this style of communication it produces a deep sense of peace, and "violent" communication starts to feel, well, violent. It's gotten to the point now where when Jaqueline and I hear people speaking with tones of judgment or power imbalance, we experience it together as an almost physical pain. It may sound silly, but I have started to see people almost like fireflies with dimmer switches, where every interaction I have either turns their light up or down based on how nonviolent it was. And my goal for my Success Character is to be a master at turning up the light of everyone I encounter. And every conversation is practice.

Anyway, you might be thinking that this passage feels like familiar ground, this idea of how we like to rush through things because we feel awkward and uncomfortable. If so, that's because it is. This is a nearly identical principle to what we discussed before in the context of learning new things, only now we find it surfacing in how we communicate. The common denominator here is insecurity and how it changes our perception of time. When we feel insecure, time seems to slow down, and the "awkwardness" we feel is to a large degree just how we perceive time when we aren't feeling comfortable. I actively train my Reticular Activating System to be repulsed by insecurity whenever I find it in myself. Insecurity is a destroyer of lives that could have been. It keeps us from learning, keeps us from communicating effectively, sabotages our best work by making us rush, keeps us from growing, keeps us settling, and will ultimately, if we let it, keep the person we were born to be from ever drawing breath.

Okay, so hopefully you're on board with me about the beauty that comes from slowing down our communication. I can feel myself wanting to stay on this subject—it produces a lot of bliss for me. But we have more to cover, so let's shake off and rev things back up.

12

The 55 Mile-per-Hour Fallacy

Trivia question: How did the concept of a fifty-five-mile-per-hour speed limit come to be?

In 1973, the Organization of Arab Petroleum Exporting Countries (OAPEC) decided to stop exporting oil to the United States and four other countries as a "punishment" for the United States' support of Israel during the Yom Kippur War. Previously, in 1969, American oil production had hit max capacity, and the United States began aggressively importing foreign oil to keep pace with the increasing demand from automobiles, so the loss of imports from Arab countries created a massive spike in prices.

So in 1974, in an attempt to reduce oil consumption and stabilize prices, the federal government enacted a national speed limit of fifty-five miles per hour. Supposedly, that was the speed where an automobile engine runs most efficiently. The idea was very popular at the time, and it was considered an act of patriotism to drive fifty-five miles per hour. But there was a problem. It turned out that an average speed of fifty-five miles per hour resulted in less than a 1 percent gain in fuel efficiency. We would have had a much bigger impact by requiring everyone to pump a bit more air in their tires. Meanwhile slowing down transportation crippled commerce for years in the United States.

Think of how important driving is to our economy. It's the cornerstone of how products and people get to work and to market, especially in 1973, and this law made highway transportation take approximately 20 percent longer. Nonetheless, the federal speed limit mandate stayed in place for twenty-one years because, even after its economic effects were completely discredited in a study commissioned by Congress in 1982, the narrative shifted to how it was keeping everyone safer. But sure enough, subsequent research (and common sense) showed it was not people driving slower that was saving lives—it was the widespread adoption of seat belts, improvements in automobile technology (air bags, alerts, etc.), and a shift toward air travel for longer journeys prompted in part by people's frustration over being told to drive so slow on the highways. In fact, in 1995 when the mandate was repealed and states were allowed to raise speed limits, traffic fatalities continued to decrease. So, when all was said and done, billions of dollars of economic opportunity cost got paid trying to impose a solution that didn't work for a problem that didn't exist. Even as a kid, I remember thinking that the most obvious hazards on the highway were not people going too fast but rather people going too slow.

I still see this effect happening all the time. There are so many ideas in society, some of them new and some of them old, that everyone seems to be on board with even though they are arbitrary, incorrect, or even destructive. What about in 1992 when the US Department of Agriculture released the food pyramid and told us to eat carbohydrates like pasta and bread six to eleven times a day? How much physical suffering has been caused by pushing carbs on America? And cow's milk? Don't even get me started on that. Clearly, we need to be careful which ideas we buy into and not just assume that because something has been around for a while or is getting pushed by those in authority that it's valid.

Case in point: the adage that "slow and steady wins the race." Older people often tell the younger generation to slow down and not be in such a rush. We hear constant reference to some fictitious race that took place between a tortoise and a hare. Does it really need to be pointed out that there is no conceivable racing scenario where a hare does not absolutely smoke a tortoise? Yes, we have identified two areas where going slow is warranted—learning and communicating—but when it comes to taking action, nothing could be worse advice. Every time we think, *I'll be less likely to make a mistake if I go slower*, we chance that going slower is itself the mistake.

Casual observation in today's dynamic and fast-paced world shows us that the swift are the ones who win the race. This is a widely recognized truth in the entrepreneurial community (often referred to as *first-mover advantage*), and in my experience, *going slow* is topped only by *doing nothing* on the list of ways to be unsuccessful. Contrary to popular advice, in the modern world, you need to be in a hurry, going faster, and ideally, you want to get wherever you're going first. As the world gets more crowded and more connected, intrinsic advantages decrease. Things like location, relationships, and access to capital are less of an advantage in a world that is more physically and socially mobile along with being more competitive. Today more than ever, time is fleeting, and since money and time are intrinsically linked for every person that means money is fleeting too, and all the more depending on how valuable you declared your time to be.

And as the race speeds up, the nature of competition changes. A hundred years ago, life was a race of Model Ts, now it's a race of Ferraris, so as the mechanics in our own lives we better be tuning our engines for speed. Next time some well-intended person with an average life tells you to pace yourself, remember the story of the fifty-five-mile-per-hour speed limit.

Years ago, when I had business ideas, my instinct was always to test the waters and get proof of concept before I moved forward. "Fools rush in" was the advice I'd been given again and again by business owners who didn't understand the emerging digital economy. I went along with it and continuously sought input from "older and wiser" (and slower) minds, but if I'm being honest, the reason I did wasn't because I agreed with the whole tortoise/hare nonsense; it was because I was scared. Slowing down, asking for permission, and wanting people to validate my ideas before I took the risk to act on them was another way of stalling, or at least trying to make risk feel less risky.

But asking for permission or approval around a new idea doesn't work. Even with normal communication there is consensus among researchers that only 7 percent of communication involves the words we say, and this will be even more true when communicating a new idea where people are likely to have biases or predilections that steer their impression.

When something is new, what draws people to it is rarely the quality of the idea; it's the confidence and other nonverbal information being conveyed by the person presenting it. Seeking validation from others about our big plans is like asking a blind person how we look in our new outfit—their answer is just going to reflect how confident we sounded when we asked the question. And anyway, seeking their approval meant we were already off to a weak start.

We all already know this; we learned it in grade school. Remember when you were in school and there was that kid who showed up one day and just seemed to leapfrog the popularity contest? Here you were, spending so much time and energy jockeying for social position (or trying to avoid that game altogether if you were me), and then some new kid shows up without a care in the world, and all of a sudden everyone wants to be their friend. It wasn't fair!

Well, if only we'd been paying attention and taken the lesson instead of getting jealous. The reason everyone gravitated to that kid is because they projected a genuine aura that they could take or leave the rest of us. They were probably affable, but never desperate in the way that most of us were at that age and many of us still are. In our default state as humans we're a walking contradiction, simultaneously craving the approval of others while being turned off when we feel other people craving ours. Even with our own kids we all know how annoying *"look, Mom/Dad, watch me do my 700th somersault"* is. What we don't respect in others we should probably try to reduce in ourselves, right? So, let's take the lesson now, better late than never, and start acting like the cool kid who didn't need other people's approval. Be always kind, but never needy. Let your confidence be so strong that you can take or leave the approval of others in all areas of life. Seriously, if you can't be the cool kid in your own life who oozes certainty and passion that your mission is valid and your ideas are good, how can you really expect others to buy into you?

DON'T BE AFRAID TO GET A LITTLE CRAZY

Passion is what people respond to and the root of passion is suffering. The Latin *pati* or *passio* means "suffering." If you've ever suffered in any way or overcome any hardship, good for you, you filled your passion reservoir and now have passion energy to tap into. So use it! Go a little nuts! Let your pain take the wheel for a minute. This isn't about being a victim. It's about giving meaning to your suffering by channeling it into something you care about. Since I started creating this blitz of content online to rally and wake up the world, I've had some feedback that I come off as too intense. It's been suggested by some (though disagreed with by others) that I'm unrelatable and there's no way that most people could do what I've done. First of all, that's fine—one of me is probably plenty—but for anyone to think they could not approach their own life with the same intensity that I approach mine is absurd. Even in the beta-reader feedback this book got there was a strong vibe of *"well, yeah, but he's just different."* Bullshit. I'm not fundamentally different than anyone reading this book. And in any way that I am different, it's only due to conscious choices—the voices I choose to listen to, fears I acquiesce to, influences I allow in my life, value I place on my time, level of effort I'm willing to give to things I believe matter, and so on. None of these attributes are hard-coded anywhere.

There is certainly nothing unique about my potential, and I contest the precept that I, or anyone, is too intense. I think the world we live in is suffering from a woeful lack of intensity. Why aren't more people in the world committed to doing what it takes to transform the things they complain about into the things they do something about? The difference between the average person and the exceptional person is just this little edge of pissed-off-ness that gets channeled into causes that matter. That dogged, refuse-to-quit gear that some people know how to shift into is something the majority have forgotten about. What about turning off Netflix, getting off the couch, and refusing to sit back down until your life is exactly the way you want it and your couch is in the exact living room in the exact house in the exact location you pictured in your dreamscape? I know that when I start talking about "average" people in a critical manner, it rubs some the wrong way, but the most average thing I could do would be to be concerned about what average thinks when it's thinking average thoughts. Isn't it time we said, "Enough"? We live in a world where things have gotten so watered down and lukewarm. But it takes a certain edge to be successful and a willingness to rub some people the wrong way. I literally don't know one successful person that everyone likes.

What if instead of trying to fit in, we celebrate the fact that none of us do, nor should we want to. It's been almost 150 years now since Alfred Adler, one of Freud's pupils who went on to outshine him, told us that the number one driver of human behavior is a need to belong, and he wasn't making the observation to explain why we are all doing so well; he was explaining what's at the core of our neuroses and psychological maladies. The need to fit in is a symptom of what ails us. Look at the world. Are people happy? No. The General Social Survey out of NORC consistently shows less than 15 percent of people being very happy. So, why are we trying to fit in with a population of unhappy people who are themselves trying to fit in with each other? Let's interpret the data logically and accept the fact that we are meant to transcend this place. We are sublime beings trapped in a world of mostly mundane experiences. That is not going to change but we cheapen ourselves when we try to reconcile it. It should always feel wrong to be here. We should always feel out of place. Yes, we must be *in* this world, but we should never be *of* this world.

That involves never settling and never being content with what you have. If given a choice between stress and contentment, take stress because that's what leads to growth. As human beings, we are either growing or dying. When we push ourselves and create dissonance between our internal and external environments, we force adaptation and growth. Personally, I am never satisfied, and I don't ever want to be satisfied because I don't know what I would do with myself. I'm not saying that because I'm greedy. I just always know that I can do more and to ever not know that would be a sign of amnesia, not maturity. I always know I can help more, I can have a bigger impact, and I can be a better role model of what is possible when you believe and act as if potential is unlimited and stress is a dare.

Of course not all stress is the same. There is good stress and bad stress. Good stress is stress that comes from within and from our own choices, stress we put on ourselves. Most people suffer from bad stress, stress imposed on us from the outside world without our consent. We all want lives of internal peace and joy, but the bad trade most of us make, which is the cornerstone of the broken system, is to accept the external stress that comes from not being in control of our own lives in exchange for a vague promise that peace and joy will come at some point. We need to be doing the opposite and ratcheting up the stress we choose for ourselves while refusing to accept the stress the world throws at us. People act like stress is this big, confounding archnemesis, but it's so easy to manage if we'll just stop trying to avoid it and focus on choosing the stress that's good for us. We should be filling our lives with so much productive, growth-promoting stress that there is no room for any stress we didn't choose to stress us out.

Think this sounds crazy? Well, good, it is. Compliment taken. Now let me prove to you how well this works. One of my favorite mentors out there, David Goggins, has something he calls 4x4x48. It involves running four miles every four hours for forty-eight hours straight. Go try it if you're doubting what I'm saying. I can guarantee you that if you accomplish 4x4x48 you will have had so much stress of your own choosing for that forty-eight hours it was impossible to be stressed by anything else.

Look at people like Elon Musk, Steve Jobs, Oprah Winfrey, Mother Teresa, Gandhi, or anyone who has built something great in this world. Do we think they were satisfied? Do we think they drove fifty-five? Of course not. They took chances. They broke the mold. They did stuff that other people doubted and judged them for. They didn't flee from stress. They were just intentional about which stresses they took on. And they never waited for conditions to be perfect before they put themselves out there. In fact, I suspect they never waited for much of anything.

Allow me a little "call you out" moment here. I know we haven't known each other long and it may be presumptuous for me to say, but whatever you're trying to do in this world, I bet you have more to give. I bet that you still have room to get a little crazier. I bet you can think bigger and stop waiting for other people to buy in before you take your shot. I'd be willing to bet that at least half of the obstacles you think are stopping you are no more real than the idea of solving a gas crisis with a fifty-five-mile-per-hour speed limit. And the other half, the obstacles that are real? How many of them would be easier to deal with if you shot out of bed every morning like a cannonball and attacked the day with fury until you collapsed into bed at night, exhausted not from external stress but from the internal pressure of being mission driven and on fire all day, every day? Before we resign ourselves to the life we already have, don't we owe it to ourselves to try a little crazy on? Seriously, be a maniac for ninety days. I dare you. For ninety days dance like no one's watching, sing your song out loud, and invite the world to politely fuck off. That's what I did on September 27, 2018, when I posted that "Let's Get Extreme" video (that said much of what this chapter says). On that day, I finally implemented the lessons from the cool kid. I finally went all in on myself. I finally stopped asking for permission or validation. I finally let my crazy out. I finally got over worrying about the opinions of others. And thanks to that I now have the fastest-growing education company in the world, a top 100 podcast, a checklist of dreams come true, and even a sweet book deal. Suffice it to say I am Never. Going. Back. And you should join me. Life is better on this side of giving a fuck.

PART IV

Live by Choice, Not by Chance

13

The 3 Ps of Success

The 3 Ps of Success is a simple heuristic for making sure we are being productive and effective with our time. There are three areas of life we must tend to and into which all productive action can be organized. They are:

1. Physical
2. Personal
3. Professional

I usually draw this as three concentric circles with physical on the inside, then personal, then professional.

We spend so much time focusing on the professional circle looking to get ahead when so often the path to our best life involves the other circles. One of my greatest joys as founder of ENTRE is the frequency with which people tell us how when they enrolled they thought that learning how to build a business or produce more income was going to be what changed their whole life, only to discover that reshaping their physical and personal habits was the real catalyst for life improvement. It's by far the most common piece of feedback we hear, to the point where we have to proactively make sure our brand doesn't get confused in the market as a fitness or personal development brand. We are a platform for professional education but so many of our students tag us in posts about things like losing weight, quitting smoking, improving their marriage, and the like, that outside observers might not even realize we actually teach business and professional skills.

Brand confusion aside, though, it's the best thing we've done, and it's how we've created not just classes that teach people but a culture that transforms people. From day one we set out to be "transformational education" rather than "transactional education," and the 3 Ps are how we've done it. Whether you're starting a business, scaling a business, trying to exit a business, trying to get promoted at work, trying to hit a sales quota, trying to change careers, or just trying to figure out what direction you want to go in this world, professional growth should always be an extension of personal growth.

To put it bluntly, most of the people who think money is their biggest problem are wrong. Money might be the most obvious symptom of their problem(s), but it's not the problem. There are a lot of people in this world trying to drive their Ford Pinto life around like it's a Porsche. Now before you get offended, hear me out. This is great news! How liberating is it to find out that if you've got Pinto habits, Pinto relationships, and Pinto confidence you don't need to wonder why you keep breaking down or not getting where you want to go. It's because you're in a Pinto. Develop Porsche habits and a Porsche mindset (hint, by doing what this book says), give yourself a couple years, and you will not be driving a Pinto around anymore.

So how does the 3 Ps framework work exactly? We break each of these areas into what we call *governing principles* and *key performance indicators* (KPIs) that allow us to quantify our efforts and progress in each area. The governing principles of each are the same for everyone, while the KPIs can vary person to person. In the sections below, I use examples from my personal life to illustrate my KPIs, but once you feel confident with the concept, you should develop your own.

Before we dive into the governing principles and KPIs, though, it's important to realize that none of this is zero sum. You are not in competition with anyone else. For you to succeed, someone else doesn't need to fail, and someone else's success has zero impact on whether you succeed or fail (and, no, that's not a political comment, but, hell yes, that's also a political comment). Life is only meant to be a competition between who you strive to be and who you might be tempted to settle for, no one else. The only question that matters is how are you doing relative to how you could be doing? Me versus me is the only basis for comparison, and thinking of life like that will help you stay in the mindset of constant and never-ending improvement. Remember the fabled words of Teddy Roosevelt: "Comparison is the thief of joy."

Bettering our previous best is the only way to be truly happy. Tony Robbins says, "Progress is happiness," and I have found this to be a universally shared truth among hundreds of the most successful people in the world I have had the privilege to interview on my podcast and hundreds of thousands of our students. Everyone seems to agree that to be happy we don't need to be the best or even be a qualified expert at anything, but we need to feel like we're making progress. The 3 Ps approach produces a massive amount of happiness for a huge number of people because it turns the entirety of life into an arena where progress is constant, expected, and easy to measure.

PHYSICAL LIFE

At ENTRE we define the physical area of life as "building, maintaining, and optimizing the body and mind." Diet and exercise are what come to mind for most people when I talk about the physical, and a lot of people will certainly prioritize how they look (fat and muscle), but that's not nearly all it is.

Physical is actually more about energy than aesthetics, and includes multiple overlapping habits and systems, such as diet, exercise, biochemistry, and neurochemistry. Generally when we talk about physical optimization we're talking about the interplay of our physical activity, nutrition (macro- and micronutrition), and our baseline habits (not challenges, sprints, or gimmicks, but the stuff we do for years that's just a part of who we are).

What also fits into the physical category is something we call *solitary spirituality*. At first glance, you might think that individual spiritual practices (religion for some people) do not fit nicely into the 3 Ps model. However, closer analysis shows that in practice most people's spirituality divides into things done alone (prayer, rituals, meditation, etc.), which we call *solitary spirituality*, and things done with others (ceremonies, services, group worship, etc.), which we call *social spirituality*. Since solitary spiritual practices tend to have an impact on our mind and body, we put them in the physical category, while our social spiritual practices involve relationships, so we place them in the personal category.

So now that the basics are defined, let's look at the governing principle and KPIs for our physical life.

Governing Principle (Physical): Balance

When working on this area, we want to improve and create balance across the six areas of physical performance: strength, stamina, pliability, mental sharpness, emotional equilibrium, and spiritual peace.

Key Performance Indicators (Physical)

Each area of physical performance can have its own KPIs. Below I list the areas as well as my personal KPIs, but again you are encouraged to come up with your own for each area.

- **Strength:** I use what I call a bodyweight heuristic to account for fluctuations in weight, meaning I perform compound exercises with reps of bodyweight. For example, how many times can I bench my bodyweight, squat my bodyweight, deadlift my bodyweight, or pull my bodyweight.

- **Stamina:** For my body, my mile time seems to be the best indicator of the kind of stamina I'm trying to achieve. I also monitor my resting heart rate.

- **Pliability:** A quick yoga class tells me if I'm flexible enough. Usually, the feedback is not positive!

- **Mental sharpness:** Extemporaneous speaking is how I measure this. I attend a Toastmasters meeting every Monday morning I'm in town (and get up an hour earlier at 2:30 a.m. to allow for it) and at every meeting I volunteer for "table topics," which are short impromptu speeches on randomly assigned subjects. The rest of the group then gives me feedback on all aspects of my communication and I get weekly real-time KPI feedback on my mental sharpness.

- **Emotional equilibrium:** I measure my emotional well-being with the principle of self-efficacy. Self-efficacy is defined as the extent to which I'm only applying energy to things in my control and giving no mind or other resources to things I cannot control. Scoring well on this front ensures that I'm operating efficiently and governed by logic, not emotion.

- **Spiritual peace:** This is hard to measure, so I measure its opposite, fear. I often rate my level of fear on a scale of 1 to 10, and get immediate and accurate feedback on how I'm doing at maintaining my practices of prayer/meditation, reflection/writing, and gratitude.

As you can see, defining these indicators is personal and subjective, so it might require some trial and error out of the gate. Have patience with yourself and try new things. When it comes to diet, my intense work pace does a pretty good job of giving me feedback on what feels good and what doesn't. I've found that as long as I keep carbs at or under fifty grams a day, go twelve hours or more every twenty-four hours without eating (intermittent fasting), and keep my hormones and micronutrients balanced with good supplementation, I am able to perform at the level I need to consistently on five to six hours a night of sleep.

This book isn't meant as an authoritative work on health and fitness or biohacking, so despite my deep passion for those subjects, I won't say much more about them, but I will at least share that anyone who hasn't tried the combination of intermittent fasting and low carb intake might want to consider it (after consulting with a health care professional, of course). It's the lynchpin for me to maintain energy levels and focus throughout the day while running on less sleep than most people. I net about an extra twenty-one hours a week of productive time with this approach, which is roughly the equivalent of an extra day and a half per week or seventy-eight days per year. So basically I get what feels like a 440-day year and have the added benefit that life is simpler because for up to sixteen of every twenty-four hours I don't have to think about or take time for food either. People often say they don't have time for self-care like going to the gym or preparing healthy meals, but I have found that these activities create far more time than they use up.

PERSONAL LIFE

The personal area of life is all about relationships and how you interact with yourself and others. It's important to include yourself because that's the primary relationship in all our lives. If you can't communicate in an honest and healthy way with yourself, how can you expect to have a meaningful connection with and impact on family, friends, coworkers, and neighbors?

Governing Principle (Personal): Collaborative Communication

We've discussed this before in the section on nonviolent or collaborative communication, but as a reminder, the goal is to create win-win relationships built on empathy, clarity, emotional transparency, and a balanced power dynamic. We break these relationships into five categories:

1. Self
2. Family
3. Close friends
4. Associates
5. Social spirituality

Key Performance Indicators (Personal)

I give myself four separate grades for each of the five categories listed above. When grading my relationship with myself, I consider the (forever dysfunctional) relationship between my ego and my Success Character.

- **Impact grade:** How much are we pulling each other toward the best versions of each other and utilizing our strengths?

- **Reciprocity grade:** How balanced is the process between the two parties?

- **Communication grade:** How clean is my communication? Is there a power dynamic? I never want to have a level of control over the other person, and if there's one embedded (like an employee), it should still not be present in my communication. Remember we're trying to turn everyone's dimmer switches up!

- **Time-allocation grade:** I try to be astutely aware of how my time is allocated to different relationships. In general, time should be most concentrated at the top of the list and descend downward. That's different from most people who do not actively put themselves at the top of their relationship priority list. This one change alone is the most positively disruptive part of this approach for many people. Also note that even though relationships of "indirect impact" live in the professional category, I consider making some sort of positive impact in the world (having an others-focused mission) to also be part of our relationship with self. Using the Robbins-Madanes model of personality, we all crave "growth from and contribution to the world" as a condition for joy, and I find it unlikely that anyone is in full harmony with themselves without this element.

PROFESSIONAL LIFE

The professional area of life is the area comprising our indirect relationships: those who are impacted by what we do but whom we may not personally know. It is where we exchange value with the world and how the world tells us what our perceived value is. It's how we get paid, what we're known for. It's our pedigree, résumé, and station in life. It's also the area on which most of us are fixated, yet as we've seen it's the outermost layer of the circle and usually the one that transforms last. That doesn't mean it's any less important, but we have the cart before the horse if we put it first. Our professional success depends heavily on our levels of physical and personal development and to act otherwise is usually an avoidance strategy, residue from the days of the old American Dream when burying ourselves in work, often that we didn't even love, was considered an honorable way to better our life.

Governing Principle (Professional): Diversified Growth

For quantifying our professional life, we developed three value channels: finance, authority, and creativity. Each value channel has its own currency, or unit of exchange, and the goal is to have strong growth across each channel. Managing our professional lives is similar to how a financial advisor manages money, only the different investment categories (finance, authority, and creativity) are measured in different currencies.

Below, I'll explain each of the value channels along with its respective currency, and then share my personal KPIs that I use to measure that channel. As you consider these, remember that just because this is the area where you get paid doesn't mean that money is the driving factor.

Value Channel: Finance

Currency: Money
My KPIs: Top-line revenue, net-income/profit margin, and passive income

This area is pretty familiar and self-explanatory. It's what we all think of when we discuss professional development, and for good reason. Here we track how much money is flowing into our personal economy, how much of that money we actually get to keep (gross versus net), and how much of that money we earn through investments and systems we've put in place that we no longer have to actively work for (active versus passive).

Value Channel: Authority

Currency: Influence
My KPIs: Social media audience (size and engagement), email list (size and open rates), Power List (who I know and who/what they know that I can access).

As you can see, these KPIs are reflective of the times we live in and also specific to me. That said, I encourage you to try them on before developing your own. You don't have to be an entrepreneur for these to be important. The value channel of authority is about respect; how much are we respected and by how many, and thus how much cumulative influence do we wield in the world? It's rare nowadays for someone to build a lot of influence without a large network, usually digital, which usually includes various lists and targetable audiences (social media, email, etc.).

Value Channel: Creativity

Currency: Energy
My KPIs: Energy levels, joy, and healthy fear

Some people are confused why I include creativity in this area, but every life begins with an act of creativity, a very particular one that is also linked to pleasure. I don't think that's a coincidence. Maybe it's the artist in me, but I believe we are created to create and to enjoy creating. This is why I consider creativity its own value channel. When I used to do a lot of coaching, I would sometimes find myself working with seemingly successful people who had what appeared to be all the boxes of life checked—successful businesses, great families, and rich lives, yet they reported feeling dissatisfied and unfulfilled. Deeper analysis would reveal they felt creatively stagnant and that their work had become simply managing or perpetuating what they'd already created rather than creating anything new. This is definitely what I was feeling from 2016 to 2018. Those were the most professionally fruitful years I'd had to that point. My agency doubled in size for two years straight and we made the Inc. 5000 list in 2017 and 2018, yet I had zero passion for the business. It had become just about growing the business, not innovating or creating anything new, and that wasn't that interesting to me. Meanwhile at home was a perfect little girl I had created that had resparked my creative instincts, and leaving her just to go sit at an office and grow a business wasn't a choice I was willing to make.

Every now and then someone pushes back when I suggest that creativity is an essential part of success and happiness. Someone will say that "not everyone is an artist" or accuse me of superimposing my personality onto the world at large. Some people seem threatened by the idea that in every one of us resides a deep longing to indelibly mark the world. I disagree, so let me make an ontological argument for why I believe we are meant to be creative in our lives and cannot be happy, or even fully ourselves, otherwise. As individual, sovereign organisms we are each endowed with a unique genetic code, chemical makeup, and energy signature, all of which interact with the world around us. As far as I know, no one disputes any of that. So just as there is no way to introduce a new variable into any chemical or energetic experiment without changing the result, there is no way a unique cluster of chemicals and energy like we each are could interact in a physical and/or metaphysical world without changing that world, that is, creating something new that did not previously exist. I further believe that sensory evidence of our unique impact in the world is one way our psyche affirms that we are awake and conscious (rather than, say, in a coma, dreaming, or simply experiencing a memory). When there is any part of our life that lacks evidence of ongoing creative contribution that could only have come from us, we will naturally start to be repulsed by that part of our life. It will feel like a dead zone in our world, a place that dims our light, and we will go to great lengths to avoid it, even sabotaging our career or relationships. I think a lot of otherwise inscrutable decisions that people make can be explained as the need to purge a part of their life where nothing new is being created.

This doesn't mean everyone needs to paint or write music, but it does mean if we are to be truly fulfilled we need to be creating things in the world that are non-fungible and could not have been created by anyone else. In any area where we aren't being creative, levels of happiness, joy, and fulfillment will naturally be low. Because for most of us our professional life dominates our time, it is the most important area in which to be creative. It can also be the hardest, depending on your job, which is one reason I am such an advocate for entrepreneurship.

Healthy fear is another KPI that can help you gauge if you're doing meaningful work. It is 100 percent natural and unavoidable to feel fear when you pour yourself into work that bears your unique signature. This is the flipside of creativity, and the essence of what Stephen Pressfield calls *Resistance* in his seminal book *The War of Art*. Meaningful work will always bear traces of the person doing it, and having our work judged will always feel like being personally judged. Thus, meaningful work will inevitably produce some degree of feeling vulnerable, hence healthy fear being a professional KPI.

Before we move on, one final note on feeling vulnerable: Vulnerability correlates to healthy fear as long as it's rooted in authenticity, while vulnerability stemming from inauthenticity is really "fear of being found out" and is not a healthy fear. Vulnerability should always be a byproduct of being open and honest in our dealings, never a byproduct of being manipulative. And how to know which type of vulnerability a feeling is? For ourselves we would already know, so no further qualifying test is necessary. But as a coach, I did sometimes find it useful to try to assess whether a client's fear in their professional life was healthy or not, and in the case of someone manipulative I could not bank on them telling me the truth about what they were feeling. So I learned to look for the accompanying presence of joy as the tell. Vulnerability plus joy, which shows up like thrill or exhilaration, is usually an indicator of someone who is being creative in their work, taking risks, and fighting the good fight that is the war of art (in the broad definition of art meaning all that humankind produces). However, vulnerability without joy, which feels more akin to dread or foreboding, is a giveaway that someone's work is not authentic, however skilled it might be.

THE FOURTH P—PURPOSE

The 3 Ps of Success are the most effective framework I have ever found for promoting balanced excellence and making consistent, measurable, and diverse progress across all critical areas of life. But on their own, they are not enough.

A life lived entirely in pursuit of physical, personal, and professional success could run the risk of being a quite selfish affair. Granted, the intrinsic needs of personality (referencing again the Robbins-Madanes model) do include "contribution" as a spiritual need that should theoretically serve as a check against wanton indulgence, but in practice I could see people suppressing this part of self and using the 3 Ps as an excuse to be pretty narcissistic. Unless there's a good reason not to, that is. Which brings us to the fourth P, the element without which the 3 Ps are just a strategy for feeling good. The fourth P is purpose. Simply said, what is the point of living the first 3 Ps? Is it just to feel happy and successful, or is it for something bigger? I believe the latter.

All 4 Ps working together flows roughly as follows. We work daily on the 3 Ps. We measure them with KPIs and treat them like little science projects to be constantly tweaked and improved, but all the while, we have in the back of our mind the idea that there is some higher end to the whole affair. Man is a teleological being (from the Greek *telos*, meaning "end," and *logos*, meaning "reason" or "plan"), and we are not going to be our best selves if we do not seek out, find, and orient toward some sort of teleological true north, a reason for doing it all. I believe our first created purpose is to find our purpose, which we referenced earlier when talking about Mark Twain's two most important days idea. But that's a process, and may take some time, so what do we do until that second day comes and our purpose becomes clear? Simple. The 3 Ps are what we do. They do not require the fourth P. Rather, they are the mechanism for discovering it.

Through daily living according to the 3 Ps philosophy we create a life of clarity and confidence in which our fourth P can come into focus. But even though the fourth P is the point of the first 3 Ps, it's not the stopping point for them. On the contrary, having a clear purpose without continuously returning to and further optimizing the first 3 Ps would be just as hollow as the opposite is selfish. The world does not need any more idealistic blowhards trumpeting grand ideas while neglecting their health or their personal relationships. Finding your cause worth serving only makes being fit to serve more important.

One thing I have personally experienced from gaining clarity of purpose is the boost of energy that comes with it. Purpose is drive. Purpose keeps us going when the going gets tough. In our most "fulfilled" state, our purpose is what we are "filled full" of. You may already be crystal clear on your purpose, or perhaps it's not yet clear. Either way, take this opportunity to evaluate it, or reevaluate it, and make sure that it checks these three requirements for being both noble and sustainable:

1. Does your purpose honor your own unique greatness?
2. Does your purpose benefit humanity in some way?
3. Does your purpose maintain integrity with the 3 Ps?

You should be regularly reviewing your mission statement(s) to make sure your purpose is clear and your life is on track. You can hit all the physical, personal, and professional KPIs you want, but they don't mean a thing if they aren't helping you get clear on your purpose and then helping you achieve it once you are.

I understand this approach might seem pedantic or overly analytical for some people, but I can say, without a doubt, that living the 3 Ps, and inevitably getting clear on and integrating my fourth P, has completely transformed my life and also, in ways too numerous to list, freed up far more time than it takes to manage. This style of living forces you to run your life like a CEO runs a business. A CEO is a steward, the person who allocates resources, tracks KPIs, directs communication, sets the strategic direction, plans the projects and workflows, and guards the mission, vision, and values of an organization. If that isn't our role in our own life, I don't know what is. We have to constantly be adapting and making changes to fix what isn't working and doubling down on what is, yet most of us don't even have a mechanism to know what's working and what isn't. There's a great opportunity here to increase your productivity and improve your quality of life, so don't pass over this section. It's not enough to have read it; do it. If you will give this framework a shot, you'll be blown away by how far you can advance. Now let's turn the conversation from what and how we measure to what we are aiming for. It's time to talk goals.

14

Planning for Success

There are plenty of people who are passionate and have an aligned head and heart, but they still aren't getting amazing results. Apparently, it takes more than just a big vision and a caring heart to do great work. So many great endeavors fail, not in ideation but in execution. Results don't come from thoughts and feelings; results happen when our heads and our hearts direct our hands and mouths to do and say things in the real world. And doing and saying the right things the right way usually involves one of the things many of us avoid the most, planning. Organizational and operational planning skills are essential for getting things done, and the lack of them are the single biggest reason most entrepreneurs fail.

And it's not just entrepreneurs who benefit from effective organization and planning. Imagine for a second just how different your life would be if you could get everything done you wanted to get done. To many, that sounds unimaginable, but I promise it's possible with the strategies in this and the next couple chapters. And in case you think you are already organized enough and don't need this conversation, let me say that (1) I don't think you can ever be too organized, and (2) I thought the same thing until I started building ENTRE.

Building ENTRE has been one of the most challenging endeavors of my life in large part because when I started I thought I was already a pretty organized and disciplined person with good habits whose weaknesses had mostly been cured or mitigated. Fortunately, I was quickly humbled and I realize now how true the adage that "what got you here won't get you there" really is. Growing a company from a bootstrapped, single-person start-up to a 200-person, nine-figure venture in less than four years has required a level of organization and planning far beyond what I had ever experienced before (bought and paid for in the form of consultants and amazing team member hires). I now recognize that I was nowhere near as organized as I thought and that getting more organized has unlocked totally new levels of possibility for my life. I've learned the difference between being organized enough to operate inside my current life (most of us are this organized) and being more organized than my current life calls for so that there is room to grow. And while this isn't a book on organizational management, I do want to share how I have applied organizational management principles to my own 3 Ps with great success.

The first of these principles is the idea of SMART goals, or more specifically, the actual use of SMART goals rather than just talking about them like most people do. If you're not familiar with a SMART goal, it means setting a goal that is:

S: Specific (you clearly know when you've hit it)
M: Measurable (based on something you can measure)
A: Attainable (not demoralizingly difficult)
R: Relevant (connected to the larger mission)
T: Time-bound (has a pass/fail completion date)

In my experience, most people have heard of SMART goals, though admittedly I tend to hang out with entrepreneurs who study these sorts of things, so I'm not sure how true that is across mainstream society. But even in my world, very few people actually use SMART goal setting in their personal lives. At least once a year, I like to revisit my latest dreamscaping exercise and consider what SMART goals I can set in each of the 3 Ps.

#1. Physical

Do you want to look a certain way? Do you have health goals you want to reach? Do you want to incorporate a spiritual practice or an artistic endeavor?

Is there some psychological or emotional issue plaguing you? Maybe thinking SMART means establishing your physical baselines by doing something like getting a comprehensive blood panel done and digging into your biochemistry. Whatever it is, set at least one SMART goal in the area of diet, exercise, biochemistry, neurochemistry, or solitary spirituality, and make sure you have a basis for measuring your progress.

#2. Personal

What's the current status of your relationships? Which relationships can you improve and what type of activities could help improve them? Is your time allocated appropriately? Do you want to schedule vacations, outings, dinners, game nights, or group get-togethers? Do you need to do a better job reaching out on special occasions? In what ways can you be more thoughtful or generous, and not just focus on what's important to you? Look for a way to build traditions so you can strengthen and keep those bonds. What new relationships do you hope to make? If you're single and spend too much time working, you might want to make sure that you have the time to date. Maybe you just want to expand your network and meet more like-minded people. These are all great personal goals.

A significant breakthrough in my life occurred when I was attending an event (ironically, a software event where I wasn't expecting any great personal insights), and one of the speakers made a half-joking comment about how he had two different modes with his kids—one he called *referee* mode, for when more than one of his kids was present, and another called *coach* mode for when it was just him and one of his kids by themselves. He pointed out that coaches are much more beloved by their players than referees, so he aimed to spend much more time in coach mode than referee mode. Hearing that hit me hard. I knew he was undeniably correct. While I love hanging out with my kids together, and my family as whole, if I really think about the moments that build and deepen those relationships, they almost always happen during one-on-one time. So, I committed to spending more time with each of my kids and my spouse individually, even if it meant subtracting from group family time, and I created a SMART goal around it.

I have found this same principle holds true with friends and even people I work with. Whether it's date night with my wife or kids, taking my daughter to school every morning, going to lunch with a friend, or even orchestrating company events so people get time to connect individually, what started as a single SMART goal has become a regular practice that pays great dividends.

#3. Professional

If you own a business, what's your vision for that business, and what do you want to see it become? Maybe you have an idea for a business you haven't started yet. If you have a career and don't work for yourself, how can you improve? If you're striving to achieve a promotion or want to make more money, don't be afraid to ask your employer what SMART goal you could set for yourself to justify what you're asking for in their eyes. And if they tell you that there is nothing you can do to get promoted or make more money, then you know to make a SMART goal to find a better job (or, ahem, start a business).

DEADLINES

The most important part of the SMART goal acronym is the last letter, T for time-bound. Take it from someone who struggles mightily with ADD and procrastination but one day was offered a book deal, without self-imposed deadlines (or publisher imposed, as in the case of this book), it is very hard to finish things, especially the big things that move our lives forward. As they say, "a goal without a deadline is just a wish," and thinking about a wish is just wishful thinking. Deadlines make us more productive by increasing the discomfort we experience around not yet having completed a goal. Deadlines suck, that's exactly the point, and the fact that they suck is what makes them effective. We hit them so we can get rid of them because we don't like them hanging over us. The same reason we resist them is why we need them. Even in writing this book there reached a point where I was desperate to finish it just so I could stop stressing about the deadline.

Another reason deadlines work is because when you know you are running out of time to hit a goal you start looking for ways to speed things up. Over the course of many goals, doing this consistently results in hitting more of them in less overall time, so it is important that all our goals have deadlines, ideally really aggressive ones that are going to put a lot of pressure on us. Many of my finest moments have been when I was clearly going to miss an important deadline unless something changed. When we set a deadline, see it approaching, and realize that we aren't going to hit it, we immediately have to seek outside resources or in some other way change the plan, and we start getting creative in ways that we wouldn't if we didn't have a deadline. A lot of breakthroughs and innovations happen when creatively trying to hit what seems like an impossible deadline. Take Apple, for example, widely recognized as one of the most innovative companies in history. Apple's culture of innovation developed under the leadership of Steve Jobs, who was known for setting what seemed like impossible deadlines. According to Walter Isaacson, Jobs's biographer, it worked more often than not, and Steve Jobs even had a term for the effect of impossible deadline. He called them his "reality distortion field," a tool that literally bent reality and made the impossible possible.

But good deadlines aren't just aggressive, they are also specific and tangible so they can be broken down into clear steps. The way you attack those steps is by starting with the bigger picture. How big? Here's an example of how I create an overall plan and use it to derive specific deadlines.

- **Five-year vision:** You may have an idea where you want to be in ten or twenty years, but so much can happen during that time, so it's difficult to plan for something that far in advance. I like to start with a five-year plan. Look at your list of goals and figure out where you want to be in five years.

- **Yearly goals:** Take that five-year vision for each goal and break down what you need to accomplish each year to achieve it.

- **Quarterly "rocks":** Now look at that first year and break that goal down into four parts. I call them rocks because they are nonnegotiable. These objectives are set in stone and have to be accomplished in three months (credit to the EOS framework developed by Gino Wickman for the terms *rocks* and *sprints*).

- **Weekly sprints:** Rocks get broken down into twelve weekly sprints, or benchmarks, that you need to hit at the end of each week.

- **Daily tasks:** What do you need to do every single day to finish each sprint at the end of the week? This is the smallest possible chunk, which allows you to stay focused and not get distracted by the bigger picture.

All you need to care about is this one task, and you'll know that you're moving closer to where you want to be in five years. Like the title of the great book by Jason Jennings says, "Think Big, Act Small." Starting with a five-year goal and working all the way back to what to do today is a recipe for success.

THE PRODUCTIVITY PYRAMID

You're probably familiar with Pareto's principle, or what you may have heard called the 80/20 rule. It states that 80 percent of output in a given endeavor generally comes from 20 percent of the input. This law is applied in terms of business or economics with 20 percent of employees doing 80 percent of the work or 20 percent of customers producing 80 percent of the revenue, but I've found it applies elsewhere as well. I think in my marriage about 80 percent of the love and trust comes from 20 percent of the activities, and I remember when I learned Pareto's principle in school thinking that about 80 percent of my grades came from 20 percent of my homework and studying. The point is that time is limited, and we get most of our results from the time spent working on the highest-yield activities, so we want to take a close look at how we spend our time.

But before we can figure out what we should be doing, it's often necessary to figure out what we should *not* do. We are bombarded with constant interruptions and distractions that can derail our productivity. Much of success involves addition by subtraction, getting rid of those activities that cause us to waste time and energy.

Don't wait to develop this skill. Knowing when to say no becomes more crucial the more successful you become because the more you become known for your results, the more people want you involved in theirs. If you are not yet at the point in your success journey where people are constantly hitting you up for advice or assistance, enjoy the calm while it lasts and use it to practice blocking out distractions. When figuring out what to focus on, you want to single out the activities in your life that produce the highest returns. You can do that by creating a "productivity pyramid." This is a simple system that breaks down your priorities into four levels.

- **Level 1:** These are the things that create true fulfillment and constant progress over time: the physical, personal, and professional things that are congruent with your purpose (or your journey to discover it) and that mean the absolute most to you.
- **Level 2:** These have a high dollar value and put money in the bank that you need to live. Until you are financially free, these must get done.
- **Level 3:** These have a low dollar value but still need to get done.
- **Level 4:** These are time suckers that don't add anything to your life and can even take you backward.

Break down everything you do regularly and place it on your pyramid. Don't skip anything, whether it's checking email, doing research, making food, taking the kids to school, going to the gym, or going out on a date with your spouse. When you lay out your activities like this, it makes it easier to focus only on those activities that move you toward your goals while avoiding time suckers that set you back. You want to fill your day with level 1 and level 2 activities (ideally doing the level 1 activities first when you have the most energy), spend as little time as possible on level 3 activities, and eliminate level 4 activities.

There is a simple framework for managing our level 3 and 4 activities called DOO. DOO stands for Delete, Optimize, Outsource. Think, *"Argh, all this clutter; what do I DOO about it?"* and you'll always remember it.

1. **Delete it:** You should be able to delete certain activities. If necessary, start with a goal of elimination for a certain number of days. If we're honest with ourselves, we know what these behaviors are in our life, though they vary for everyone. One person's vice can be another person's harmless indulgence, but for most of us the behaviors we'd do best to delete or restrict tend to center around the conveniences of the modern world—video games, social media browsing, Netflix, online shopping, processed foods, and the like. You can create rules of moderation to scale back these activities if it's too hard to go cold turkey. And keep in mind the ripple effect that some behaviors can have on productivity. Take drinking, for instance. Even just a few drinks at night can make you sluggish the next day and result in an entire day

of subpar performance. Of course, just deleting certain habits is easier said than done and you may require more support than what's in this book for breaking certain patterns or cravings. For me, the book *The Power of Habit* by Charles Duhigg was ground zero for reprogramming some of my toughest habits to break.

2. **Optimize:** For behaviors you want to reduce but not eliminate, look for ways to make them more efficient or valuable. Take video games as an example. Instead of cutting them out altogether, you could plan to play them at the end of a long day as motivation to get all your other work done. Or you could incorporate them into quality time with one of your kids. I personally like combining activities when possible as long as they do not cannibalize physical or cognitive capacity from each other. Examples of this are listening to an audiobook while I do cardio, dictating social media content captions while I drive, or sipping a protein shake while I work.

3. **Outsource:** See if there is a way you can pay someone else to do certain tasks for you, particularly for level 2 and 3 activities that you can't cut out or restrict because they are functionally necessary. When I was a kid, my mom struggled with being late to work after taking me to school each morning (the school did not have a school bus). At first, she tried carpooling with other moms, but she wound up being even later on the days she drove. So, she called a private bussing company, got a bunch of other working parents together, and organized the school's first bussing system. Sadly, my mom passed a year before this book was written, but the bus route she organized still runs to this day and thousands of parents across multiple decades have benefitted from her knack for outsourcing.

If you find that you have a lot of level 4 activities, it might be overwhelming to cut all of them out at once, so start small. Each week pick a new activity to eliminate. For those big ones you might struggle with, try writing a reminder and taping it onto your monitor (or even better, write down the value of your time). If every time you open up your computer you see, "$1,000 an hour: it's *your* choice," you're bound to think twice before you get sucked into the comments thread on someone's controversial Facebook post (the kind the algorithm loves to serve you up).

Another great technique we'll discuss in a later chapter is using commitment and consistency. If you're struggling to cut out a particular time-sucking behavior, tell people that you've given it up; the louder and more publicly the better. Personally, I like to up the ante on this strategy and post commitments on social media along with regular updates on how I'm doing to increase accountability.

The plan is the first step, and you can't move forward without it, but now that you know what you have to do, how can you make sure you get it all done?

15

Mastering Time

A good friend of mine who is also a business coach talks often about "the tyranny of the urgent." Not everything that feels urgent is truly important, and too often the things that are most important feel like they can wait because they are grounded in "timeless" principles so resist the pressures of time. If we're not careful, we end up living lives in which we're always working on the urgent things and neglecting the stuff that is truest to the mission—hence "the tyranny of the urgent." The antidote to all of this is one of mankind's oldest and least sexy inventions: the schedule.

Many people resist scheduling, and I did too for a long time. It was my piano teacher Mike Lowe (who you may remember from chapter 5) who changed that. Not only did he encourage me to do a lot of practicing in my head, but also he taught me how to schedule my practice. The idea was that improvement doesn't take place during the act of practicing, but in what he called "learning intervals," which were the gaps between practice sessions. If you've ever practiced something intensely, and then come back the next day to notice improvement, you have experienced a learning interval. Our strategy was to increase both the quantity and frequency of learning intervals by practicing lots of different things in shorter stints. Side note: approximately twenty-five years later I heard Elon Musk talking about a similar approach and how he teaches himself things in multiple small breaks between other tasks—he calls it "interstitial learning." So Mike and I laid out a plan for me to practice four hours a day in preplanned five-minute intervals. That meant that every day I could practice forty-eight different aspects of playing the piano, so every night my brain would be rewiring and improving at all forty-eight of them. It worked so well that I got kind of addicted and upped my practice to six, eight, and even ten hours a day, but always in five-minute chunks. I would have a hundred or more concepts rewiring nightly, and honestly my youthful pride got pretty wrapped up in people constantly asking me how the heck I was improving so fast. I wasn't the best pianist in Houston but on the daily I was being told I was the most improved, and that felt pretty good for someone who was never supposed to have a career as a professional musician. Ever since the success of my learning experiment with Mike, I have been obsessed with schedule optimization and am a believer that we are capable of far more than most of us are taught we are based on how we manage our time.

A well-run schedule is a force multiplier that can supercharge all our efforts in life. Breaking down every aspect of life into five-minute intervals might be too neurotic for some (and I know my wife would agree), but if someone wants to try it, I'd definitely advise it. Note this doesn't mean you have to "context switch" (basically to lose momentum) every five minutes. You can always string multiple segments together to work on the same thing. But having done it this way I'll tell you it feels different—thinking of an hour spent on one project as really twelve consecutive five-minute work intervals gives a sensation of control and freedom you don't feel when working with larger chunks. And supposedly, Elon Musk plans his entire day in five-minute increments, so this level of meticulousness is apparently doable.

While many might think that what I'm describing sounds stifling, I could not feel more differently. A well-constructed schedule is where the rubber of discipline meets the road of freedom. Time is our most valuable asset, so optimizing it is going to be some of the most valuable work we can do. Personally, I work in fifteen-minute intervals, with every minute of every weekday from 3:30 a.m. (2:30 on Mondays) to 6 p.m. accounted for. This type of hyper-scheduling reduces stress and gives me confidence that during every moment I'm doing exactly what I'm "supposed" to be doing based on the goals and priorities I had in mind when I made my schedule. This confidence keeps my mind from wandering or questioning what I'm doing, while allowing me to stay present and engaged. Every time we ask ourselves, *"Am I doing what I should be doing?"* we context switch, which costs time and invites errors. As a hack I recommend an app called Horo for your computer and the use of cell phone alarms and calendar alerts so you are always prompted when it's time to switch. Even checking the clock unnecessarily is a form of context switching.

I use a looser version of this strategy on weekends as well that uses larger chunks of time (mostly because it makes things easier to plan with my family). As I'm writing this, I'm twenty-seven minutes into a three-hour block on a Sunday morning with family lunch coming up in two hours and thirty-three minutes (thanks, Horo). If you're thinking you couldn't possibly be this disciplined, trust me: anyone can get scheduled, and once you do, you'll never want to go back to whimsical living with its constant anxiety about what to be doing and tragically squandered potential.

Let me say this as emphatically as possible: this section right here is the climax of this part of the book ("Live by Choice, Not by Chance"). Carefully crafting a robust schedule for ourselves based on detailed plans, SMART goals, and a detailed dreamscape of the life we are building is the essence of living by choice. Said another way, living any less scheduled than what's possible is living less by choice than what's possible and leaving more to chance. Imagine the relief of knowing that every moment of every day you are doing exactly what you have objectively determined is the most effective and direct path to achieve the life you want. That feeling can be yours every minute of every day. But let me guess: you're still hesitant?

This isn't my first rodeo. I've taught this approach to hundreds of people and heard every excuse imaginable for why it's impossible and have seen types of schedule sabotage that boggle the mind. I've heard people invent nonexistent neurological conditions to explain why they can't stick to a schedule. I've seen people miss scheduled appointments because they spontaneously decided they needed to shoplift and got arrested. One person told me that his cat ate his schedule (I guess the dog had the day off). I get it, most of us have baggage around being "boxed in" or feeling like we are "giving up our freedom," but that's not what this is. For most of us the thought of operating from a strict schedule brings up resentment and resistance because it's historically been associated with school or work—areas of our life where we lacked control and where our schedule was one of the tools used to control us. But this book is the beginning of the end of all that for you. From now on, "clocking in" or "staying on schedule" means creating the exact life you want and executing on your meticulous and glorious plan for achieving it. This is no longer about being boxed in; you are breaking free.

In my experience, our willingness to make changes has much less to do with the changes themselves and more to do with our reasons for making them. Remind yourself why you want to do all this. Anyone can reprogram virtually any part of themselves if they are clear on and believe in their purpose for doing so. I used to sleep until noon when I was a musician after being out all night; now I get up at 3:30 a.m. I used to be 30 percent bodyfat; now I run about 10 percent and haven't missed a workout in six years. I used to struggle to finish two-thousand-word papers in college; now I'm writing an entire book. If you find yourself resisting change, remember, it's not about willpower, it's about finding your purpose and letting your Success Character lead the way. Speaking of willpower, there is much more on that subject still to come.

So now let's assume you're ready and willing to construct the ultimate schedule. How do you begin? Simple. Start with those daily tasks that you absolutely have to get done. These tasks are directly related to your bigger over-all goals, and they overlap with the level 1 activities in the 3 Ps. These are the most important things in your life, so they should take priority every single day. These are the "daily deposits" that constitute "The ENTRE Way," which we referenced back in the dreamscaping section—the specific activities that move us meaningfully forward in each of the 3 Ps. And make sure to schedule all of them, every single one. If it's worth being in your life, it's worth sched-uling. If it's not worth scheduling, then it's not worth being in your life. And want to know something exciting? You never have to forget anything again. When living your most organized life, "I forgot _____" can really only mean "I forgot to schedule _____" because if it had been on the schedule it would have gotten done.

Most of us tend primarily to schedule appointments that involve other people, or one-off commitments that don't recur. But what message does that send to ourselves? If success is primarily built on smaller tasks done consistently over time, then why are we not scheduling the most important parts of being successful? Are we more worried about missing a date with someone else than we are about missing a date with ourselves? It's been said that most of us would never be friends with someone who treats us like we do, and I think schedul-ing is one place this shows up. Schedule what matters most—your recurring commitments to yourself. Everything else can start squeezing around those for a change, rather than the other way around. Unless we start scheduling "the mundane," our quality of life gets eroded by the sickly sweet temptation of short-term excitement. Soon the morning gym commitment gets bumped because we stayed up late with our friend planning a cruise. We forget to prepare our healthy meals for the week on Sunday afternoon because the Super Bowl is on, so Monday at lunch, instead of our fifteen-minute healthy ritual followed by a productive afternoon, we're taking thirty minutes to go buy fast food and then crashing an hour later. Every time we bump a small but important thing for a big, exciting thing, we displace what matters most and send a negative ripple through our life. It's the tyranny of the urgent all over again, only now it's worse because nothing was urgent, we were just easily distracted and undisciplined. How easily we forget that it's the little stuff, the stuff that needs to be unbumpable, that creates our life. In a perfect world, our schedule would have no "exciting" stuff at all, and we'd never have to worry about anything mission-critical getting displaced. In this world there are no Super Bowls, no after-hours cruise planning sessions, no unplanned drains of time—everything happens inside its scheduled window. It's bliss, I promise you, and you won't miss dawdling because once you've broken free and are living the exact life you want you won't need temporary escapes or diversions anymore. The point is to create a life that is so saturated with the joy of progress, growth, and purpose that you won't want to miss a second of it. When your schedule is a masterpiece of organized 4 Ps living where you know every box of life is getting checked and every stressor is one you chose with intention, you stop looking for escapes and start trying to avoid them. Even sleep gets annoying when the life you wake up to every day is this on track. On that note, if you take nothing else from this chapter, please let this quote reverberate in your mind. *"Show me your schedule; I'll show you your future."*

On that note, one of my greatest joys is having a solid batch of my daily deposits done every morning before my work day starts at 8:00 a.m. That's why I wake up at 3:30 a.m.; listen right away to an audiobook (personal deposit); organize my vitamins and supplements for the day (physical deposit); hit cardio, stretch, and lift weights starting at 4:10 (three physical deposits); practice piano at 5:30 (personal and physical deposit); and take my daughter for breakfast at 6:45 (personal deposit) every day. And on top of that, sometimes I create social media content during my cardio, or go live on Instagram while practicing piano, so I even get some personal brand building (professional deposits) done early as well. For more on the idea of doing essential tasks first, I recommend a great book called *Eat That Frog* by Brian Tracy.

Starting well is the biggest part of doing well, and so many of the obstacles I've seen with people I've coached are the troubles they have getting started. One of the greatest fallacies in coaching and in life is that "it's not how you start, but how you finish." I think that's a little reductive. We do our best work when we have the time, flexibility, and freedom to be creative, not when we're under the gun. Pick any sport, and you'll see it's a lot harder to play from behind. You won't see any basketball or football teams intentionally applying a strategy of lollygagging for three quarters and then pushing themselves to win in the final quarter because of an it's-not-how-you-start-but-how-you-finish philosophy. That coach would be fired really fast!

The best predictor of future behavior is past behavior, so the best predictor of how you'll play the second half is how you played the first half, and the best predictor of how you'll finish the day is how you started. Get obsessed with strong starts. Really, when your day starts off chaotic, does it really ever get better? Or do you just chalk a bad day up to "waking up on the wrong side of the bed" and hope the next day goes better? Mornings are the critical time each day when we get to establish choice and not chance as the determining factor in our lives, and the earlier we get up and the harder we attack the day when we do, the more certain we can be that it was our choice to do so.

For most of my twenties, I lived a double life—aspiring entrepreneur working on various businesses by day, and beatnik musician by night. When the money gigs were over at 2:00 a.m., that's when we got to be artists. By 3:00 a.m., we would gather at the afterhours clubs for jam sessions that would last until five or six in the morning. I'd get home around 7:00 a.m., eat breakfast (dinner?), and then go to bed. Although I was very scheduled in the afternoons, evenings, and night times, I clearly didn't have a morning routine since I didn't even have a morning. And even after I switched careers and wasn't a working musician anymore, I would still stay up late working and sleep in the next day. I thought if I just did the right work when I was awake, it didn't matter when I did it. I now believe I was wrong for two reasons. The obvious one is that for most of us the hours before 6:00 or 7:00 a.m. are likely the only chance we'll have all day to be alone. There is also a certain way the world vibrates when the sun is just coming up that we miss when we sleep in. I think one of the reasons I did as well as I did when I was a musician was that my schedule was so extremely shifted that I still got to experience sunrise most days, even as a prelude to sleep. This question of whether it's just quantity of sleep or if which hours you sleep matters is one I have been really interested in for the last several years. After probably a hundred conversations with night owls on the subject (including computer programmers, artists, musicians, writers, and even some night nurses at hospitals), I've concluded that most people agree there is a power in getting a jump on the day before sunrise, even among those who don't do it. And certainly, almost every great author or authority on success has said as much.

It was one such author who inspired me to once-and-for-all rip the Band-Aid off and become a before-sunup riser. In the book *The Miracle Morning*, author Hal Elrod opens with an account of a car accident that left him dead for six minutes. After waking up from a subsequent six-day coma, Elrod had to rebuild his life from the ground up, starting with learning how to walk again. His morning routine was the foundation of that process. In *The Miracle Morning*, he teaches his life-saving morning routine through an acronym called SAVERS.

S: Silence
A: Affirmation
V: Visualization
E: Exercise
R: Reading
S: Scribing

The Miracle Morning came out in 2012, and I read it the following year. I was thirty-four years old, and I was angry the whole time I was reading it because I could feel what was happening; I was losing my ability to deny in good conscience that staying up late and sleeping in was costing me my full potential. So, I began the arduous process of resetting my body clock from waking up as late as noon to my initial goal of 6:00 a.m.

At first, it was awful, and I wrestled with doubts that I could do it. Then, my own miracle happened. I was looking through the notes from a seminar I had attended back in my affiliate marketing days, and I stumbled across what I wrote after watching a presentation given by a gentleman I've since become friends with named Wayne Allyn Root (who is also a world-class sports handicapper, and once ran for vice president on the Libertarian Party ticket—a super interesting guy). His presentation was titled "Positive Addictions," and one of his positive addictions was a morning walk. In the talk, he shared what he had done when he decided to start getting up an hour earlier every day to go for a walk. It was as genius as it was simple. He just set his alarm clock one minute earlier every day, so every thirty days, he was getting up a half hour earlier without ever having to shock his system and adjust. So that meant I could shift my wake-up time from noon to 6:00 a.m. in 360 days, or just under a year. It worked like a charm, and I even started pushing the envelope, sometimes waking up not just one but two whole minutes earlier than the day before. (Crazy, right? I was really living on the edge.) After a year, I was a 4:00 a.m. guy, and then two years later when my fourth child was born, I decided I needed to push it a little more, and after an easy thirty-day push, it was 3:30 a.m.

Today, I'm officially a full-on morning-routine addict. My morning routine energizes me for the day, allows me to check off some level 1 activities and 3 Ps deposits, and also gives me something I really can't live without as a bona fide introvert—alone time.

But routines aren't just for mornings. Most high performers I know also have nightly routines. And I don't mean things like brushing your teeth or putting on your eye mask; I mean things related directly to productivity and performance. Just like we should begin every day with the end in mind, we should end every day with the next day's beginning in mind. My nightly routine consists of two parts, one involving things I stop doing and one involving something to do.

The first part of my nightly routine is called the 10-3-2-1-0 formula (which I learned about in a book called *The Perfect Day Formula* by Craig Ballantyne), and it's become second nature. Here's how it works:

- 10—Cut out caffeine ten hours before going to bed.
- 3—Cut out all food and alcohol three hours before going to bed.
- 2—Stop working two hours before going to bed.
- 1—Stop looking at all screens one hour before going to bed.
- 0—Hit the snooze zero times when your alarm goes off in the morning. To ensure this I use the five-second rule and make sure my feet are on the floor within five seconds of consciousness.

The second part of my nightly routine is a simple two-step process we developed at ENTRE as part of the ENTRE Day called Nightly Assessment & Planning (just remember NAP, for short, as in "do your NAP before you can take your nap"). This shouldn't take more than a few minutes, but if done correctly and consistently, it can make a significant impact. Here's how it works:

1. Reflect on your day and analyze how well you executed your plan for that day. You should be able to identify a significant deposit you made that day in each category of the 3 Ps. Give yourself a grade (I use a 1–10 scale) and make notes on what you can improve the next day. I do it on my phone, so I use blue-light glasses, since I'm usually within two hours of bedtime, but you can easily do this in a notebook.

2. Plan the next day. When will you check emails, make sales calls, eat meals, have meetings, work out, see your kids, have a date night with your spouse, work on your book, change that light bulb, and cancel your unused satellite TV subscription? Plan everything like we've talked about. This may take a while if you've never planned your days meticulously before, but after some regular practice, you'll have consistent cadences established for each day, and the nightly planning process will involve only making tweaks.

Do this every weeknight (and weekends if you want), and then on Sunday night make sure you not only look at Monday, but also review the entire week ahead. The peace of mind that comes from knowing every base has already been covered for the day before you even wake up in the morning cannot be described; you just have to experience it. If you do this regularly, it will completely transform your life. (And yes, I know I say that about multiple things in this book, but I stand by all of them.)

Don't put off or underestimate the importance of planning ahead. There is a Navy SEAL saying that sums it up—"By the time you need to be ready, it's too late to get ready"—so get ready now.

SCHEDULING AND PRODUCTIVITY HACKS

In my consulting, I often come up with plans to fix problems or scale a business that get met with a rebuttal to the effect of "there's not enough time to do all that in the time frame given." So I call their bluff and we do a time-usage analysis, and not once has it ever turned out to be true. I am completely convinced that every one of us has more time than we recognize. The key is knowing where to look for it, getting ruthless about the process, and sometimes reframing how we look at time.

Day Chunking

Most people break their work day down into two segments—morning and afternoon—but I chunk my work day into four smaller segments—early morning, mid-morning, midday, and afternoon. It's kind of a trick I play on myself, but it works, and thinking about it this way feels like magically creating more time and opportunity.

Peak Timing

What's your peak time—the time you feel the best? For me, it's in the early morning, but whatever that time is for you is when you want to focus on your most important daily tasks. This is often influenced by food—what you eat and when you eat it. One of the reasons people tend to feel so good in the mornings is they have gone so many hours without carbohydrates. I said it before and I'll say it again, beware of carbs if you want to be as productive as you could be.

Time Chunking

For me, it's fifteen-minute intervals. For Elon Musk, it's five-minute intervals. I cannot overstate the importance of setting a predetermined amount of time to accomplish each task on your calendar, and blocking out all other distractions. If you aren't regularly in the habit of putting your phone on airplane mode, closing all of your browsers, and putting your head down and focusing for regular intervals, you'll be blown away by how much you get done.

One method I'll pull out for larger projects is the 60/60/30 method. This involves chunking tasks into two sixty-minute work blocks (with a ten-minute break in between) and then a thirty-minute work block (followed by another ten-minute break). This comes out to a total of three hours with two and a half hours of work and the third work block feeling easy because it's only half as long as the other two. Pair this with four-part day chunking, and you can have a 60/60/30 block in the early morning, one in the late morning, one midday, and one in the afternoon (or shifted later, depending on your wake-up time). That's ten hours of real work spread across twelve hours in one day. Compare that to the American average of two hours and fifty-three minutes of real work spread across eight and a half hours of the day (according to the Bureau of Labor Statistics). With this method you can accomplish in one day what the average person does in a week.

Project Chunking

This is a similar concept, but instead, you group together tasks that are connected and attack them all at the same time. If there's something related to what you just finished, don't wait to do that other thing later—do it now. So, if you just made a video, don't put off finding a platform to host it on, sending out an email to notify people about the video, setting up push notifications for the video, cross-promoting it on other platforms, and building the auto-responder sequence to notify people about future videos. Those are all related tasks, so chunk them together and do them all at the same time while you're in that mindset and have momentum.

Take Breaks

We aren't machines. We will all eventually run out of gas and hit a wall. What's great about the 60/60/30 method is that it has built-in breaks. You can actually be more productive working for an hour, taking a break, and then working for another hour than you could be working two hours straight, because you have time to reset and refocus. Be sure to make a clear time to stop, and have breaks built into your schedule.

This can be difficult for those of us who always have something else we could be doing, but if we don't take a break, our bodies and minds get tired, and our productivity decreases. And move around on your breaks. Don't just sit in the same chair looking at your phone. A neurological and physiological "flushing" occurs when we get our blood and lymphatic fluid circulating even a little from moving around, and that helps us feel fresh when we start working again. For bonus points throw in some push-ups, wall sits, or a quick plank on every short break. You won't even notice the time spent, but over the course of a year these little interstitial exercise sets will make a massive change in your body.

Mix and Match

Certain deposits can be combined, especially physical deposits with other types. For example, if you're married or in a relationship, you can combine a Physical deposit and a Personal deposit into a gym date! Every single Saturday and Sunday, I have a standing gym date with my wife. It's sacred, and we only miss it if I'm out of town. It's indescribable how powerful this habit has been for our relationship. We get to spend quality time together, away from the kids, supporting each other in doing something hard. And by watching the person you love push themselves, and them you, you actually become more attracted to each other. Look for times during your day when you can kill multiple birds with the same stone. Do you have a commute? That's a great time to listen to podcasts or audiobooks. Need to stretch? Grab a book and read while you hold it. I sometimes write social media posts while planking on my elbows. Get creative and find ways to get fit while doing other things.

Don't Ignore Pockets of Time

During my busiest year as a musician I played almost four hundred gigs, while also teaching lessons, writing a musical, going to school, and trying to get a business off the ground. With all of that going on, it was hard to find time to actually practice the piano and continue to improve. Fortunately, piano teacher Mike had prepared me well.

I got really creative. For example, if I felt myself needing to pee during a class, I would excuse myself to go during the class instead of waiting to go in the ten minutes between classes. That way I could always use five of the ten minutes between each of my classes to run up to a practice room. I kept flash cards in my car with chord progressions, song lyrics, weird harmonies, and rhythmic patterns so that, sitting at stoplights, I could practice music in my head. And between every piano lesson I taught, when the other teachers would mill out into the break room and chat, I would squeeze in five more minutes of practice.

All this may sound a bit silly and manic, but it added up. You can make a lot of progress in just a few minutes here and there if you quiet your mind and concentrate. Remember the rewiring and improvement happens between sessions anyway, so having more frequent sessions of work or practice, even five-minute sessions, means more constant improvement. If you have a couple of minutes before a phone call or a meeting, don't just waste it by scrolling through your phone or waiting around. See what you can get done. Get disciplined enough at this, and it's like discovering an eighth day of the week that was there all along, peppered throughout the other seven days.

Audit Your Habits

In *The Power of Habit*, Charles Duhigg explains how all habits operate on the same three-step loop—a cue, followed by a routine, then concluded with a reward. This loop, repeated over time, forms "neural grooves" in our mind, similar to how running water creates grooves in the earth. As the grooves form and deepen they become the path of least resistance for our thoughts to take and it gets harder to resist them. Once cued, we are now stuck in the groove and the more we engage in a particular habit, the deeper the groove gets. This is true for everything from checking your email to your morning routine. Most of our habits are on autopilot, so we aren't even aware of what we're doing. The catch is that it doesn't matter if a habit is positive or negative; they all work the same way. We are triggered by a cue to perform a routine because of the psychological reward we have trained ourselves to receive. If we're ever going to change our habits, we have to understand what they are.

What you can do right now is look at your current habits. Find one that occurs on a consistent basis that is not yielding the result you want—a level 4 habit. Maybe it's drinking soda, maybe it's idle chitchat with a coworker, or maybe it's a Sudoku obsession that's gotten out of hand. Whatever it is, figure out the cue, routine, and reward, and then change one of them. If the dog barking in the morning cues you to take it out to pee and then you reward yourself on your return with a donut, don't try to discard the whole habit; just exchange the reward. Maybe initially it's half a donut, maybe it's a sugar-free snack, maybe it's eating the donut while you do a wall sit. The point is incremental progress that minimally alters the neural grooves you have rather than trying to break entirely out of them. That approach usually backfires. It will take some time, but if you work within your neural grooves, you can slowly reroute them.

This work is imperative. Be merciless about rewiring your negative habits and addictions and replacing them with ones that help you achieve the life you want. One of my favorite quotes is by Will Durant when paraphrasing Aristotle: "We are what we repeatedly do. Excellence, then, is not an act, but a habit." Be habitually excellent!

Free Up Your Brain

True self-awareness is both humbling and empowering. Admitting how fragile and, frankly, screwed up we all are as human beings is the first step in discarding the flawed idea that our brains can really keep it all together or should even bother trying. None of us are responsible enough to remember everything we need to do. None of us are organized enough to remember where everything goes. None of us are disciplined enough to do exactly what we need to do when we ought to do it. Obviously, we need to allow for grace and be kind to ourselves, but what about actually overcoming our flaws and performing beyond our natural capacity? Enter the external brain.

It was Ari Meisel who came up with the concept of the external brain in his book *The Art of Less Doing*, and it's an impactful way to improve your productivity, accountability, and creativity. In many ways our brains are our own worst enemies. We learn so much and we have so many ideas, opportunities, and obligations that our brains get full and it's easy to get overwhelmed. Then, our self-preservation instinct kicks in, and our brains start to act as a sort of governor to make sure we don't get exhausted. We stop retaining new information, we start coming up with excuses, and distractions become more tempting.

What if there was a place outside our brains where we could put all the ideas, opportunities, and things to do that pop up, so our brains never hit capacity? That's the external brain. Just like using a schedule ensures we never forget to do "the little things" that determine our life, our external brain ensures we never forget "the little stuff." It's the place where we can dump everything that's thrown at us so we can later organize it all without anything slipping through the cracks. Obviously not all little stuff is worth keeping, but you never know unless you have an opportunity to go back and sort through it all. And you expend a lot less energy over the course of a day if you don't have to evaluate things that pop up in real time but can just store them for a better time.

The term *external brain* sounds like it's straight out of science fiction, and maybe a couple decades ago it would have been, but now it's really just a combination of utilizing digital tools like notetaking apps (I use the Notes app on my phone, but my business partner, Adam, who's even more organized than me, uses Evernote), to-do lists (there are a zillion apps for this), cloud storage (Google Drive, for example), etc. You can have access to all of that on your phone, and it can be synced to your computer, where it will always be accessible and easy to share with anyone who might need to view it. Use these devices and apps to organize your life and make things easier. The less you have to remember yourself, the more you can focus and concentrate on executing the tasks at hand.

Don't Skip Weekends

Some people get touchy about this, but I strongly resist the idea that two out of every seven days must be taken off. Intentionality shouldn't only happen some of the time. Do the math. Saturday and Sunday make up about 28.6 percent of your life, and when coupled with holidays, most of us end up being unscheduled and unaccountable for a third of each year or more. That's like budgeting a third of your income to blow at a casino. Think of how much time and opportunity you lose if you only make progress five out of seven days a week. I'm not saying you can't relax or take time off, but continue to be organized and strategic about your scheduling and your progress. Don't take your foot off the gas and lose momentum for nearly a third of your days.

I know this can all be a lot to start incorporating. That's why it's so important to do the nightly NAP process and analyze how you did at the end of each day. Examine what was easy and what was difficult. What strategies worked and what didn't? Doing this allows you to spot your own patterns and blind spots that you might not notice if you weren't looking closely. If you see that you struggle to get the same tasks done or are continuously less productive during a certain time of day, you can adjust accordingly. Figure out what works and stick with it, but always be evolving to become more effective and more efficient.

We're all wired differently and have different goals, so different techniques work for different people, but there is one thing that works for everyone and that nothing works without—taking action. That's where we head next.

16

The 3 Legs
of Successful Action

Whether coaching individuals, consulting with small groups, or leading online training, I've worked with thousands of people, and the biggest challenge I deal with is not figuring out what people should be doing; it's figuring out why they aren't doing it.

My work has shown me there is a troubling lack of clarity in the world surrounding what action taking needs to look like if it's going to have a high likelihood of success. When I first started ENTRE, I knew that I would be teaching thousands of people how to start taking action as entrepreneurs, so I became obsessed with understanding the nature of successful action. I studied dozens of people throughout history from different areas who have achieved great things—athletes like Michael Jordan, business titans like Sam Walton, world changers like Gandhi, and innovators like Thomas Edison—and I found three common characteristics in every person I studied. We now teach these 3 Legs of Successful Action as a core principle at ENTRE, and it is one of our most powerful concepts that people often credit with helping them get clarity on why certain things have not worked in their lives after years of frustration.

Leg #1: Knowledge

Mike Dillard is a legend in the online business space and used to host one of the most influential entrepreneurial podcasts on the air. He was also one of my early mentors I met as part of that group huddled backstage in Lake Tahoe. I've learned a lot from Mike, but one of the most significant things he has taught me is that there are only two ways to create opportunity: to expand your network or to acquire new knowledge. We've talked about the first way; now let's talk about the second.

Remember when you were a kid? Think about how much energy and curiosity you had. There were times when it felt like anything was possible. When we're kids, our default state is high energy, high achievement, high learning, and high belief. It's not until we become adults that we lose energy, and those possibilities dwindle in our minds. I believe that acquiring new knowledge helps us renew our child state. The more we discover and learn, the more we can tap into that vast pool of energy that has remained dormant since our youth. As adults, we have the added benefit of being able to utilize that knowledge. Kids may be great learners, but they don't have the maturity or life experience to understand the context and apply what they learn. Once we've been through the trials of life, we now have much more context and can learn in a richer way than we did when we were younger. That's extremely powerful when trying to create change and do awesome things in our lives.

They say knowledge is power, but I think it goes beyond that. Knowledge is like a superpower that allows us to do extraordinary things, even defy the laws of nature. Take the second law of thermodynamics, which says that, over time, energy in any system becomes more random or disordered via a force called entropy. And yet we human beings use knowledge constantly to construct, organize, and bring order to energy. The laws of nature did not forecast the existence of a power grid, or a hydroelectric dam. Human knowledge did that. What we've come together as human beings to accomplish is astonishing; we just need to remember to astonish ourselves individually too. Falling back in love with learning like when we were kids unlocks our ability to do incredible things in our own life and taps into the energy we will need to do them.

The good news is that there are almost infinite quantities of information out there. Knowledge doesn't only provide us with more information about what we need to do and how we can do it, but it provides us with a sense of progress because learning happens sequentially. And remember: *progress is happiness.* This is so important because when you go into business or try to do anything new in your life, it can feel like a long time before you see any tangible results. Learning to enjoy the learning process that precedes the results is often a prerequisite for sticking with something until the results come.

The two most successful businesses I've had to date, Xurli and ENTRE, both involved a solid year of laying groundwork without turning a profit. During that time, it was learning new things and feeling a sense of progress that made the work fun. Remember Alex? He was the NASA scientist turned entrepreneur who talked about how big things happen three times—once in your mind, then in your life, then in the minds of others. Well, the knowledge-gathering phase is usually when the seeds of big things get planted, so learn to love learning if you don't already!

Leg #2: Environment

The second leg of successful action is our environment, including our surroundings, physical location, community, and culture. I think it's pretty obvious what I mean by physical location. It's not just the geographic coordinates of where we are but the décor, the temperature, the noise level, the number of distractions around us, and especially the people in our proximity, but let me quickly define the other two terms. Community basically means all the people we're connected to. It can mean family, friends, coworkers, clubs, groups (online or offline), and the like. And by culture I mean everything that shapes our default beliefs and attitudes—a mix of family, neighborhood, town or city, country, religion, schooling, and so forth.

Obviously the part of our environment that influences us the most is the people around us. In historical times our biggest environmental influence might have been the weather, or the cave we lived in, or the bears we were hoping didn't eat us, but in the twenty-first century, I think we can agree it's the people. The root of the word *community* is the word *common*. In the literal sense, your community is just the people you most commonly see.

If we look up the word *common* in the dictionary we find what we would expect—unspectacular language like "whatever's prevalent, whatever is of ordinary quality, whatever is the most widespread or typical." I don't know about you, but I don't like the sound of that for my community or my life! What if instead of accepting a common community we build ourselves an *uncommunity*, a community populated with the uncommon? Doesn't that sound better than ending up with whatever's prevalent, ordinary, widespread, and typical? The way it is written now the word *community* feels like it's just a synonym for whoever we settle for having around us and if this book is about anything, it's about not settling in any aspect of our life.

One of the books I've reread a few times since college and been deeply influenced by is named *Candide*. In it, the author Voltaire refers to the essential need of every man to tend his garden. This "not settling" is what he was writing about. If we don't choose to be the gardeners of our own lives we just end up a plant, wondering how we got stuck in whatever garden we find ourselves in, planted there by circumstances we didn't choose. And the more you study human beings the more you will realize I am not being melodramatic here. We must tend our garden with great care because anything less will let the weeds destroy our life. Our environment affects us deeply and we human beings can go sour really fast if we're subjected to the wrong environment and influences.

Case in point: the Milgram experiments. In 1961 Yale psychologist Stanley Milgram brought people together for an experiment. He told participants that his experiment was studying the correlation between negative reinforcement and human performance (which, in a strange way it was, though not as he was describing). He put the participants in pairs where one person would play a word game while their partner would shock them with electricity when they got an answer wrong.

Now, these were not real electric shocks, but the participants believed they were, and were more than willing to apply them. The dark implications of the experiment were quickly obvious. "In the name of science" (meaning because there was a guy with a lab coat and a clipboard telling them to do it) people were willing to shock innocent strangers over word games.

After each shock was administered the voltage was turned up. Each pair went through thirty rounds, and though some refused to continue eventually, no one objected from the outset. Every single participant in the experiment showed willingness to shock a partner using up to 300 volts, which can cause a heart attack. Sixty-five percent of the subjects went to 450 volts, which can kill a full-grown man. The experiment organizers made it vivid and realistic, complete with sound effects of people gasping, clutching themselves, banging into furniture, and thudding dead to the floor.

Eighteen different times they conducted this experiment with different groups and always saw the same result. Eventually they were told they couldn't do it anymore over ethical concerns as clearly embarrassed participants started complaining to the Yale psychology department about having been confronted with their own capacity for evil.

So why did people shock each other over word games? Why didn't they just leave? This happened in a free country in the 1960s, the era of "free love" and the civil rights movement when humanity was supposedly in a high-consciousness state, and this was being done at Yale University, one of the most prestigious institutions in the world. All the participants were free to leave any time they wanted.

Well, they did it for two reasons, both terrifying. First, they had been paid a whopping $4.50 to be there (about $42 in today's dollars), and second, some grad student in a lab coat who they'd never met and who had no legal authority over them told them that science demanded they continue. So assuming human beings haven't fundamentally changed in the last sixty years, fifty bucks, a decent actor, and some cheap props are all it takes to turn an ordinary person into an accomplice to murder. Yikes!

This is obviously an extreme example, but it illustrates why we have to be so careful what we allow to influence us. And there have been other experiments too that reached similar conclusions: The Stanford Prison Experiment conducted by Philip Zimbardo at Stanford University in 1971, the Third Wave experiment conducted by Ron Jones at Cubberley High School in Palo Alto in 1967, and of course countless actual experiments conducted by demagogues and dictators throughout history who induct ordinary citizens into horrifying atrocities. Any student of history can see how easily swayed humans can be into moral compromise. We can get really dark, really fast if we're in the wrong environment with the wrong community of people around us, and not one of us is fully inoculated. So if we admit we can be swayed to murder innocents by hanging out in the wrong company, do we really doubt that the people around us are affecting other attributes like our work ethic, motivation, and habits?

Thankfully, though, the news is not all bad. It turns out we're also capable of incredible things and our environment can be a hugely positive influence! The Pygmalion effect, also known as the Rosenthal effect, is a psychological phenomenon in which high expectations from the environment around us leads to dramatically improved performance.

This has been proven across hundreds of educational settings where experimenters will go into schools and universities and tell teachers they have identified a certain group of students in their class who have unusual potential for intellectual growth. Basically, they set a higher expectation for those students in the mind of the teacher.

Of course, there's no truth to it and the group of students identified are chosen completely at random. But guess what happens when they come back at the end of the school year and test those students. Those who the teachers expected more out of get significantly better test scores than the other students, because first the teacher and then the other students, picking up cues from the teacher, started treating them like they were smarter and expecting more from them.

The Pygmalion effect has been demonstrated across students of every age, from preschool through postgraduate, as well as in continuing education programs for adults. We never age out of being heavily influenced by our environment, so we need to be intentional about what's in it.

Leg #3: Resources

The third leg of successful action is our resources, meaning any part of our environment that can be used to accomplish our goals or create some sort of leverage to make accomplishing our goals easier. Resources can mean capital (the money we have or the money we can access), tools (which can be physical tools like a hammer, digital tools like a piece of software, or even intellectual tools like a problem-solving method), and relationships, particularly strategic relationships (meaning people who can help us get stuff done or connect us with those who can).

It's important to realize how much broader the term *resources* is than just referring to capital. I'll bet if you think about your life, you've known someone who had a lot of knowledge yet never became successful. In these instances, people will often blame a lack of capital for why they never got ahead. We must be on guard that money does not take on undue weight in the resources conversation. Yes, it's great to have a lot of money to work with, but resourcefulness will always be the greatest resource at our disposal. When I started my financial turnaround at age twenty-nine I didn't have much money, so I had to work extra hard to find great tools to work with and to create high-leverage relationships. These overcame my lack of money and eventually helped me get it.

So that covers the 3 Legs of Successful Action: knowledge, environment, and resources. But knowing how to take action is not the only thing we need to get clear on to achieve our best life. For many of us, it's time to get clear on what is stopping us from taking action in the first place.

ELIMINATING PROCRASTINATION

I believe human beings are not meant to die with regret and I can think of no bigger regret than failing to live up to our potential. So given that the number one saboteur of human potential is procrastination, I'd say it's a problem worth attacking.

What's the source of procrastination? One word: fear. Fear of what? Well, that can vary person to person, but I believe that most of us actually have a deep fear of success, or at least too much of it, and that is the common root of most procrastination. We can never stop reminding ourselves that the first driver of human personality is **belonging,** and the more successful we become, the less we belong. Marianne Williamson captured this perfectly in one of my favorite quotes from her book *Return to Love*:

> Our deepest fear is not that we are inadequate, our deepest fear is that we are powerful beyond measure. It is our light, not our darkness, that most frightens us. We ask ourselves, who am I to be brilliant, gorgeous, talented, fabulous? Actually, who are you *not* to be? You are a child of God. Your playing small doesn't serve the world.

In a nutshell, procrastination is generally the fear of how great we could be if we immediately took action on what we know we're capable of achieving every time action was called for. Procrastination is a nefarious mechanism we use to keep ourselves from succeeding without the shame of any obvious failures or quitting outright. You could say procrastination is how we quit without anyone noticing because it spreads our failure out over too many small incidents to be obvious. Procrastination is the murder of who we could become by a thousand tiny cuts.

If you struggle with procrastination, here are four techniques that can help you better live up to your potential.

#1. Reframe the Issue

Procrastination isn't something you're going to fix overnight. You won't suddenly have an epiphany that will change your behavior. It takes discipline and consistency, so you have to work on it, and you have to pay attention every day. The first step is to change how you frame procrastination. Don't think of it as a disease you're going to cure, but a tendency you have to change. You do that over time by creating a habit. Much like going to the gym and seeing results can break you out of a rut, you can get addicted to the feeling of no longer procrastinating. Even just procrastinating a little bit less than usual is still a victory, so make a game out of it. If last time you procrastinated for eight hours, this time set a seven-hour timer and do something fun until it goes off. Then the next time allow yourself six hours of procrastination. Just like any other addiction or bad habit, reducing the shame around it is half the battle.

#2. Stop Making the Same Decision Multiple Times

It takes energy to make decisions. If you make too many, you're exhausted and less likely to follow through on them. This is called decision fatigue and the first step to reducing decision fatigue is to make sure you're only making each decision one time. And the way to do that is through goal setting and scheduling. When you map your days out ahead of time, you collapse all the decisions you would have had to make about what to do with every hour and minute of your day into a single session of decision-making that only has to happen once for each period of time being planned. Breaking bigger goals down into smaller chunks that get scheduled in reasonable intervals makes bigger goals feel less daunting, and you'll be less likely to procrastinate. Once your schedule is set, there are no more decisions to be made; you're now propelled entirely by routines and habits. You wake up with a scheduled list of things to do and you spend your day getting them done, giving no time or energy to thinking about which ones to do.

#3. Don't Wait for Perfection

One thing entrepreneurs say to each other all the time is that "imperfect action beats perfect inaction every time." You can't compromise action in pursuit of perfection. Go back and watch some of my early videos, and it's clear that I was far from perfect. If I had waited until everything was perfect or near perfect, I never would have shot a single video. I needed things to be messy because that was the only way I was going to learn. And perfection is impossible anyway. Even calling ourselves perfectionists (which is thinly veiled code for "procrastinator") moves us further from perfection because it pledges us to an idea we know to be not only imperfect, but destructive.

#4. Treat the Rules as Laws

When I wake up in the morning and give myself five seconds to have my feet on the floor, that's a rule I made for myself. That's all it is: a self-created, self-imposed rule. No one will know if I break it and there's no actual penalty for doing so, other than what I may self-impose. I have to be the one to create consequences for breaking the rules. Obviously most of us would have no problem getting up early if we knew there was a $10,000 fine for sleeping in, so we just have to create that kind of pressure for ourselves.

As human beings, we are more motivated by the avoidance of pain (like fines) than the pursuit of pleasure (like a sense of fulfillment from getting up early). So, create some laws, complete with penalties for breaking them, and rule over yourself like a sadistic overlord who loves penalizing bad behavior. Have fun with it. Indulge yourself in a healthy "mwahahaha" after imposing a particularly harsh penalty on yourself. And enlist some help if needed. Tell your spouse that for every time you oversleep, miss a workout, or (insert goal here), you'll give them a thirty-minute back rub, or do one of their household chores for a week, or make a donation to a charity. Make the penalties things that benefit someone else and you'll win either way.

THE WILLPOWER FALLACY

We love the idea of willpower. And why not? Willpower allows us to take credit for our wins ("I mustered the willpower to do _____") and let ourselves off the hook for our losses ("My battery was drained; I just couldn't do _____"). There's just one problem. Willpower isn't real. It's been scientifically disproven.

The technical term for what we call willpower (or, more accurately, the term for its absence) is *ego depletion*. Remember we talked about how in

Freudian psychology the ego is the moderator between our id (basic instincts) and our superego (sublime idea of self)? Well, the way willpower generally gets explained in psychological terms is that as the ego gets tired from wrestling the id, it starts to wear out and our basic instincts start to overpower us. Next thing we know it's 9:00 p.m., we're gorging on ice cream, and yelling at our kids. After all, it's been a long day, right? This thought model stems from experiments done in the 1990s at Case Western Reserve University, where subjects were made to sit in front of plates of food without eating the food and then given various problem-solving tests. The evidence showed that subjects who had to resist more enticing food (like cookies) scored worse on the tests than subjects who were not tempted by the food in front of them (a plate of radishes, for example). The conclusion was that resisting cookies drained the willpower tank and made people less mentally acute, while resisting radishes did not.

That study has been referenced in over three thousand scientific journals, and its conclusions were widely taught in psychology classes until about 2010. However, additional research has called these conclusions into question and shown that the Case Western studies proved only correlation, not causation. Additional studies and analysis conducted by Evan Carter at University of Miami, Carol Dweck at Stanford, and several others since 2010 have shown something quite a bit more interesting—that willpower, aka ego depletion, is essentially a placebo effect for what we believe about ourselves and human beings in general. If we believe that being tired or having recently resisted temptation makes us more susceptible to future temptation or making bad choices, then that is exactly what happens. But if you don't believe in ego depletion, if you don't believe that you are more likely to make a bad decision just because you're tired, it doesn't happen. Scientific consensus has shifted and now we know that willpower is just another way of describing how we feel about ourselves, a self-fulfilling prophecy. Unfortunately, the old-wives-tale version of willpower is still making the rounds and most of us still think we have some imaginary tank of gas that keeps running out. To quote Nir Eyal writing for *Harvard Business Review*, "It appears ego depletion may be just another example of the way belief drives behavior. Thinking we're spent makes us feel worse, while rewarding ourselves with an indulgence makes us feel better. It's not the sugar in the lemonade that produces the sustained mental stamina, but rather the placebo effect at work."

This has far-reaching implications. How many of us grew up with parents blaming their lesser behaviors on stress or long days? So many of us subconsciously think that we are less capable of things than we really are because we often find ourselves tired or stressed. How many dreams have failed to take flight because the dreamer thought they were too tired or overworked to pull it off? And this whole time it's been a fallacy—the willpower fallacy, nothing more than poor self-image strategically paired with blame shifting. And another excuse bites the dust.

We shouldn't be surprised, though. We've already seen many fallacies that outlive their usefulness in our culture (like speed limits saving gas, the food pyramid, and one of my favorites, the persistent idea that entrepreneurship is more risky than employment). Willpower is just a hypothesis that we accepted and never bothered to test, and if we had we would have found that when we ignored it, it disappeared. So, let's discard this disproven external force that used to let us off the hook and instead talk about a very real internal force that puts us back on the hook. Let's talk about self-control. Most of us are deficient in this area and have been covering that deficiency with this bogus idea of willpower, but with willpower now stripped away we come face to face with self-control and our struggles with it.

So how do we develop control of self? According to the research, it comes down to two things: incentives and beliefs. If we really want to succeed, we must create for ourselves a system of incentives and beliefs that can help us better achieve our intended outcomes. The best way I have found to apply this concept is to understand the desire for self-control as an attempt to exert **influence** upon ourselves. And for how to do that we turn to the seminal work on influence called—wait for it—*Influence* by Robert Cialdini. In it, he breaks down the factors that influence human personality by laying out six principles of persuasion.

1. **Liking:** If people like you, they are likely to say yes.
2. **Reciprocity:** People tend to return favors.
3. **Social proof:** People will do things they see others doing.
4. **Commitment and consistency:** People want to be consistent. If they make a voluntary public commitment, they'll follow through.
5. **Authority:** People defer to experts and to those in positions of authority.
6. **Scarcity:** People value things if they perceive them to be scarce.

I originally read this book during my turnaround year of 2009 to learn how to better influence prospects in my internet business into becoming customers.

But when I reread it in the spring of 2017, it hit me a different way: *What if I turned these principles on myself?*

In particular, I focused on two of the principles. These principles are so useful because, unlike our flawed concept of willpower, they don't deplete or diminish and we can access them at any time as they are baked into our DNA. The first principle is social proof, or the idea that we tend to do what we see others doing. You probably already connected this to its origin in our natural desire to belong, which is why we want to find communities of like-minded people who are already doing the things we want to do.

The second principle I've already referenced as well: commitment and consistency. Do you remember when we talked about how it's easier to eliminate time-sucking habits if you tell others upfront what you're doing? That's the commitment and consistency principle at work. As human beings, there are few more important things for the health of our society, and our own self-preservation, than the ability to believe what other people say and have what we say be believed. This is at the core of mankind's basic social contract. Throughout history, people who don't do what they say have been shunned, and if we go back to our tribal origins, consistent failure to keep our word was pretty much a death sentence. What band of hunters would want to go into battle with a tribe member that couldn't be relied on? So, we have a pretty deep-seated fear of being seen as inconsistent with the commitments we make publicly. Thus, there's a very simple hack for increasing the likelihood that we'll actually do something we know we should do—publicly declare what we're going to do and do it in a way that is easy for others to verify. Not wanting to be embarrassed is a great motivator.

Once I started applying these two principles to myself, my results increased exponentially. I got more discerning about the company I kept. I surrounded myself with people who provided me with positive social proof and were already doing what I wanted to do. If that wasn't possible, I'd often opt to be alone rather than around people who did not align with my goals. And I started cornering myself through public declarations—making commitments that I had to follow through on or be embarrassed. That's basically how I created ENTRE; I started shooting videos, and in the videos, I kept referencing this big mission I was on. Eventually it would have gotten silly and embarrassing to be talking about *the mission* but not actually building it.

So there you have it; the warm-up phase of the book is complete. You might be thinking, *Say what, Jeff? This was just a warm-up?* Yup, this has all been a warm-up—getting your head right before we dive into the opportunities that exist in the modern economy and looking at how those kitchen-table millionaires are actually doing it. Consider everything up to this point as a sort of boot camp for getting you ready to learn what comes next.

And if you're thinking, *Geez, Jeff, that was a lot of boot camp!* just know this isn't my first time showing people what I'm about to show you. I have taught hundreds of thousands of people how the new economy works and explained exactly what I've done to make it work for me, despite starting out as a high school dropout with a half-million dollars in debt. And yet most people I lead to water, so to speak, don't drink because what I'm showing them is so cognitively dissonant from what they've known and been told their whole lives.

Or maybe they're just scared of what they're going to tell their spouses. "Honey, I've decided to level up in all areas. I'm going to start building a new income vehicle so I can quit my job and build generational wealth for the kids. Also, every night I'm going to do a planning ritual called a NAP. And my day is now chunked into fifteeen-minute intervals. Also, I think we should homeschool our kids while we're at it to get them out of the broken system. And let's stop eating processed carbs because they reduce our potential. And can you meet me at the gym Saturday morning?"

Or perhaps the entire basis for this conversation (the failure of existing systems, inability to ever retire, all that time and money wasted on traditional education, etc.) is just too big and unnerving to want to confront. Whatever the reasons are, it's the single most frustrating part about my otherwise pretty amazing life—the number of people I can't help because they either won't listen or they aren't willing to *take action the right way* and *become the person who succeeds* with these types of opportunities.

I sometimes feel like Cassandra from Greek mythology. Cassandra knew the future but was cursed that no one would heed her warnings, so she was forced to watch people around her, who just wouldn't listen, suffer needlessly. It's not as bad as that for me—after all, hundreds of thousands of students have been through ENTRE, and my videos online have been viewed by millions of people—but millions more need to get the message, and the mainstream media pipes are clogged with stuff that sells advertising rather than stuff that really helps people. This is why I had to write this book.

The world now is so crowded and competitive, the new economy is so unlike what came before it, and the traits we need to be successful today are so different from what they used to be, yet schools are still teaching us to aspire to be good employees while employers are holding on hoping you don't get the memo about the better options out there. The reason this book opens with so much indoctrination is because the hardest thing about defying conventional thinking is believing it's okay to defy conventional thinking.

But you have to do it! Conventional thinking is based on a world that has officially been sunset, and in the new world life is pretty binary. Depending which side of the modern shifts you're on, life is either getting easier or harder than before, with very little middle ground (the whole "death-of-the-middle-class" thing). In this regard, the new world has some dystopian shading that we can't be in denial about if we want to come out ahead. If you aren't winning in this world, you're losing. Badly. I want you to win, and I've spent twenty-five years outside the system learning what that takes. That's what this book has been about up to this point—how to be habitually excellent enough to have a shot at using the info that comes in the rest of this book to win your personal race in a world that is unprecedentedly crowded, dehumanizingly competitive, rapidly changing, and built on a system that does not deliver on its promises.

To summarize, I took all this time to set up what comes next because I am tired of leading horses to water that can't or won't drink because it's too scary or challenging. Yes, I've helped thousands of people pivot their lives and escape the broken system, but I've also seen just as many run away once the facts and their implications were made clear. I trust that will not be you, so thank you for coming this far with me. I hope you're now suitably thirsty and ready to drink the water I will now lead you to.

PART V

Creating Surplus Income

17

Preparing for Your New Future

All right—it's time to move beyond the conversations about personal growth, lifehacking, performance optimization, time management, psychology, and other "soft" stuff. From here on, we'll be talking about the pragmatic stuff—money, credit, business models, investments, tangible opportunities, income vehicles, systems, and tools—all the things you should be jonesing for at this point that directly answer these three questions:

1. How do I control my own time (i.e., make enough money to pay bills so I don't have to rely on the broken system anymore)?
2. How do I take care of future generations (i.e., go beyond just paying bills and build true wealth)?
3. How do I retrain the way I think about money and risk in a world dominated by misinformation about both (i.e., a world that is still pretending the system isn't broken and can make you feel a bit nuts for thinking it is, even though the evidence is right under your nose)?

Just think how awesome your life will be once those three answers are crystal clear!

So that's where we're going from here—*practical* and *actionable* information you can use to manage your money better, stretch your money further, grow your money faster, and, most importantly, make more of it, period. I'll be detailing ideas, strategies, and tactics that are not taught in mainstream financial circles but are widely utilized by successful entrepreneurs and the ultrawealthy. I'll also discuss specifics on how from 2008 to 2018 (before I started ENTRE or made a single dime from selling how-to information) I went from broke and nearly bankrupt to generating approximately $55 million in online sales without borrowing any money, without collecting any sort of a paycheck, without ever having to clock in or be anywhere at a certain time, and without wearing a uniform, following a dress code, having a boss, being tied to a particular location, or ever needing more than a laptop and cell phone.

But first, regarding that claim—$55 million in ten years from home on a laptop—let me address the elephant in the room—*how do you know I actually did that, and, more importantly, how do you know I did it with methods that anyone else could learn from or potentially emulate?* Well, you probably wouldn't have read this far if you didn't have some degree of confidence that I am who I say I am and I've done what I say I've done, but I know people are skeptical. Every day I get emails, direct messages, and social media comments from people wondering if my story is real.

Well I have nothing to hide—and everything I've done has to be provable anyway. ENTRE is currently one of the fastest-growing companies in the world (4,000 percent growth in 2020) with scrutiny coming from the media, potential investors (who email me almost daily wanting to invest in us), the mainstream public, hundreds of thousands of our own students, my book publisher, and numerous regulatory agencies (the education industry is the second most regulated industry in America behind health care).

Nonetheless, skepticism is still natural and hard to overcome for many people. I don't blame them, nor am I offended (it doesn't change what I eat for dinner), but it's a shame when people don't take action on my message because of unfounded doubts about the messenger. I do understand that, based on how most of us were raised and what we've been taught, the idea that some guy dropped out of high school to play piano, failed at nearly a dozen different businesses, ended up half a million dollars in debt, and then abruptly turned it all around and generated $55 million from a laptop with businesses that were nearly free to start and widely available to millions of people sounds, well, a little far-fetched! I'd probably doubt me too if I hadn't lived it!

So while I'm tempted to brush off such skepticism by saying simply, *"Yeah, that's my point. When you embrace the ideas we've covered up to this point, you become capable of things that seem impossible to most people,"* I will instead address some of the questions that I know people have when my story gets told.

Question #1: *Are you saying you profited $55 million online before founding ENTRE?*

Answer: No. Obviously, generating $55 million in *revenue* is not the same as earning $55 million in *personal income*. You can think of the businesses I built just like any other small businesses. There are bills to pay, and the owner only gets to pocket what is left, if anything, after they are paid. The difference between the businesses I ran and more traditional small businesses is that mine were generally more efficient—more profitable, simpler, and less costly to operate. They didn't require physical space, they didn't stock physical goods so no money was tied up in inventory, they only sold products and services that could be delivered at large scale without requiring proportional man hours or logistical complexity (meaning they had low employee count relative to revenue), they were not geographically constrained and could operate all over the world, and they were insulated from the vicissitudes of the traditional economy. I'll talk more about these businesses as a category, but for now, here's the list of the individual businesses I ran during that stretch, my ownership interest in those businesses, the revenue they generated, and the approximate profit margins (meaning how much was available for me to take home as income).

1. 2009–2012: Affiliate marketer (100% owner)
   Gross revenue: *~$10 million*
   Profit margin: *~30%*
   Profits: *~$3 million*
2. 2013–2018: Digital agency owner (100% owner)
   Gross revenue: *~$30 million*
   Profit margin: *~25%*
   Profits: *~$7.5 million*

3. 2016–2018: Online direct sales (50% owner)
   Gross revenue: ~*$15 million*
   Profit margin: ~*30%*
   Profits: ~*$4.5 million (x 50% ownership = $2.75 million)*

Total revenue: *$55 million*
*Average profit margin: ~*27.27%*
Estimated profits (2008–2018): ***$13,250,000***

*Total of revenue times profit margin for each business divided by total revenue for all businesses:

($10M x .3) + ($30M x .25) + ($15M x .3) / $55M

So, all told, these businesses generated for me over $13 million in profit on $55 million in revenue over a span of ten years—while working my own hours from wherever I wanted and answering to no one. Sounds like a dream, right? It is. I pinch myself every day. And it is a dream made possible by the new digital economy and the opportunities that emerged from it. All the business models I have participated in since 2008 fit into a category that goes by different names (digital business, online business, internet business, "IM" or internet marketing, business 2.0, etc.), but regardless of their label, they embody what makes the modern economy so exciting—unprecedentedly low startup costs, higher-than-traditional profit margins, low-friction scalability, high revenue per employee, high maneuverability and adaptability, and so on.

A note of caution—for obvious reasons these businesses are enticing, but I'm not saying everyone should start a business in this category. In my experience, there are people who are well suited for "the laptop lifestyle"—being alone a lot and spending hours a day at a computer—and others who thrive on more traditional stimuli like face-to-face interaction and local connections, but as far as I'm concerned, *any* business worth running in today's world should leverage digital technology and take advantage of whatever characteristics of the modern economy are relevant to it. Even businesses that might seem to resist modernization (say a hardware store or a candy shop) can take pages from the digital business playbook to find much more secure and profitable ways of functioning.

Question #2: *If you were $495,000 in debt, how did you have any money to start a business?*

Answer: The two franchise restaurants I operated in 2007 and 2008 didn't collapse in a day. There was a sequence of events that lasted several months where my focus was always covering payroll while I made peace with the other fires burning in the business that I couldn't put out. I knew a point would come where I would be far enough behind on lease payments that the landlords would padlock my spaces. And I knew that when that happened and the lending bank got wind of it, they would freeze my accounts since they would know my loan default was imminent. So right when things were about to collapse completely, I did something desperate that saved me—I let as many people go as possible, and I did my best to keep the stores going with just myself and a skeleton crew. I paid everyone who remained each day in cash so there would not be outstanding payroll checks that needed to clear when the bank froze the accounts, and instead of doing nightly bank deposits, I let cash build up in the safe. Basically, I was going down in a blaze of glory and siphoning off what I could so that I could have something to live on when the dust settled. The day the padlocks went on the doors (once I was ninety days late on my rent), I had accumulated about $14,000 in cash. The plan was to live on that for several months while I figured out my next move. I didn't have any rent since my soon-to-be-ex-in-laws were being kind enough to let me (and their daughter who I'd soon be divorced from) live in their house. I figured I had six months. As it turned out, I didn't. Within a couple months, I would invest the entire $14,000 into launching my affiliate marketing business—which became, up to that point, the best financial decision I ever made!

Question #3: *Are you one of those "gurus" who made all his money from selling information about how to make money?*

Answer: No, though that's a smart question to ask, given that 99 percent of the people in the market today who talk about making money make their money by talking about how to make money. This is especially prevalent on the internet, where you've no doubt seen ads featuring twentysomething "bro marketers" in beachside mansions with fast cars in the driveway talking about how they pay for their beachside mansions and the fast cars in the driveway. But it's not just an internet phenomenon. I won't name names, but many of the people whose books sit on shelves next to this one made their money by writing books about how to make money (or using those books to land keynote speaking gigs, media appearances, etc.). Not so here. That's why I took the time to detail the list above of the actual businesses I ran profitably before I ever got in the business of teaching or sharing knowledge.

Question #4: *If these businesses are so lucrative, why do you spend your time teaching, writing a book, hosting a podcast, creating content, and so on? Why not just keep running these businesses?*

Answer: I'm an entrepreneur, which means two things—I like solving problems, and I seize opportunities. There is a massive problem in this world of misinformed and disempowered people, which is probably why you are reading this book. The vast majority of people do not have the information they need to level up their lives because of a coordinated effort to keep them ignorant called *the broken system*. That is not only a huge problem worthy of being solved by a willing entrepreneur, it's also one I have strong personal feelings about. The powers that be who perpetuate this misinformation know what they're doing, and I hope for their humanity's sake that in their quiet moments they are ashamed, but I have no doubt that they will salve their guilt if ever asked by disavowing direct responsibility. The broken system is vast and involves so many people that it's easy for anyone who's part of it to play it off like we're all just helpless participants (the "what was I supposed to do?" defense). Regardless, whether someone's participation is willfully destructive (think greedy bankers who sell financial products they know they would never put their own money into), coerced by intimidation (people scared to lose their jobs if they speak out), or just naive (the majority), it's not likely to change until we the people force it to by pulling our capital, energy, and other resources out of the broken system and create a new one built on entrepreneurial values, individual responsibility, and self-mastery.

As for the second entrepreneurial quality, seizing opportunity, well I won't apologize for carpe-ing the diem! The best chefs eat their own cooking, and in my case, I am taking my own advice—when opportunity knocks, answer.

Since it became obvious to me that I was in a unique position to help solve one of the biggest problems on earth, I have dedicated my life to solving it. So far, I've helped hundreds of thousands of people, and I have plans to help millions more, which is exactly what good business and good entrepreneurship are supposed to do. As Elon Musk said, "You get paid in direct proportion to the difficulty of the problems you solve." Not surprisingly, I am now getting paid the most I ever have, a fact I wear with pride as evidence that what I teach works.

Question #5: *If you're so successful, why don't you have a bigger social media following?*

Answer: I don't actually get this question that much anymore, but I got it a lot when I started this crusade. On those lines, let me share some data you might find interesting, especially if you plan to do anything yourself online. This is my experience of approximately what size of following, by platform, you must reach before people stop using the size of your following as an attack on your credibility.

I found that the "small audience" criticisms stopped at roughly:

- Instagram: 10,000 followers (this one was the most obvious)
- Facebook business page: 5,000 followers
- YouTube: 1,000 subscribers
- LinkedIn: Never came up
- TikTok: 10,000 followers

Anyway, again, I don't get this question much anymore, but I mention it because it speaks to a larger point of ignorance many have in the modern world. The size of someone's social media following is not a basis for evaluating their credibility. Many successful people will have a large social following, but many will not. And a large following does not, by itself, indicate a successful person. I know many more people with big bank accounts and small social followings than I do people with big bank accounts and large social followings. And on the flip side, I know more people with big social followings and small bank accounts than I do big social followings and big bank accounts. Seriously. The number of people who become truly successful at private enterprise and also take the time to make the investment required to build a large social following is not that big (I'm guessing maybe a few thousand entrepreneurs, not counting those who were already celebrities before they got into business). Contrast that with the hundreds of thousands of people on social media who are making factitious claims of success, paying to inflate their follower count, and trying to make a buck selling information on how to make a buck, and we need to be very careful who we learn from.

No exaggeration, going behind the scenes into the world of "lifestyle influencers" is Kurt Vonnegut–level absurdism. When I first started reaching out to people about how to grow my following and get my message out there, I was shocked at what I discovered. I discovered a world of "growth pods," groups of thousands in shared channels on Telegram and WhatsApp who all agree to like, comment, and share each other's posts. It's like an incestuous collective-bargaining agreement between hordes of aspiring influencers trying to gain favor in the social media algorithms by colluding to engage with one another's content. So bizarre.

I've met dozens of "professional influencers" (mostly on Instagram but also on TikTok and YouTube) who love to talk about how they earn six or seven figures a year but omit the fact that they spend most of what they earn on videographers, photographers, copywriters, editors, travel, rented houses, rented cars, rented planes, and so on, to make themselves look rich and successful.

I've met high-priced consultants and "talent managers" who (in their words) "can turn anyone under forty who isn't fat into a celebrity" in exchange for 50 percent or more of every sponsorship deal. It'd be entirely laughable if not for the tragic toll being exacted on the psyches of those who beat themselves up comparing their real lives to the fake lives they see in their feeds every day that this grotesque industry is manufacturing.

Want a quick, tangible example that will give you a healthy cynicism about everything you ever see again on social media? Do a quick Google search for "fake private jet photo studio" and see how easy it is to rent a studio set of a private jet to take pictures. For just $64 per hour, you can fool everyone into thinking you're a baller. Don't forget your hashtag cliches like #Ibizahere-Icome, #jetlife, #nosecuritylines, or #whatdayisit!

In a word, ick. If all my crusade accomplishes is to help inoculate people from social media envy, I will still have done good work in this world.

Anyway, moving on (sorry for the rant; clearly this subject touches a nerve). Hopefully, any lingering doubts you had are allayed, and we can get to the matter at hand—*you* and your financial future.

Here are some questions I want you to consider as we go through the remainder of this book. What are you building? If you drew your life on a piece of paper, what would it consist of? In particular, what parts of the picture represent things you have built that will outlast you? What's your legacy? What are you going to leave your children? What will your children remember you for? What will their children remember you for? And what about those who are born after all memories of you have faded? Will there be anything for them to know you by? Will your having ever existed fade over time or will it become a living, tangible legacy?

Let's get real for a minute. Grab a pen and something to write on and actually write out the beneficiary section of your will. Do this for every beneficiary.

> "I, [your name], upon my passing, do bequeath to [name beneficiaries] my [list of assets]."

How did that make you feel? Are you satisfied with the inheritance you're on track to leave your beneficiaries? Is your legacy where you want it to be?

I am obsessed with legacy, both my own and the legacies of my students. If giving is the best part of living, then isn't it also the best part of dying? Especially with where the world seems to be headed. At the risk of offending, I don't think it's enough to just leave your children great memories. Obviously, there is more to life than assets and investments, but life is also a lot more with assets and investments, and the same is true for our children's lives.

Do you have a plan to build that legacy? How's it going? Most people don't like to think about their legacy because the broken system makes it difficult to save enough to retire, much less leave anything meaningful to their kids. But there is an easy way to think about building your legacy that I call the 3 Phases of Legacy. You could just as easily call this the 3 Phases of Getting Rich, but I just prefer the term *legacy* because it reminds us why we should want to get rich in the first place.

- **Phase 1: Income.** This phase is about increasing income to create surplus, or money that is unused for daily living. Once there is sufficient surplus income, we can look to the next phase. Most people are in this phase already (or need to be) and the question here is, *What is your income vehicle to get you through this phase?* I believe that for most people starting a business is the best income vehicle for growing their income fast enough to ever graduate beyond this phase. I teach a target of getting your income to be five times your cost of living in this phase (I call this your *Awesome Life Number*). We'll talk about why that number is the target later.

- **Phase 2: Growth.** This phase involves leveraging surplus income from the income phase to create predictable, bankable, and sellable cash flow. For most, this means expanding their income vehicle (usually their business) into larger and/or more diverse income streams. The goal of this phase is making your income predictable and futureproof. The best way to think about it is to ask, *Would a bank or investor lend on or invest in my cash flow?* For that answer to be yes, that cash flow has to be highly stable and secure.

- **Phase 3: Wealth.** This phase involves diversifying into assets that are outside your primary business or income vehicle, and which are stable, low-risk, tax advantaged, and heritable. Ideally, during this phase, the majority of your income shifts to passive sources, so you are no longer having to work for money.

For the purposes of this book, we will spend the most time talking about the income phase, since that's where 99 percent of people are or should be. All the chapters here in part five will be focused on the income phase, while part six will cover both the growth and wealth phases. Keep in mind that you only have a finite amount of time to move through each phase, and that timeline is different for everyone. You might have sixty years left, or you might have twenty, so you'll want to consider how much time you think you have and try to attack the phases accordingly. If you're already thinking you are short on time, you're probably right. If you think you have plenty of time, you're probably wrong. I estimate that 99 percent of America, and an even higher percentage of the world, is not on track to complete these three phases unless something dramatic shifts. This is not the time to go fifty-five miles per hour!

WHAT'S YOUR AWESOME LIFE NUMBER?

You may have heard about the concept of the "magic number." Anyone who's ever sat through an MLM pitch probably remembers the presenter talking about hitting some amount of residual income and never having to work again because all your bills will be paid. That amount of monthly income is sometimes referred to as your magic number. I used to believe in the magic number and thought nothing would be greater than just achieving that so I could relax and not have to worry.

The one time I joined an MLM in my early twenties, my bills were about $4,000 per month, and I was obsessed with getting to my magic number of $4,000 a month in residual income. But looking back, my life at $4,000 a month wasn't that great, and it wasn't because of what I had to do to pay my bills; I actually liked playing the piano. The problem was that it wasn't enough money to enjoy most of what this world has to offer, be able to retire well someday, support a family in comfort and security, build multigenerational wealth for my family, pay for unexpected but urgent expenses that might pop up, or even have the basic peace of mind that comes from knowing you can survive a disruption in your income.

In hindsight, there was never going to be anything magic about swapping $4,000 a month in active income for $4,000 a month in passive income. Either way I would still be living on $4,000 a month and that dollar amount is what sucked, not how it came in. Since that time, I've learned it takes a lot more than just covering your bills to live a great life. Here's the harsh truth (and the point where some of the beta-readers got too offended to continue): in the modern world, if you're not what most people consider rich, you're poor. That's why, instead of a magic number, I like to talk about an Awesome Life Number, which is the amount of money you need to be on the path to true wealth. As a starting point, I suggest five times whatever you need to pay your bills. That way you can set aside 40 percent of your gross income for taxes, invest another 40 percent, and live off of the remaining 20 percent.

I didn't know it at the time, but falling $495,000 in debt was the best thing that ever happened to me. It was like I was cornered in an alley and found myself in the fight of my life to get out. I had creditors calling me, the federal government hounding me because I defaulted on a Small Business Administration loan (which meant my creditor was the US Treasury), massive real estate conglomerates suing me for tens of thousands of dollars because I had signed leases for multiple locations that still had years left, the State of Texas wanting its unemployment and payroll taxes, and so on. In that situation, I had to think drastically differently about my income goals. It wasn't going to be nearly enough just to replace the $4,000 a month that I made as a musician. I had to quickly find a way to make five to ten times that amount just to avoid bankruptcy, pay off my debt, and survive. For the eighteen months it took me to pay off my debt, I didn't get to enjoy a dime of it, but once my debt was paid off, I finally got a taste of life without financial stress. The amount of my debt and the level of income I had to reach to pay it off forced me to experience what I never would have otherwise—that generating five times what you need to live is the starting point of building wealth, and anything less is just prolonging the feeling of lack and compromise that most of us call daily living.

Most people hide from this conversation, but the reality is that if you have even an average financial situation, you aren't even close to experiencing what this world has to offer. I'm not talking about filthy rich luxuries like yachts and private islands. I'm just talking about knowing you can provide for all the people you love at a level of comfort and security you want to and that you can weather any storms that come.

If this were even a hundred years ago, I would understand wanting to bury our heads in the sand to avoid this conversation. Back then, socioeconomic mobility was limited, and the position you were born into was usually the position you died in. But the world has evolved so much for those who are open-minded. Opportunities exist that were inconceivable a few decades ago, so if you don't like your position today, you can actually do something about it. And it doesn't matter how old you are. I once coached a ninety-six-year-old woman who, in the last chapter of her life, was able to create an online income greater than what she was getting from her widow's pension and social security.

At the time of this writing, the median annual wage for an American worker is roughly $35,000 per year, with median household income at $67,000. So, assuming most people and households are able to pay their bills, and we're looking to get five times that, the average Awesome Life Number for an individual worker is $175,000 per year or $335,000 for a household. Obviously, this is way beyond what mainstream education or financial planners teach most people to aim for because they don't want to scare you away. But trust me, it is doable. I would never have thought I could have done it until I did. Don't worry, I will give you multiple ways that you can go about achieving this. The good news is that even if you fall short of your Awesome Life Number, you will still be way ahead of where you would have been otherwise. I hesitate to even say that because I don't want you to expect anything short of that number, but as they say, "Shoot for the moon, and even if you miss, you'll land among the stars."

The important thing is to keep going. The more you stretch your mind to accommodate such an ambitious target and keep working toward it, the more natural it will start to feel. And eventually, you'll expect it and feel like something is amiss when you're not making that amount. Remember when I talked about putting a $1,000 per hour value on my time? And how instead of thinking I was making $20 per hour, I thought of it as losing $980 per hour? This is the same principle. Start expecting your Awesome Life Number and feeling like something is wrong if you're not hitting it. Let the frustration build and drive you. Now let's talk about how to hit it.

18

Debt, Credit, and the Rat Race

The vast majority of Americans today are not good stewards of their money. Despite the fact that the United States is the wealthiest country in the world (with a GDP more than 50 percent bigger than number two China, and by far the highest GDP per capita of any country in the world over 10 million people), Americans are among the worst at handling their wealth. In 2019, the average US "consumer unit" (i.e., the 2.5-person average household) spent $63,000, which is 94 percent of the $67,000 median household income figure we saw in the last chapter. Considering the average tax rate paid by US income earners is 13.29 percent, this means that the average American household spent 107 percent of its after-tax income, and that was in a year when incomes had gone up almost 7 percent from the year before. Even in 2021, after the COVID-19 pandemic should theoretically have shocked people into being more conservative, consumer spending rebounded much faster than incomes. Americans just love to spend money and they couldn't wait to get back out there after the pandemic, even if they were still collecting unemployment.

Conventional wisdom tells people to make two major investments early in life—a college education and a home—and those two investments sit at the core of why so many people, both in the United States and all over the world, end up stuck in the rat race, unable to pivot or eventually retire. The average American will carry student debt until they are in their mid-forties, despite well over half of all those college degrees having zero impact on the long-term earnings of their holder. Student debt is the most cited reason that people between the ages of twenty-five and forty-five give for not being able to do things they want to do (switch jobs, move cities, get married, take a vacation, invest for retirement, etc.). Not content to let people get out of debt by their mid-forties, the broken system tells people that, as soon as possible, they need to also buy a home and lock themselves into a fixed monthly payment for another fifteen to thirty years. Personally, I believe the decision to buy a home, long considered the cornerstone of the American Dream, is one of the most misunderstood and manipulated conversations in society, and one on which the rat race depends to keep people stuck. I know from many arguments that I've had on social media that this is not a popular opinion, but hear me out.

Of course, we all need somewhere to live, and that will cost us money. But until we graduate into the wealth phase of legacy and are well past the point where we're counting money at the end of each month, the goal should be to live as affordably as possible in a way that meets our basic needs and nothing more. A simple analysis of the real estate market in most cities around the world shows that not only is renting a cheaper way to meet most people's needs, it also offers much more flexibility and doesn't disrupt cashflow with large unplanned expenses. The goal all the way through the wealth phase should be to keep our money as fluid as possible and deploy it into investments that generate cash flow (assets). Despite what banks and traditional financial planners would have you believe, your home is not an asset; it is a liability, one that eats up nearly a third of all money earned in America after taxes. I've had numerous people argue this point with me over the years, but whenever we break out the calculator and do an actual cost-benefit analysis based on rental versus ownership costs in their city, we find that if they had rented instead of bought and consistently invested the money they saved (mortgage payments, taxes, insurance, home improvements, maintenance, unanticipated repairs, etc.), they would have come out ahead and likely could have purchased an actual real estate asset (a cash-flowing investment property) within ten years.

Between student debt and mortgage debt, millions of us get snared into the rat race from graduation to retirement. And adding insult to injury, in 1961, the financial industry debuted a new debt vehicle called a reverse mortgage, sold under the diabolically simple premise that you could use your home equity to retire without a mortgage payment. So let me get this straight: If I take on sufficient liabilities (i.e., purchases that deplete my cash flow like a home) such that I am unable to invest for retirement, I can now refinance my home, deplete whatever equity I did build, and create an even bigger liability I can leave to my kids? I don't think that's the legacy most people are going for. I think I'll pass; thanks, Mr. Banker.

Let's give credit where it's due (no pun intended); it's an ingeniously vicious cycle that the banks, schools, employers, and government have spun into a heck of a brochure. And it all depends on one central assumption that making a lot more money is not an option for most people. Well, the reality is that without generating additional income, most people will never move through the income phase, never accumulate a meaningful retirement, and never leave a tangible legacy for their children. In 2021, the average annual raise was 2.9 percent (for the people who kept their jobs, that is) while the consumer price index rose 5.3 percent. It was the worst year to date in an ever-worsening trend of annual raises being less than the increasing cost of goods, a trend that I believe will be recognized years from now as the canary in the coal mine that showed anyone who wanted to look how broken our system truly was.

Once most people wrap their minds around basic economic data and the obvious conclusions it points to, I don't usually get much pushback on the idea that they need more income if they want to have a shot at a great life. And most will even agree that starting a business is the best way to do that. But there seems to be a widespread belief that starting a business is highly risky, too much so for the average person to reasonably entertain, even if the facts suggest they should. It blows me away what a brainwashing our society has done on people's confidence. For centuries of human history, starting a business or going into the family business was what you did, or if you were not of a class that had that right it was what you wished you could do. But the modern world has so disempowered and frightened the average person that they think betting on themselves is riskier than betting on their boss. We'll talk more about the various ways this has happened, but one of the most obvious has been to hijack the very useful business tool known as debt and turn it instead into a drug that's given to people to self-harm. Imagine if 99 percent of all usage of saws was people cutting off their own limbs? In that world one might understandably be scared to become a carpenter. Well, that's what has happened with debt—so many people hurt themselves with it that people are scared to use it the way it was intended. So let's start there.

For most people, any real shot at building wealth has to begin with clearing out bad debt. Bad debt is money borrowed for anything that isn't producing a return greater than the interest being paid on the money borrowed. If you have a $300,000 mortgage that costs you $2,000 per month to service, then unless your home is producing at least $2,000 per month in income, that is bad debt! Ditto for cars, credit cards, and student loans.

Bad debt is a parasite, stealing whatever financial nourishment you try to feed into the body of your life. Getting rid of it by whatever means necessary will accomplish two things: it will give you an instant increase in cash flow and also reduce your fears around taking strategic and intelligent risks, like taking on good debt, or starting a business. You should have a strong game plan for eliminating bad debt if you find yourself in this situation (which about four out of five Americans do). There are two common methods for paying off debt, and I don't have anything better to offer. They are:

1. **The debt snowball:** Start by paying off your smallest debt by dollar amount, and then move on to pay off the next smallest.
2. **The debt avalanche:** Start by paying off the debt with the highest interest rate, and then move on to pay off the debt with the next highest.

So which one is better? Depending on which finance guru you listen to, you'll get different opinions, but if we lean on the actual mathematics of the question, the answer is pretty clear. The average household earns roughly $4,000 per month after taxes while spending roughly $2,500 per month on essential expenses. The question is how to best utilize as much of the remaining $1,500 per month as possible to pay off debt. The answer is easy—the debt avalanche method pays off your debt quicker. It just makes sense. Interest is wasted money, so you want to pay off the debt that's wasting the most money faster. When you pay off the higher-interest debt faster, you pay off the total debt faster. So why would any professional even recommend the debt snowball if the avalanche is proven to pay off debt quicker, you ask?

The reason is basic human psychology. As human beings, we derive inspiration, motivation, and momentum from what we call in both marketing and finance "small wins." When you win a battle, no matter how small, it creates a sensation of progress (happiness) and momentum that reduces resistance to the work needed to achieve subsequent bigger wins. This is a close cousin of commitment and consistency, both of which have beneath them a basic tendency to want to keep things going once we get some momentum. By attacking the smaller debts first, you're fighting a smaller battle, which allows you to get that first win faster. Psychologically, that will propel you forward and provide you with the discipline needed to continue to fight the fight and win the subsequent bigger battles.

The problem with attacking the smallest debt first is that the interest piles up on your other debts. Your principal balance will decrease further with the avalanche strategy, but you have to accept it taking longer to get that first debt knocked out. Psychologically, that might make it difficult for some people to persist because they don't have the reward of getting something accomplished, but hopefully, after coming this far with me, you are tougher than that and do not need to be paying unnecessary interest to offset a lack of discipline or persistence. We must be disciplined about our financial lives. If we were to sum up the entire American attitude about personal finance into one word, it would be *undisciplined*, and that is what the broken system is banking on (literally).

We have to be better. We can't be emotional about money. Most of the financial dysfunction in this world stems from people's emotions ("must keep up with the Joneses . . ."). Feelings are the enemy of financial discipline. The way to be more financially disciplined isn't to kowtow to our low self-image by overpaying in interest, it's to do the work in the first part of this book—get clear on your mission, vision, and values; develop your Success Character; commit to a standard of balanced excellence; and reshape all your habits, not just your financial ones. The fact that mainstream financial gurus can tell people to use the Debt Snowball method without getting laughed out of town says a lot of negative things about our society. We can't be giving ourselves permission to make less intelligent decisions because we doubt our own likelihood of following through. That's two wrongs not making a right. Low self-confidence doesn't somehow make up for being bad at math. Just pick your highest interest rate debt and put every non-essential dollar you earn toward getting it paid off as fast as humanly possible.

HOW TO IMPROVE YOUR CREDIT

If you've been saddled with debt, the odds are you also have some issues with your credit. It is time to fix those. Without good credit it is much harder to acquire good debt, which is money borrowed for anything that produces a return greater than the interest being paid on the money borrowed. Using that definition, it's easy to see how good credit makes it easier to acquire good debt—it's easier to invest in things that produce a return greater than the cost of interest if the cost of interest is less because the borrower's credit is good.

In a perfect world, we would teach credit to children, and everyone would have grown up proactively building their credit and staying out of trouble. But we all know that's not the world we live in, and the average credit score in America is below 700, which means the average borrower is paying more interest than necessary on any debt they take on, good or bad.

I made a ton of financial mistakes in my twenties, but one of the things that I did right was focus on my credit. I must have gone to the right school, right? Wrong. I learned about credit from a late-night infomercial, of all things, and it paid off big time because it created possibilities that I'm still benefiting from today. Because I was able to establish good credit in the early 2000s, I acquired a couple rental houses, even though I was a low-paid musician. I did what I advocate above—renting to live as cheaply as possible and focusing on acquiring real estate assets, not real estate liabilities. My rental properties became literal lifesavers and there were times during my string of business failures in my twenties when my rental property income was the only way I could pay for groceries. My point is that learning to properly handle debt and credit can improve your financial picture long before you are making millions of dollars. If you need to improve your credit, here are three things you can do immediately to get the ball rolling.

#1. The Authorized User Technique

Whether you're trying to repair poor credit or just getting started, arguably, one of the best ways to get moving in the right direction is to become an authorized user on other people's credit vehicles who have already established good credit. This is also called piggybacking because you find someone with good credit and let them add you to their account.

There has to be a certain level of trust between you and the other party, so it's best to ask a close friend or family member. However, this is not the same as cosigning, so there is zero liability. That's the cool thing about this. You can inherit someone else's good credit without them having to take responsibility for your poor credit, or you for theirs if their credit suddenly turns. If the other person is reluctant, tell them you don't even have to use the card. It doesn't even have to be in your possession. You just need to have your name on the account.

Keep in mind that this won't solve all of your credit woes. Creditors can do some digging and see what you're doing, and not every card reports activity to the authorized user's credit reports. But if you do a little research, this can be a great way to get established.

#2. Credit Repair

When I was $495,000 in debt, I had to work out all of these scenarios with different creditors. It was really hard work because I was hamstrung. Even when I had cash, I couldn't get a loan because of my debt. That's when I aggressively pursued credit repair, and it helped me out tremendously. Many people are reluctant to utilize credit repair services—some even think they're a scam. I can tell you that the right ones are not, and they are a tremendous asset when it comes to dealing with the bureaus. So if you're in a hole, work with a professional to help dig yourself out. But you do have to do your homework. Watch out for companies that offer a slow pace of dispute with high monthly fees because that company could be trying to string you along. Often, the best course of action is to consider what you eventually want to accomplish with credit, and then turn to an expert in that field. For example, if you want to buy a rental property, talk to a real estate lender and see who they recommend, because they work with people to fix credit all the time. If you're looking for a personal or business loan, turn to people who specialize in those areas and ask who they recommend.

#3. Raise Your Credit Limits

To maximize credit you want open credit lines with the highest limit you can get. Call up the credit card company and ask them how to increase your limits. If you're younger and don't have a long credit history, there might be certain spending patterns you need to establish. The goal is to get as much of a credit allowance as possible while keeping your utilization low. That means having high limits while carrying low to no balances from month to month. This will be essential down the road when it comes to borrowing other people's money.

#4. Get a Secured Credit Card

If you're starting from scratch or trying to improve poor credit, you want to focus on building healthy credit, but that can be difficult if you don't have good credit or any credit to begin with. If you're in that situation, you can start by applying for a secured credit card. This is a card that requires a cash deposit that is often equal to your credit limit. So, if you don't pay your bill, it will come out of the deposit. It's not an ideal scenario, but it's right for people who can't start anywhere else.

You can't run or hide from bad credit. You have to fix it. But credit is not built in a day. It's constantly flowing, so you want to continually monitor and work to improve your credit.

Once you have either fixed your credit or established a positive credit history, the best way to keep building and improving your credit is through credit cards. Every six months, you not only want to raise your credit limit, but also lower your interest rates on that card. Put an appointment on your calendar for every six months to call your credit card company and request a balance increase and a rate decrease. I recommend you start by focusing on one card and try to raise that limit as high as it can go before moving onto the next card. Eventually, once you have four or five cards, each with limits of $30,000 or more, you can go out and get premium cards like American Express Platinum or Chase Sapphire Preferred, which carry extra weight on your credit report and have lots of other perks too.

Quick reminder on discipline: just because you have higher lines of credit doesn't mean you get to use them. Use the cards to pay your bills, and don't spend more on them than you can pay off each month. And if you do end up charging a large expense and having to carry a balance, make sure it is less than 30 percent of the credit limit on that card or you can hurt your credit score.

Never close an account with an outstanding balance or missed payments. This can destroy your credit score and your borrowing power. On that note, just plan to never close an account if you can help it. It's better to keep the credit available to buoy your scores and just get rid of the card if you don't want it. And make this all easy on yourself by following these steps:

- Call all your creditors and request the payment due dates be on the same day of the month for all your credit lines. Now you don't have to remember a bunch of due dates and can budget to make all your payments on the day that works best for you.

- Set up an automatic payment through each credit card company for the minimum payment of each card on the due date so that if you ever miss paying off the entire balance you still at least pay the minimum and don't get a late payment mark on your credit report (you do still want to pay the entire balance every month; this is just for backup).

- Set a reminder on your phone to pay your credit card bills a few days before the due date so that when the due date hits, the card balance is zeroed out. You might have to play with the dates, but the goal is to figure out what date the credit card company is calculating your balance and reporting it to the credit bureaus. If you time the payments right you can get the card companies reporting a zero balance, which boosts your score.

- Schedule and track all of this in your external brain so you never forget it. Missing a single payment can take years to fully recover from.

Now that we've covered the basics of debt and credit, let's get into some clever strategies to stretch our money further!

19

Leaning Out Your Life

Toward the end of 2010, I had been doing affiliate marketing for two years. My $495,000 debt had been paid off for about six months, I was consistently generating between $40,000 and $80,000 a month in affiliate commissions, and I had completed my improbable financial turnaround. Unable to repair my marriage, I had gotten divorced and moved to New York City, where I was now living a bachelor's life in TriBeCa, a swanky neighborhood in Lower Manhattan. But all was not well. The decade of struggle as well as the emotional fallout from my divorce had taken a toll, and I was being fairly reckless with the money I was bringing in. I wasn't a big partier or anything; I just liked traveling (first class for a change), buying cool stuff, and taking people out to eat. The SoHo Shopping District was a ten-minute walk from my apartment, I could be at three airports within half an hour, I had a new BMW and could be off the island in ten minutes, and I had no job to fill my time. What's that saying about idle hands? Well, it's true.

Having coached lots of entrepreneurs now, I can say that my reckless-ness was not unusual. I now refer to it as *lifestyle creep*, where your income starts to go up significantly and your lifestyle expands right along with it. I was just being an average American, albeit with an above-average income, so thankfully I wasn't quite spending 107 percent of it. But we aren't going to let this happen to you. Before we worry about how to generate more income, I want to make sure that you're doing everything possible to utilize the money you have and create good habits. Notorious B.I.G. taught us "Mo Money, Mo Problems," but I have learned that isn't true. If we're disciplined, mo money, less problems is how it works. It's up to us and financial discipline can start well before income rises.

There are simple things you can start doing today that will help you find hidden pockets of money you didn't know existed. I'm not even talking about forcing yourself to live on a shoestring budget. We often don't realize how much money we waste until we take a closer look. Even after you start making more money, these are hacks you can continue to benefit from. I started implementing a few of these ideas years ago and continue to do so because, honestly, it just feels good to live lean. You may have heard the saying that we tend to attract more of whatever we focus on. Well, respect is a form of focus and for this reason I find that when we respect money, we tend to attract more of it. These behaviors show respect for money.

#1. Food

The number one way to save money on food is to stop eating out. You've heard this before, so it should be no surprise, but this applies to takeout as well. Use of takeout apps doubled during the pandemic and, as of 2021, 60 percent of Americans order takeout at least once a week, while some people order out as often as every single day. This is ridiculous.

The average American has $500 in savings and nearly two-thirds of us live paycheck to paycheck. It is absurd for most of us to be paying people to bring us food. I'm not saying it's absurd for everyone, but there are enough people doing it who can't really afford it that if they stopped, these apps would probably shut down. In February 2020, the *New York Times* published a report on the cost of using food delivery apps. Four apps were tested (Grubhub, DoorDash, Postmates, and Uber Eats) and multiple items were ordered from popular restaurants. A Subway sandwich cost between 25 percent and 91 percent more via the apps versus ordering in the restaurant. A Panda Express family value meal's price changed between 37 percent and 49 percent (in both cases Uber Eats was the worst). Bear in mind, this is all just the cost of having the food delivered, not the higher cost of the food itself.

The Bureau of Labor Statistics reports separately on the higher cost of food purchased from restaurants. The average American spends an additional $2,700 per year on food from restaurants versus what it would cost to prepare meals at home. So, we have Americans spending almost $3,000 extra per year on the food itself, then paying a 25 percent to 91 percent markup on that food if they have it delivered, all while the average American has $500 in savings and two-thirds live paycheck to paycheck. Put all this together and the average person barely scraping by could afford a down payment for a rental property in a decade if they did nothing more than eat at home. Couple that with renting instead of owning and now we're talking two rental properties in the next decade, and we haven't yet earned a dime of extra income.

Most people already know that they can cut down their budget by spending less on food, but very few do it. Implementing changes to your diet can be difficult for some people, but it really isn't as big a lifestyle change as many anticipate. Most of the resistance we feel around making changes to diet or food prep is emotional, not practical, and, like we said, feelings are the enemy of financial discipline. With food it really just comes down to planning ahead and cooking at home. Food is not life; it's fuel for life. Approach it as such and recognize that higher food costs and delivery fees are like a tax you are voluntarily paying for not planning ahead. What if instead of being billed in the moment you got a tax bill at the end of the year based on your lack of food discipline? How would you feel writing a $5,000 check because $14 hand-delivered Subway sandwiches are so much more convenient than $2 sandwiches we make for ourselves?

#2. Banking

The amount of money banks generate from fees has tripled in the last thirty years. According to the Bank Fee Finder Summary Report by Chime, published in 2018, the average person pays $329 per year in bank fees. That's a huge hit. Bank fees alone can drain the average person's life savings in around eighteen months (read that again). Think about it like this: $329 a year in fees translates to $27 a month, which is roughly what you'd pay for three streaming video services (Netflix, Hulu, Amazon Prime, etc.). Between ATM fees, over-draft fees, and hidden service fees, banks make a fortune charging you for accessing your own money! Here are a few things you can start doing today to cut back on unnecessary fees.

- Use only your bank's ATMs. The $2 to $5 fees for using other banks' ATMs to withdraw your money can quickly add up.
- Call your bank and opt out of overdraft protection. Two-thirds of people don't remember the moment when they opted *into* overdraft protection.
- Consolidate accounts. Many accounts have minimums and will penal-ize you if the money in your accounts falls below those minimums. If you fall into that category, it's better to consolidate accounts so you can stay above the minimums.

Don't be afraid to call your bank and ask. It's often older people who pay more in fees because fees are waived for many student accounts. At the end of the day, banks want your business more than they want fees, so if you threaten to switch banks, they will most likely waive any unnecessary fees. You might also learn of any perks. For example, some banks are willing to waive fees if you sign up to have your paycheck directly deposited into your account.

#3. Your Car

Banks love car loans. Why? Let's say you buy a car for $30,000. A year later, it's likely only worth $22,500 because the average car loses about 25 percent of its value in the first year, but you likely still have $25,000 or more remain-ing on the loan. Now you're paying interest on more than what the car is worth. I love being able to use other people's money, but *only for good debt*, which we defined earlier as "money borrowed for anything that produces a return greater than the interest being paid on the money borrowed." Unless you're an Uber or Lyft driver and your car generates income, a car loan is not good debt! I always recommend people buy used cars and finance as little as possible (unless they borrow it from their own "private banking system," a super cool strategy we'll look at later). Here are three things to consider when purchasing a car.

- **Negotiate:** Always negotiate. Car salespeople are good at making it sound like they don't have wiggle room when it comes to price, but there is always room, especially at the end of the year or month when they need to clear the lot and make their numbers.
- **Bundle insurance:** It's cheaper if you can bundle your car insurance with homeowner's or other insurance all from the same company.
- **Raise your insurance deductible:** On average, Americans spend four times as much money on insurance as they would on auto repairs. Raise your deductible and pay less for insurance.

#4. Tip Yourself

If you're like most people, when you go out to eat at a restaurant, you scan the prices on the menu and do the math in your head to anticipate your bill before you order. But most of us do not account for the tax and tip that we will have to pay when the check comes (at least according to my highly scientific survey method of having asked a bunch of people).

Sales tax and tip are part of what I call "the dressing" of our financial life—little extras that cost us greatly but that we don't really account for (like how people eat salad and think they're eating healthy but don't account for the 900 calories' worth of ranch dressing they slather all over it). Amazingly, even though we don't budget for tax and tip we always still manage to come up with it (bad tipping aside).

What if instead of costing ourselves "the dressing," we paid it to ourselves? If every time we eat out (or valet our car, stay at a hotel, or pay any other "dressing" transaction) we match all taxes, tips, and other fees with equal contributions to our savings and investments, we accomplish three things: we save money, we heighten awareness of these extra costs, and we do less of these things by making them more expensive to do. Full disclosure: I've personally never tried this because by the time I thought of it I was past the point of saving my way to wealth, but I have taught it to numerous people and gotten great feedback from those who did it for any length of time. A year after I shared this idea with the staff of my agency, one woman, who was twenty-four and made about $40,000 a year, told me she had saved $1,000 and was so excited. It was a great moment. Of course, I was let down to learn that she was the only one who'd tried it, but as I always say, if one person's life changes because of the work I do, it makes it all worthwhile!

#5. Utilize Apps

Another great way to live lean is to "keep yourself poor" by automating your savings. The idea is to pull money out of your checking account at regular intervals before you have a chance to spend it and thus reduce the amount you have available for bills or extras. This forces you to make sacrifices you might not otherwise make if the money was available in your checking account for you to spend. This is a tactic I have been using since my early twenties and it's how I was able to consistently save up funds to try out my business ideas throughout my twenties, even though I only averaged about $40,000 a year in income that entire decade. Even still, I keep a low enough balance in my checking account that if I'm tempted to make a large impulse purchase, I'll probably have to transfer money from somewhere else or pull it out of an investment, an inconvenient extra step that stops me from a lot of impulse buys. Many banks will allow you to set up automatic transfers from your checking account to a savings account and there are also many apps built around the same idea. Digit is one of the multiple apps out there that I started using a couple years ago because rather than relying on you to set a fixed savings amount, it uses machine learning to observe your spending and deposit patterns. Simply connect it to your checking account and once it learns your patterns it will automatically withdraw any extra money you are unlikely to need before your next deposit comes in. You can set it to be more or less aggressive and earmark different savings buckets for different purposes. I currently have money coming out daily into accounts set up for each of my kids along with a separate rainy day fund. It's really cool to have money being saved on autopilot that you forget about until you need it.

Recently, a buddy asked if I had heard of a certain cryptocurrency investment he was eyeing. I had not, but it sounded interesting. The problem was I had just done a couple real estate deals and did not have much cash lying around, and then I remembered my Digit account. I logged onto the app, checked my rainy day fund, and, sure enough, there was $110,000 in it. With only a few taps of my phone screen the funds were back on their way to my bank and two days later they were placed into that crypto investment. That was three months ago at the time of this writing and that investment is now worth over $800,000. Now, depending on where you are in the phases of legacy, I am not necessarily advising you to place your savings in cryptocurrency, but this anecdote illustrates the power of having a storehouse of cash for when you need it. When opportunities come along, it's often the person who can strike the fastest who gets the win. In business, this is called first-mover advantage (FMA), and it usually goes to the person with both the confidence and the cash to make a deal happen.

#6. Credit Card Rewards Program

Credit cards get a bad rap, but like in our saw analogy, they are just a tool that when wielded properly can be highly useful. Learning to responsibly cycle money through credit cards can earn you substantial rewards, especially if you have recurring business expenses (yet another perk for entrepreneurs). You just have to make sure that you're using your cards responsibly and paying off your balance each month because if you carry a balance, the interest charges will cannibalize the potential rewards. Find cards with good rewards programs and use them responsibly. There are numerous blogs and other resources that review credit card offers in the market and can tell you which ones have the best perks. Just make sure whatever resource you're getting your recommendations from is unbiased and not owned or controlled by a bank or credit card company.

Personally, I do this with two cards: one for personal use and one for business. I put most of my family's personal expenses on a Costco Rewards Citicard that gives us enough cash back each year in the form of a Costco voucher to allow me to pay for two months' worth of Costco runs. For a household with four kids that usually has another eight to ten friends grazing at any given time, this is not unsubstantial. For business, I have historically used an American Express Platinum card and absolutely cleaned up on rewards, especially for travel. Recently I switched to a credit card program through my bank (they made me an offer I couldn't refuse), but from 2008 to 2021 I ran every dollar of online advertising I did through my AmEx card. For a decade I have flown free and first class using points as long as I book my flights through AmEx's travel platform. It's seriously amazing. Just recently ENTRE had an event where we flew ninety-five people in (including several from other countries) and paid for every one of those flights with our points.

#7. Implement the 30-Day Rule

Anytime you get the urge to spend money on something outside your typical budget like a vacation or Jet Ski—in other words, something you want but don't need—instead of impulsively forking over the money, give yourself thirty nights to sleep on it.

There are two reasons why this is so important. First, there is a power in delaying decision-making about things we want to do but don't have to. It allows us time to make sure that we aren't giving into a dopamine craving and are really making a decision we won't regret. My dad once told me, "If someone asks you to make a financial decision right away, the answer should always be no." That was great advice.

The other reason we wait a full thirty days is that most of us operate in monthly financial cycles. On whatever day you are considering the decision, you might feel like you have plenty of money, but it's important to make sure it won't have an unintended consequence at a different time of the month when your financial situation may be different. By waiting a full month, you have an entire cycle to observe whether or not the purchase would have put you in a tight spot on a different day of the month. If you go the entire thirty days without your account ever dipping below the cost of the item you were considering purchasing, then you know it was something you could afford and can buy the next month. Back when I was a struggling musician, I ran into this issue a few times when I would get paid for a gig and immediately blow the money on some new piece of musical gear I just had to have. Then, sure enough at the end of the month, I'd be scrambling for basics, like paying rent or my cell phone bill. I learned to wait a month and make sure that every one of those thirty days wouldn't have left me missing that amount of money.

Thank heavens those days are over. Obviously, all this "living lean" talk isn't the most exciting part of this book, but for most people it's the place to start while implementing the other tools and techniques to move into the more fun parts of increasing income and building wealth. On that note, let's turn the conversation to making extra money, not just saving it.

START A SIDE HUSTLE

Similar to how there are easy ways to save money that you didn't realize you were wasting, you also might be able to use your skills and resources to make a few extra bucks as well. We'll go deeper into starting a full-fledged business in later chapters, but even as part of just living lean, starting a part-time side hustle is a worthy subject. I often hear people bemoaning that money is hard to come by. These fifteen ideas are not meant to be an exhaustive list of every way to make money, nor are any of them likely to make you rich, but you can use this list to get your own creative wheels turning as you figure out how to make some extra money and get a taste of entrepreneurial life. In addition to the sites listed for some of the options below, a quick Google search will yield you numerous options for all of them.

1. **Sell stock photos:** If you love photography or have great photos, you can post those to stock photo platforms to earn extra income. They could be travel photos or just photos you have around your house. So many people need to publish images on their websites. Bloggers and online marketers always need photos that obey copyright regulations. As a result, sites like shutterstock.com and depositphotos.com are constantly looking to expand their portfolios of copyright-free images.

2. **Transcribe audio:** Are you a good typist? If so, you can earn at least twenty dollars per hour transcribing audio—probably more if you have legal or medical experience. Sites like TranscribeMe allow you to cash in on that skill, and you can typically do as much or as little transcription work as you want.

3. **Uber or Lyft driver:** This is a go-to way to earn extra cash if you have a decent car that gets good gas mileage and live in a well-populated area.

4. **Rent your car:** If you don't want to drive others around, you can rent out your car on a site like relayrides.com, just like you would your house or apartment on Airbnb. You become the competition for the car rental company. There are obvious risks, but, depending on your situation, it can become quite lucrative. A client I worked with rented out his car two days a week and generated enough income to pay off his car note and insurance, while still having a bit of profit left over.

5. **Deliver food:** As we discussed, during the pandemic, takeout orders skyrocketed, and they aren't slowing down. While I don't advocate being a frequent customer of these apps, being on the fulfillment side can be a nice, flexible side gig. This applies to groceries too. Whether it's Uber Eats, DoorDash, Postmates, Grubhub, Instacart, or more than one, there is extra money to be made.

6. **Housesit pets:** If you like pets and enjoy caring for them, a site like dogvacay.com allows you to become an at-home kennel for those who would rather leave their pet in a home instead of boarding it at a kennel.

7. **Sitting:** Housesitting, babysitting, or petsitting is a simple way to earn extra cash. This is one of those areas where there is a lot of competition, but it is possible to build a reputation and post your services. If you can build up a good list of reliable clients, this can be a great source of extra income. If you're in college, you also might be able to proctor tests, which allows you to get paid to monitor other students.

8. **Product testing and research studies:** You can get paid extra money for giving your opinion. There are many market research companies out there looking for people to test products, fill out surveys, and provide their opinion on a wide variety of consumer goods.

9. **Mystery shopper:** Some people consider this a dream job, which is one reason why it's in high demand. You're shopping anyway, so why not get paid for it? Mystery shoppers are hired by market research companies to rate the quality of service in various restaurants and stores.

10. **Sell your old stuff:** If you live in a house or have a storage locker with a lot of old furniture, appliances, or collectibles, you can try to get rid of it on an app like OfferUp. You can even do it professionally for others and make a commission.

11. **Hauling junk:** Every decent-sized town seems to have multiple services offering to come haul away junk. This one can grow into a sizable business too. Most people know of 1-800-GOT-JUNK, but that's not the only example. College Hunks Hauling Junk started as a summer project in Washington, DC, for one college student and is now in over one hundred cities across the United States and Canada.

12. **Résumé writing:** This can be an especially lucrative gig if you're in college because every college student, whether they graduate or not, will need a résumé. Employers constantly complain about not getting well-written résumés and cover letters. And once you build a track record, you can begin advertising your services and charging more.

13. **Creating playlists:** Every good party needs a good playlist. Did you realize that people pay for access to other playlists? And musicians who want to get their music known will pay to get their songs on playlists. Sites like playlistpush.com are designed to help independent acts get their music heard by Spotify playlist curators and YouTube content creators.

14. **Making beats:** Yes, musical beats. If you have a YouTube channel or produce ads, you can't just use popular music without getting flagged or possibly sued. That's why there is a big market online for beats that content creators can use without worrying about copyright issues. The term for this is "Creative Commons" music and it is big business.

15. **User testing:** You can get paid to test out websites. Sites such as usertesting.com and whatusersdo.com allow you to download their testing software and record yourself with a webcam during the test. Clients want to see and hear you interact with their website. If you're good and they like what you do, opportunities may arise to do live tests where you can interact with clients in real time.

I realize that these aren't the sexiest or flashiest business ideas. Many aspiring entrepreneurs dream of inventing the next killer app or becoming a viral social media sensation, but succeeding at business isn't about flash, it's about doing the work day in and day out. You have to decide what's important to you. Do you want a lifestyle that looks flashy but you're broke all the time (like the underworld I told you about of six- and seven-figure lifestyle influencers who spend all their money on looking rich), or do you want to sacrifice now to become successful so you can earn the time and money to do truly cool stuff and live life on your terms? As someone who spent a decade as a broke jazz musician, I will tell you that life got a lot better when I stopped trying to make life so fun and carefree. Case in point: I now spend more time playing the music I actually want to play than I did when my job was to play the music other people wanted me to play. We'll talk in future chapters about some bigger and more glamorous ideas for businesses, but don't dismiss the idea of starting small with a side hustle and developing the right habits. Without the right habits, no big idea will be successful, and the last thing we should worry about is appearances in deciding what business to start.

Self-awareness is at the core of the income phase. Make yourself more aware of the amount of money you have coming in and going out of your personal economy. Most people think they know, but when they sit down and look at the actual numbers, they are shocked at what they find.

How closely do you look at your bank and credit card statements? This month, go over each of them and see what you're being charged. There are so many people out there who pay for gyms, streaming services, and other recurring charges for services they aren't using and forgot to cancel. If this is a problem for you, or you struggle to cut expenses, keep track of every single thing you buy each month and then take a closer look to see what you don't need and how you can become more efficient with your spending. Apps like Truebill and Trim can also help do an audit of unwanted subscriptions or unnecessary expenses.

One of the first steps to becoming a successful entrepreneur is to become adept at identifying real-world problems that people deal with and solving them. While you go through this process of personal financial optimization, take note of your challenges and make sure to document them (remember to always "document the struggle"). You'll be glad you did for all the reasons we discussed earlier, plus you might just identify the next problem that *you* can be the one to help others solve. Take it from me: helping people solve their problems in finance or other important areas of life can turn into a great business!

Now that you're doing the conscientious things that financially savvy people do, let's make sure you're thinking about things the way financially savvy people think.

20

How Rich People Think

But Jeff, if I'm living paycheck to paycheck. I can't save money."
Every time I hear someone say this, it frustrates me, but not because I don't understand where people are coming from. On the contrary, I get it. I spent an entire decade making $40,000 a year living in a major city where the cost of living was not cheap. I know what broke feels like and how it grinds on you month after month and year after year. But in hindsight I can see the truth of a simple perspective shift—the problem is not *living* paycheck to paycheck; the problem is *thinking* paycheck to paycheck. In a different era, sure, maybe we really were *stuck* and had no options, but this isn't our grandpa's world, and we don't have our grandpa's money problems. In the modern world, there are always opportunities to make more money, good money, and people who complain about living paycheck to paycheck either are not aware of those opportunities or have too much doubt (of self or of others) to go after them. This is tough love, and it's true. I don't care if you're a single mom with two jobs; there is a way to do it. Remember the section on the willpower fallacy; being tired only changes our options if we believe it does. With the right mindset, anyone can overcome living paycheck to paycheck.

In the 1980s, *Forbes* did a study that revealed one-third of the million-aires in the United States were self-made, while the other two-thirds came from privilege and either inherited their wealth or the business they used to build it. That isn't the case anymore. Today, according to Fidelity Invest-ments, 88 percent of millionaires are self-made, and even more astounding, almost 70 percent of those with a net worth of $30 million or more are self-made. Almost nine out of ten millionaires, and over two-thirds of the ultra-wealthy, are people just like the rest of us who weren't born with a sil-ver spoon in their mouths but rather just got fed up with the status quo and committed to living differently than most people do. At some point for every such successful person, the fear of living a mundane, average life outweighed the fear of betting on themselves to live boldly and take calculated risks, so that's what they did.

So, what are the commonalities in these millions of millionaire stories (and the 1.5 million new ones that get written each year according to *Forbes* maga-zine)? There are as many ways to make a lot of money as there are people with a lot of money, but we can start by studying one thing that every wealthy per-son is deeply familiar with and uses every day. For many people, the day they begin getting wealthy is the day they get obsessed with this one word. It was definitely the thing I got obsessed with that made the shift for me. That word is *leverage*, and there are seven different types of it, any one of which can be used to create outlier results in this world.

THE 7 TYPES OF LEVERAGE

I learned a lot of different things as a piano player, including a variety of ways to screw up your life. When I started getting gigs, I was living my dream, but a decade later, I had played three thousand gigs, was earning roughly the same income as when I started, had arthritis in my wrist, had a teaching studio that was a mix of kids who didn't want to be there and adults who were too busy adulting to ever have time to practice, had a second divorce in the works, was living at my in-laws' house, and was half a million dollars in debt with eleven failed businesses. In many ways, I was just like every other schmoe who ends up stuck in the consequences of their life choices, and in some ways I was worse off than most, but there was one thing that made me a little different: I held an unshakeable faith in the power of entrepreneurship. Even with eleven business failures my belief that starting the right business was the vehicle of my salvation never wavered. I had met too many millionaires and billionaires and heard too many entrepreneurial success stories to ever give up on that dream. Plus, I knew the data. I knew that 45 percent of all business owners end up as millionaires, while only 4 percent of employees do (I suggest rereading that stat a few times, by the way). So I kept going, and in 2008, my fortune started to turn. I finally started "the right business," which became the first of three eight-figure businesses, followed by the nine-figure business I'm running now (and for the record the plan is to have to reprint this book to update that to "ten-figure" in due time).

Okay, so what *exactly* is the difference between "the right businesses" and "the wrong businesses"? To date, I've still started more wrong businesses than right businesses and that will probably still be true at my funeral. But, like Mark Cuban says, in business it only takes one winner to make up for all the losers. So are "right businesses" right because they are online? Not necessarily. I know plenty of people who have online businesses that don't get very far, and plenty of people with offline businesses that crush it. Was it because they had low overhead? That was certainly a nice feature of my first business that allowed me to get started even though I was broke, but I know plenty of people with low overhead businesses that struggle to turn a profit (they're usually called hobbies) and very high overhead businesses like construction or IT hardware businesses that do really well. Was it because I have some Herculean work ethic? Definitely not. I do have quite the work ethic but I also have just shy of a dozen examples of my work ethic not equating to success.

The answer is that in 2008, for the first time, I started a business that actually gave me some *leverage*. That's the magic word right there. Prior to November 2008, most of what I did involved trading my time for money at a fixed rate. As a pianist, the gig determined the value of my time. How well I played might have determined if I got hired again, and it might have even meant I could charge more the next time, but it never meant I could get paid in any way but by the hour. Even most of my businesses were low leverage. Let's review my eleven failed business ventures through the lens of leverage. And as I'm doing this, consider any businesses you have tried or considered and look at them through this same lens.

1. **Booking agent:** Book one band, get paid one fee. Spend hours going back and forth between bands and club owners to hopefully get paid *if* the gig goes well, people show up, and everyone is honest. Leverage = none.

2. **Party promoter:** Promote one party, earn one commission. Sure, the parties could be big, but so were the risks. And it was zero-sum—either the party hit its numbers and I got paid, or it didn't and I didn't. Leverage = none.

3. **Sandwich shop owner:** Sell a sandwich, make a dollar. Sell two sandwiches, make two dollars. Sell a million sandwiches . . . I'll never know because we never scaled, and we never scaled because we never had any leverage. Leverage = none.

4. **MLM:** This one was sold to me on the basis of all the leverage I could create by recruiting others to build the team—then I learned about trying to get cats to fight like dogs. I recruited twenty people I knew who could afford to buy into a business opportunity. Unfortunately, since my musician friends were mostly broke, that meant I was recruiting from other friend groups and mostly targeting people with jobs. It was the mid-2000s, during an economic boom when people with jobs thought they were the smart ones and had no interest in recruiting for our team. I learned quickly there is no leverage in building a team of people in which you're the only one working. In this case the leverage was worse than none—they were expecting me to do their work. Leverage = negative.

5. **House flipper:** I *love* real estate investing, but flipping houses is the least interesting type of it because it's the type that has the least leverage (especially when you're starting out broke and trying to use credit cards that eat you alive at 20-plus percent interest rates). Even if you can get a lender to help you, you're buying distressed properties, so the interest rates are high, the loan-to-value ratios are low, and all the risk is on you because the asset is producing zero income while you hold it and costing you taxes and insurance on top of loan interest and rehab costs. If you successfully flip it, sure, you can make some money but that's a big *if* that depends on a lot of things going right, especially if you've never done it before. I could write a whole book on why

flipping is the worst way to do real estate, but for now, I'll just leave it at this—of all the ways to do real estate, flipping has the least leverage, so don't unless you're willing to make it a full-time job. Leverage = minimal and can go sideways fast.

6. **Loan officer:** Originate one loan, earn one commission. You front all the marketing expense and time to land a deal, and then only get paid if it goes through. Also, the better deal you get for your client, the less you get paid. Leverage = none.

7. **Campus coupon marketer:** Walking around college towns trying to find local business owners (who would rather be found by a rattlesnake than a solicitor) and sell them a $400 product one time that would pay me 20 percent profit if I sold thirty of them per market in the two weeks I had in each town. If I hadn't been doing this business with a friend of mine, I would have gone insane. Actually, I'm not sure we didn't both go insane. Leverage = none.

8. **Campus text message marketer:** We're starting to get it. At least, we were leveraging a new technology to make the sales pitch easier. But it was too new and involved too much educating and not enough selling. And we still had to find the local business owners. Leverage = none.

9. **Real estate marketer:** This one sounded great until we actually got into it. I can now report there is no lower leverage activity than paying to bring lunches to real estate offices to try to sell stuff to the subset of agents who can be found hanging out in the office instead of being out on listing appointments. Another red flag was attracting anyone who does anything for a free lunch. Leverage = none.

10. **Mobile marketing agency owner:** I actually love the agency business as a concept because there is a ton of leverage in signing clients to retainers, but this was the mid-2000s, mobile marketing was too new, and clients were unwilling to sign long-term contracts. Every sale was a test, and we never got to build any leverage. Leverage = none.

11. **Restaurant franchise owner:** Same as #3—sell a sandwich, make a dollar. Only, now, I have to sell a few hundred thousand sandwiches to pay off my bank loans before I ever get to pocket anything. Leverage = none.

If this book accomplishes one thing, I hope it's to encourage people to get obsessed with creating leverage in their life. I would consider that a great contribution to society. At the risk of being politically incorrect and perhaps a little dramatic, a lack of leverage is the real pandemic in our world. Diseases kill thousands, or even millions, but a lack of leverage relegates billions to lives of drudgery. Getting obsessed with leverage is the single mental shift that can do the most good for the most people. Here are the seven types of leverage you can start looking for.

#1. Other People's Work

Failure to hire the right help soon enough is the number one reason I see businesses stagnate. Most entrepreneurs are control freaks because they love their "baby" so much and they're scared to entrust the work to anyone else. That's a fine approach to raising an actual baby, but it is a recipe for burnout and wasted opportunity. And it's not just entrepreneurs who need to leverage other people's work. Often, the person in a job who gets the raise or promotion isn't the person who does the most work. It's the person who creates the best systems for harnessing the work of others.

#2. Other People's Skills

Obviously, I'm a big fan of learning—I've labeled knowledge as a superpower, after all—but we are fools if we try to learn it all and do it all ourselves. The most successful people in any given endeavor are the ones who get the right information and put it to use, whatever it is and wherever the information comes from. Nothing has taught me this more than ENTRE. We grew 4,000 percent in one year, and that growth would have sunk our ship if we hadn't brought in consultants and executives who had much more specialized knowledge than we did.

Even if you're not running a business, it still pays to build relationships with people who are smarter than you about various subjects. Take my buddy who tipped me off to a profitable crypto investment. That's a relationship I had cultivated in part because my friend is knowledgeable about something I'm interested in but don't have time to master myself. Life is short, and time is precious. Choose your relationships wisely. Just because someone lives next door to you or has the same last name as you doesn't mean they are the best people to devote your relationship energy to. Curate your relationships like a museum director building a collection—seek out the rarest, most interesting, and most valuable people to invest your relationship energy into, and your life will leap forward in wonderful and unexpected ways.

Many people feel bad about being selective when it comes to distributing relationship energy. A lot of my fellow musicians thought I was aloof or even rude because, instead of hanging out with them on the breaks, I would often seek out the most interesting people I could find at the event to talk to. It wasn't all of them who felt that way, but it was enough that I heard about it. At one gig, the bass player even told me I should stop mingling with the guests because I looked like a "wannabe." He said other musicians would be less likely to hire me because I thought I was better than them. I replied that I already spent most of my time hanging out with musicians but on these gigs we had a rare opportunity to be around some of the most successful people in the world and I'd be damned if I was going to squander that chance because my fellow musicians were offended I wanted to talk to the billionaire instead. "Why don't you want to talk to him?" I asked. And for the record "hanging out on the breaks" usually meant standing in a backyard or a stairwell watching one or more bandmates smoke a cigarette they'd been fiending for during the last set. Pass.

#3. Other People's Network and Resources

Every single successful person I've ever talked to speaks of the value of relationships. It is often said our net worth is tied to our network, and I believe truer words have never been spoken. If you haven't started building your Power List yet, what are you waiting for? The cool thing about a Power List is that everyone on the list has their own Power List too. Networking with successful people puts you one degree of separation from their entire network of successful people. I have found that in any environment, whether it's an industry, a city, or an interest-based community, the number of really successful people is fairly small and they are also the best connected. Usually, a few of the right relationships can connect you with all the people you could ever need to know in a given environment. Just like with finding a mentor, you have to find ways to offer value in return. It doesn't have to be anything crazy; just being known as a person of integrity who keeps his word goes a long way with successful people, who are usually more interested in people's intangibles than their pedigrees.

Another thing I've learned from networking with successful people is that they usually have a lot more to offer than you even realize. In 2020, I attended an event called WebinarCon and wound up seated next to a gentleman named Perry Belcher. If you don't know the name, you probably aren't in internet marketing, because Perry is one of the greatest direct response marketers in history and cofounder of DigitalMarketer.com. After a few minutes of fan-geeking, I composed myself and made a proper introduction. An hour later, I had learned that not only was Perry a really nice guy, he was also an expert on something I never expected based on work I didn't even know he'd done. The subject was franchising regulations, and, at the time, I was involved in a potential deal to franchise a concept that a friend of mine had created. The advice I gleaned from Perry during that hour ultimately changed my whole approach to the deal and, in the end, steered me away from it. I would estimate that single conversation saved me hundreds of hours of time and having to learn the hard way.

#4. Other People's Money

This one is so common that financially savvy circles refer to it simply by its initials, OPM. If you have ever borrowed money from a bank, you have used OPM. When a bank makes a loan, it's not actually the bank's money that gets loaned out. It's either money from the depositors at the bank or money the bank borrowed from the Federal Reserve, which itself is funded mostly by interest income generated through its own operations in the capital markets—or, more OPM. OPM is pretty much how the world goes around, and it's definitely how the rich get richer. It's often said that it takes money to make money, but that saying misses the point. The real saying should be, "It takes either money or credit to qualify to get other people's money to make money." Most wealthy people generate as much or more income from OPM than they do from their own money, but having their own money makes it easier to get OPM because they have credit and/or collateral.

OPM is the essence of the topic we covered earlier about debt—in particular, good debt versus bad debt. If you are going to buy something that will depreciate, for goodness sake, do it with your own money so you aren't paying interest on top of the depreciation; this is why you should never borrow money from a bank to buy a car. But if you're going to buy something that will appreciate, then I say with equal fervor—please do it with OPM so you can buy more of it, assuming it will appreciate and/or generate a return greater than the interest cost on the OPM!

Most people are familiar with the idea of using OPM to buy real estate, but it can go way further than that. For example, I don't pay for the ads I run—OPM does. At present, I spend about two million dollars a month advertising on platforms like Facebook and Google, but, as I said earlier, I put it all on credit cards, so technically, I never actually pay for those ads. The credit card companies do using, you guessed it, OPM. I then have thirty days to sell products and services before I have to pay them back with, you guessed it again, OPM (the money I earned from my customers). Me personally? I never spend a dime on ads. Every online business I've built to date works the same way: use credit cards (OPM) to buy ads to make sales to bring in revenue from customers (OPM), and then use that OPM to pay for the ads and other expenses, and then (and only then) convert what's left of OPM into MM (my money). And on top of it all I'm earning credit card rewards the whole time that are subsidized by more OPM because those incentives are paid for by the credit card companies' profits, which are disproportionately generated by less responsible card users who don't pay their full balance each month.

Thinking about business this way is useful because it keeps me from thinking that just because money is in my bank account it's actually mine. I don't consider money to be mine until I've used all the OPM revenue from customers to pay back all the OPM expenses to credit cards or other capital sources.

OPM is key to one of the trickiest problems in business—managing cash flow timing. It is commonly known in business that most businesses fail because they are undercapitalized, but that statement is really an oversimplification of the challenge most businesses have with cash flow timing. Most businesses, given enough time to pay their debts, could work, except that creditors like to put these pesky conditions on their extensions of credit called due dates, or "terms." As one of my old bass player friends used to say (not the one who nagged me at that gig), "The man doesn't just want his rent, but he wants it on time! Damn the man." Managing how long it takes to see a return on expenses, such as marketing, inventory, and payroll, and making sure that return comes sooner than the bill is due, is the art of running a successful business. And having OPM lined up in case you need it is the insurance policy that will keep you alive to fight another day in case you miscalculate.

One of the greatest entrepreneurs of all time, Richard Branson, once said, "Learn to raise capital by any means necessary. That is your primary job as an entrepreneur. You must continue to raise capital from family and friends, banks, suppliers, customers, and investors." That quote highlights the importance of OPM. Whether you're a business owner or not, every day you need to be in the business of attracting money. Every human life is a business. Whether you operate a separately organized business or not, you have assets, liabilities, income, and expenses. This reality has led to a popular concept in entrepreneurial circles known as "You, Inc." Everyone on earth is the CEO of their own instance of You, Inc. As CEO, your number one job is attracting capital, and a major piece of that is credit, or the ability to access OPM.

And here's the most important lesson there is to learn about credit, one that you don't want to learn the hard way. It's a hundred times easier to line up OPM when you don't need it than when you do. Start now working on credit and building up relationships with banks so that when the time comes to borrow money you have an established relationship and have already been approved.

And a final thought on OPM, or really more of a quick temperature check. How does the OPM conversation make you feel? Does it upset you? There are entire world religions dead set against the idea of lending OPM and charging interest, so if it upsets you, you're not the only one. But this is the world we live in, and this book is intended to teach you how to get ahead in this world. I do not make the rules and personally I have no qualms about a system in which people allow their money to be loaned out at interest while participating in that interest. I do think most people should be more informed about how the system works, which is part of my reason for writing this book, but the system is not responsible for the ignorance of its participants. Bottom line: if you're going to hate, don't hate the player, hate the game. But unless you're prepared to opt out of the game altogether (and going off the grid is a very different book than this one), you might as well play to win. Losing is not defiance, it's surrender.

#5. Other People's Time

Time is a limited resource; it doesn't matter who you are. We all only have twenty-four hours in a day, which is why you absolutely must learn the science of time management. Those with a millionaire mindset have learned how to manage their hours in a precise, analytical way and are always working to improve their efficiency by asking how they can do things better and faster. A major part of that equation is knowing how they can offload the tasks that aren't the best use of their time (the outsource part of the DOO framework from chapter 14). This goes back to those level 3 tasks that are necessary but aren't top priorities or moneymakers. Successful people don't use their own time to complete menial tasks. Laundry, cleaning the house, maintaining the lawn and your property—you could do all of this yourself, but if your time is more valuable and you can make more money doing something else, you're literally losing money by not paying other people to perform these tasks.

One of my favorite quotes is by Antoine de Saint-Exupery, who said, *"Perfection is achieved not when there is nothing more to add, but when there is nothing left to take away."* That is how I think about life, constantly asking how much can I offload so I can focus on the most important things only.

#6. Other People's Ideas

Similar to leveraging other people's skills, we also have to learn to leverage other people's ideas. This is one of the most powerful forms of leverage there is, but we often make it harder than it has to be. We tend to resist other people's ideas, seeing them as being in competition with our own. Idea leverage threatens our ego in a way no other type of leverage would. We are not offended at the idea of using someone else's money instead of our own, nor using their labor, time, or skills instead of our own, but to use someone else's ideas, or even to admit to their value, we might feel like we have to give up something. But we must be willing to, and here's why.

There is a phenomenon called the Dunning-Kruger effect that deals with how people of limited comprehension (which all of us are to some degree) struggle to understand the limits of their own comprehension. Through a series of studies, social psychologists David Dunning and Justin Kruger proved a concept called *illusory superiority* where the worse people are at a thing, the more likely they are to overestimate their abilities at that thing. Have you ever had an argument with a person who was so clearly wrong, but so convinced they were right? If so, you may have been experiencing the Dunning-Kruger effect, though as an aside I can't help but think we should take care not to judge in such a situation, given that by its nature the Dunning-Kruger effect is experienced mutually between parties whenever it is present. One might say that in Dunning-Kruger terms we all live in something of a glass house.

That said, whether we are the victims or the perpetrators, if illusory superiority is true then it logically applies when inverted as well (if x increases when y decreases, then x must decrease when y increases, right?). Thus, if the Dunning-Kruger effect states that the less competent we are at something, the more likely we are to overestimate our ability, then the inversion would state that the more competent we are, the less likely we are to overestimate our ability and the more likely we are to seek help. This is a potent and humbling realization—that thinking we need help is actually an indicator of high ability, or at least high awareness. Wow! If that were more widely understood, imagine how it would change society. Imagine a world of people who felt confident asking for help! Well, in my experience, the most successful people are those who are not just confident, but excited, to ask for help and seek out other people's ideas, which supports the idea that the Dunning-Kruger effect works both ways.

The simple point here is don't be afraid to seek out other people's ideas; rather, be afraid not to. Thinking you already have all the ideas you need is likely to be evidence that you don't.

#7. Automation and Systems

Leveraging automation and systems is at the core of the external brain concept we discussed in chapter 15. Technology, specifically the internet, is a huge lever we must learn to pull on. When you learn to harness it, the internet is like having a dedicated employee who knows everything, can do almost anything, and never takes a sick day or complains. This is why we must lean into technology in any business we operate, or even just our You, Inc. business.

Automation extends to so much in modern living. Obviously, internet businesses are highly automated and that's what makes them so cool, but there's a lot more to automation than just online sales funnels and email follow-ups. What are the things you do on a regular basis that are repetitive and could be automated? When I lived in New York City, I had an almost entirely automated life and it was one of my most productive periods. My bills were paid on autopay. My groceries were delivered once a week and the cleaner unloaded them and stocked the fridge and pantry. My laundry was picked up from my front door and delivered back clean and neatly folded the next day for the cleaner to put in the dresser and closet. My Google calendar alerts told me where to be, automatically created map links to tell me how to get there, and texted them to me at my departure times. I even used automated bots to trade stocks. Today, life is a little messier with four kids, but I still use automation and lots of it. Even my kids have embraced it. My five-year-old daughter has a recurring alarm set every night that tells her to come get me for "dolls and tickles." A ten-minute ritual then ensues involving a four-minute timer for dolls followed by a six-minute timer for tickling her back in bed. She absolutely loves it and it is the highlight of her day (clearly the apple didn't fall far from the tree). And far from being concerned about her, I am ecstatic that she is already leveraging automation and systems to create routines that make her life more predictable, efficient, and successful long term.

The right technology in our life can make everything so much easier. Always remember your external brain is smarter than a hundred of you could ever be, so don't fall prey to the Dunning-Kruger effect and think otherwise. We'll dig deeper into how automation and systems can create leverage in business later, but for now, go ahead and embrace it across your whole life.

———

Leverage doesn't come easily. Throughout human history, most people have done low-leverage work. It's a relatively new concept, at least in its availability to the masses, and there are lots of ways it can apply to life. It's the single biggest lever you can pull to exponentially improve your life, so much so that the word *lever* is the root of it. And just like a literal lever, it takes more force to get it going than to keep it going, so be willing to do the hard work to acquire every type of leverage you can in your life. Any one of these seven types of leverage can create massive results, and when you start combining them, watch out.

Take a minute to go through the seven types of leverage and make notes on how each of them is currently being utilized in your life and where more is needed (hint: more is needed everywhere, always). Don't worry if you don't see a lot of opportunities at first; perspective is a muscle you have to develop. It all goes back to the reticular activating system—that part of the brain that controls what you notice consciously and what gets filtered out. Scanning your environment for leverage opportunities takes practice, but it is the key to seeing the world the same way as a wealthy person.

Next, we're going to talk about a particular type of asset that has forever changed my life and can change yours too. It's the foundation for most of the businesses I operate and the highest leverage asset I've ever discovered, especially for those who don't have a lot of money to start.

21

Your Anomalous Cash Flow Phase

For most of human history, limited socioeconomic mobility was an accepted fact of life. If you were born a farmer, you worked the family farm. If you were born a blacksmith, you worked the family smithy, and so on, but there has always been an out for anyone who was committed to it. That out is sales. The ability to get people to buy stuff has been a way to cut ahead in line for as long as man has been trading between settlements, at least in terms of income if not in social class. And this has only gotten truer as civilization has evolved and distinct commercial industries have emerged. The advertising industry has been around for hundreds of years, with the first actual advertising agencies dating back to seventeenth-century London. And ever since 1855, when a Baptist preacher named James Robinson Graves founded the Southwestern Companies (the world's first door-to-door sales company), anyone who wanted could strike out on their own and make great money for themselves if they were committed to mastering the persuasive arts. And while in 1855, anyone didn't really mean *anyone*, it does now. In the modern world, anyone can get ahead if they learn to sell.

Did you know that numerous billionaires cut their teeth with door-to-door sales? John Paul DeJoria (Patrón, Paul Mitchell) sold encyclopedias door-to-door, Sara Blakely (Spanx) sold fax machines door-to-door, Reed Hastings (Netflix) sold vacuum cleaners door-to-door, and Mark Cuban (Broadcast.com, Dallas Mavericks) sold garbage bags door-to-door. The list goes on and on. A LinkedIn study found that one of the most common early jobs on the résumés of Fortune 500 CEOs was sales manager, which is almost always a role held by a former salesperson since salespeople usually resist being managed by someone without sales experience.

With such an established body of evidence that sales is the single best skill a person can learn to attract future success, it raises the question: Why doesn't school teach sales? Out of nearly four thousand colleges and universities in the United States, only 3 percent of them have a degree path related to sales, and a review of the Department of Education curriculum guide for high school shows no mention of sales at all. Yet, we persist as a society under the idea that it is impossible for most people to dramatically increase their income. Sales is the superpower of successful people in any industry. Dreaming of being a rapper? Take a page out of Kanye West and Jay-Z's playbooks and get started in sales. Want to be an actor? Do what Johnny Depp and Jennifer Aniston did and build your confidence with sales.

Ultimately, we all know why sales isn't more prevalent in schools; it's because most people don't like it and are terrified at the thought of doing it, specifically having to deal with the rejection that comes with it. But that's not a good reason to avoid doing it, or not teaching it for that matter. On the contrary, learning to deal with rejection and worrying less about what other people think is a great life skill we should all be learning and practicing constantly. I'm not trying to convince you to go get a sales job (although for many people that would be a good start to making more money and pushing through the income phase), but I am trying to win you over to the entrepreneurial axiom that holds this: because money is only made when things are sold, the people who deserve to make the most money are the ones who get them sold. Hopefully, this book has you so fired up and ready to ignore what people think about you that you would be willing to get an old-school sales job if that was your best option for escaping the broken system, but, fortunately for you, in the last twenty years something has emerged that is even more powerful than human-to-human sales, and that is internet-to-human sales. And just as human-to-human sales take place in specific agreed-upon environments (showroom floors, car lots, front doors, phone calls, etc.) there are places on the internet where sales are understood to happen (Amazon carts, Etsy stores, blogs, sales funnels, social media links, etc.). Collectively, I refer to all digital assets involved in commerce as "digital real estate" and those who build these environments as "digital real estate developers."

In some ways this is the climax of this book, the big reveal. Learning to develop digital real estate is how I finally built a sustainable life outside the broken system. I believe that learning to develop digital real estate is the most powerful skill of our time. More than any skill or innovation in human history, digital real estate development levels the playing field for the average person and offers the majority of people a shot at pushing through their income phase to build real wealth in the modern world.

Technically, digital real estate simply means any location in the digital world that people can visit or "land" on (websites, mobile apps, software, databases, NFTs, and even land and structures in the metaverse), but I use it intentionally to mean those digital properties where products and services get sold or that lead people to such sales activity. Digital real estate has the same properties that make physical real estate development attractive, the ability to generate cash flow and own assets that appreciate in value over time. And the beautiful thing about it for anyone with "sales reluctance" is that digital real estate bypasses the physical act of selling, so insecurity should no longer inhibit people from taking economic control of their life. If you embrace it, digital real estate is the single greatest thing to ever happen to introverts like me, misanthropes, shut-ins, agoraphobes, and anyone else who fancies themselves not a "natural salesperson." Digital real estate takes many forms, and every dollar I've generated since November 2008 (approaching $150 million now) has involved digital real estate—even my phys-ical real estate gets leased or rented through digital real estate. In fact, when this book comes out, it will be the first physical product I've sold in a physical store since I closed my restaurants in 2008. And still, the largest percentage of sales will come from Amazon, the world's largest digital real estate development, and the second largest will be audiobooks, more digital real estate.

Einstein once called compound interest the eighth wonder of the world and said, "Those who understand it earn it, and those who don't pay it." I think we can say something similar about digital real estate. "Those who understand it earn from it, and those who don't pay for it." To understand why digital real estate is the key for most people to push through their income phase and start building real wealth, we have to talk about something I call the "anomalous cash flow phase."

An anomalous cash flow phase is the phase of your life when you *increase* your income rapidly, at a rate many times faster than either the rate of inflation or cost of living increases. Normal income growth, for example, the average annual American raise of 2 to 3 percent, usually gets absorbed by either inflation or lifestyle creep, so for most people there must be a phase where income increases abruptly and dramatically if it is ever going to exceed expenses and reach the critical mass of surplus needed to become wealthy in our lifetime. Einstein also said, "Insanity is doing the same thing over again and expecting a different result." If you want to double, triple, or even quintuple your income (remembering that the goal of the income phase is to earn five times your expenses) it's not going to be by putting in more hours at the job you already have or making modest cuts in your day-to-day life. This kind of change to your income-to-expenses ratio is probably not going to happen doing anything that seems normal or reasonable to most people (hence calling it *anomalous*). I'm not saying working overtime and cutting expenses aren't good things to do. After all, I wrote a whole chapter on living lean. But if you've been making $100,000 a year at a job it's going to take more than small measures to get that to $500,000, which would be one of the ways to complete the income phase.

To be clear, there are only three ways to get through your income phase:

1. Get your living expenses down to one-fifth of your income (living off $20,000 a year in our $100,000 income example)
2. Increase your income to five times your expenses (earning $500,000 per year in our example)
3. Combine the two approaches (for example, cutting bills to $50,000 while increasing income to $250,000)

Surely, you can see that none of these scenarios are likely to happen unless something dramatic happens, something "anomalous."

START YOUR OWN DIGITAL BUSINESS

The harsh reality is that even if you're a doctor, lawyer, engineer, or have any other "good" job (other than sales), you probably lack sufficient leverage to increase your income rapidly enough to reach your Awesome Life Number through your job alone. And that's doubly true if you have a family. The model of getting a job and working your way up the ladder is not a formula for building wealth, and it's only going to get worse in years to come. Already only 4 percent of employees historically become millionaires (6 million out of 157 million employees in the United States), with a much lower percentage than that becoming multimillionaires, which is what it takes to retire comfortably nowadays. But that's just historical. Moving forward the odds of building real wealth through a job are declining quickly. Here's why. In the two years prior to this book being written, the US money supply increased by an average of 25 percent per year (compared to historical averages of 3 to 7 percent). Once that massive increase in available dollars has time to percolate through the economy, the buying power of the dollar will be significantly impacted (aka, rampant inflation), and the government shows no signs of easing off on diluting the money supply. This will result in increasing prices on consumer goods for a long time, making it nearly impossible for people to improve their income-to-expense ratios by cutting expenses. In my opinion, the absolute best way for most people to create a five-to-one income-to-expense ratio, hit their Awesome Life Number, and graduate from their income phase is to start a digital business (i.e., create digital real estate) and get completely obsessed with creating anomalous cash flow unlike anything they've ever seen before.

So why is a digital business so powerful? For starters, we live and transact in a digital economy. In 2020, the global digital economy surpassed $20 trillion, nearly 25 percent of the entire world's combined gross domestic product, and the numbers get really crazy in the United States, where the digital economy hit $13.6 trillion in 2020 (65 percent of the $21 trillion US GDP). Yet, of the approximately 30 million MSMBs (micro-, small-, and mid-size businesses) in the United States, only about 2 million of them (6 percent) transact online.

Simple math shows there is an opportunity window wide open right now, but not forever. Anyone creating digital real estate right now, and I estimate for the next ten to twenty years, has an enormous advantage over traditional business owners. Based on today's numbers there is an opportunity to be part of the 6 percent group of business owners who are doing 65 percent of all the business in the United States. This is classic FMA (first mover's advantage). Don't be that person twenty years from now wishing you had struck while the iron was hot! And it's not just the size of the opportunity that makes this opportunity so appealing, it's also the smaller size of the downside risk. A digital business owner doesn't have the same expenses, overhead, operational friction, labor issues, and other headaches that come with running a traditional brick-and-mortar business. You don't have to deal with employees clocking out early, calling in sick, and needing health insurance. You aren't going to get an OSHA violation if an employee falls on the job.

The digital economy doesn't keep hours or need to sleep. It goes 24/7, and you can put it to work for you in a way that human beings aren't capable of. And customers? My word, there are a lot of customers waiting for your wares online. Today, there are 4.3 billion people who have access to the internet, and they can all shop across borders. Over the next ten years, that number is projected to increase to 7.5 billion. Right now is hands down the best time to build something online, and if you do it well and put in the time, it's only going to grow. Starting a digital business today is like becoming a real estate developer in California in the 1800s.

Real estate has been the foundation of wealth throughout human history, and that hasn't changed, but it's time to expand the definition. There's a saying in real estate—don't wait to buy real estate; buy real estate and wait. Well, I'd say the time has come not to wait to develop digital real estate, but to develop digital real estate and wait!

There are different types of digital real estate, and I'll break down five of them below. There are others, but these are the main ones that generate most of the success that I see online. I have personally used all five of these to generate at least seven figures, three of them eight figures, and one of them nine figures.

#1. Affiliate Marketing

When I say that digital business is what turned my life around, I'm talking specifically about affiliate marketing. I'm not saying affiliate marketing is the best digital business model, nor am I saying it's the one you should start with (there is no one-size-fits-all recommendation for where to start), but it is the one I happened to discover back in 2008 when I was at my lowest of lows. And the early mentors I met at that three-day event in Lake Tahoe were all affiliate marketers. Affiliate marketing is how I paid off my half-million dollars in debt in eighteen months and went on to generate approximately $10 million in commissions in my first five years online. In 2010, when I was ranked number

281 on the list of the top 500 independent home business earners in the world (a list maintained on a website called businessforhome.org), it was from affiliate marketing (most of the list was MLMers at that time, though now I suspect that has changed). Suffice it to say, affiliate marketing was very good to me, and it can be good to you, too.

Affiliate marketing is a great place to start because you don't need startup capital, you don't need to create your own products, you don't need to employ anyone else, and you don't even need to deal with customers. It also has the long-term potential to compound if you do it the right way.

So what is affiliate marketing? It's basically a fancy term for being in the referrals business. You find products that other people might want and refer them. The difference between affiliate marketing and an old-school, warm-market referral is that affiliate referrals happen through hyperlinks (those little links you click to open up web pages). Affiliate hyperlinks have personalized tracking codes in them so merchants know you are the one who sent the referral, and then they pay you a portion of whatever gets sold. It's that simple. Virtually anything you can think of to buy or sell online can be promoted as an affiliate, and there is an entire industry built around making it easy for you to find good "offers" and get paid for promoting them. You can go to a site like ClickBank.com to find thousands of different products to sell in all different niches (like health, gardening, clothes, finance, travel, books, etc.). ClickBank is just one of dozens of affiliate networks that supply ready-to-be-promoted offers by affiliate marketers. Anything you can think of to market, you can likely find. I recently counted the number of niches on ClickBank—it was 279.

How about a little site called Amazon? I'm confident you've heard of it. Well, sign up for the Amazon Associates Program (they call their affiliates "associates," but it's the same thing) and you can now create a trackable affiliate link for any product on Amazon and get paid if someone buys it, along with getting paid on anything else they add to their cart in the same checkout session. Walmart, Best Buy, Nordstrom, and Target all have affiliate programs. Want to promote travel offers? Priceline, Travelocity, Hotels.com, Orbitz, Airbnb, and virtually any other large travel site you can think of have affiliate programs. And again, this is just a new twist on the age-old business of referrals. In travel a referral business used to be called having a travel agency, and you used to have to have a license for it, only now it's all done online and anyone can get set up as an affiliate for a dozen different travels sites in minutes. Individual product companies have them too. A few years ago, I bought my wife a Tesla, and guess what? When I installed the Tesla iPhone app, up in the top right corner was a little treasure box icon. Sure enough when I clicked it, I was given a link to share with friends that would track back to me as the referring affiliate if someone clicked it, scheduled a visit to a Tesla store, and ended up purchasing a car. If I remember correctly, the commission offered was $500 and I was unimpressed. Even Amazon averages a 4 percent commission per checkout and I'm used to promoting items that pay 20 percent or more in commissions. Only $500 for helping sell a Tesla just made me chuckle, but nonetheless it proves the ubiquity of this type of marketing.

Think about it: businesses have been creating referral programs for ages, so why wouldn't that continue in the age of the internet when referrals are easier to track than ever? At ENTRE we have an affiliate program. Heck, we'll probably make an affiliate offer for this book so you can share it with your friends and get paid. There are literally thousands of affiliate programs and millions of products you can sell.

How does it work? When you sign up as an affiliate, they give you links for products or services to which you can refer people. The links take those who click on them to offer pages containing information about whatever is being offered and how to get it. You, the affiliate, then share your link through any one of an almost infinite number of ways to get content out online—social media, writing a review or a blog post, creating a video on YouTube, running an ad, etc. When people buy the product using your link, you earn a commission.

The key as an affiliate marketer is to create good-quality content that successfully refers people to affiliate offers for a long time, not just for a day or temporarily. If you can create a quality video or blog post or something that "sticks," you have created a long-term, cash flow–producing asset you can earn commissions from for years. Think of a YouTube video, for example. YouTube videos often have affiliate links in their description, something you'll start noticing now that your reticular activating system has been clued in. And since YouTube is the second largest search engine, and is owned by the largest search engine, Google, a well-made YouTube video can get traffic for years. I know multimillionaires who got that way just by making YouTube videos with affiliate links in the descriptions. Obviously, YouTube is just one way to promote affiliate links, but it is one of the best.

Once you learn the basics, you can also use paid ads to drive people to your links, and even build an email list, giving you the ability to send more links to people in follow-up emails. Affiliate marketing is a powerful way to grow your income over time because you can push as many people as you want to as many offers as you want over as much time as you want. Obviously, there's a lot more to it than just this brief description, but hopefully you get a sense of how powerful it can be. If you want to go deeper with affiliate marketing training, I have free training videos on my YouTube channel.

#2. Create a Course, Coaching Program, Newsletter, or other "Knowledge Business"

A lot of people are freaked out by this idea at first because they don't think of themselves as experts who are qualified enough to teach people about something. What they don't realize is that all you have to do to get started is know just a little bit more than the people you're talking to. There are thousands of subjects that people want to learn about online and many of them will gladly pay you to help them shortcut their own learning process by doing the research for them and reporting your findings. You don't have to be the world's greatest expert at a subject; you simply must be willing to research and document that subject and patiently teach it to others. You might be surprised by the demand for online learning. Online education is a $350 billion industry, and it is by far the fastest-growing segment of the trillion-dollar education industry in the United States. There is a massive shift occurring away from traditional education toward self-directed learning online. Teachingguide.com estimates that about 40 percent of online classes have made over $5,000. I have personally created multiple courses that have generated millions of dollars each and I've done it with software that ranges from free to a couple hundred dollars. The biggest investment in creating a knowledge product is your time.

First, you find a topic that you know well and are passionate about. There are literally thousands of topics—basically the same list of niches as affiliate marketing. If you're a great cook, create a cooking tutorial. It can be anything. I have a friend who has an awesome YouTube channel where she analyzes crimes that involve food and then cooks the meals that were involved. Say there was a

Mafia shooting at a restaurant and the victim was eating chicken parmigiana. She would tell you about the crime while she cooks chicken parmesan. Just pick a subject that someone else in the world might be interested in and start doing research. All you need is a phone and a microphone. You don't even have to be on video if you don't want to. You can create a slideshow and remain hidden off camera the entire time. Then you can go on a site like Udemy or Skillshare to begin building the course. Like affiliate marketing, your online course can become passive income if you market it well because you can continue to earn money on it long after the work is done.

Aside from just selling a course directly, you can turn it into multiple streams of income. If you're doing a cooking tutorial, for instance, you can also become an affiliate for the products you use and put links to all the cookware you use in the course, so you get paid again if anyone purchases those items using your links. You could take this same material you utilized for your course and turn it into an e-book or an audiobook. You could host an online class where you cook with viewers live. You could offer private or group cooking lessons. The possibilities go on and on. I've been in the knowledge business for a few years now, and it's not only lucrative, but it's the most rewarding work I've ever done. If you're like me, you might get into this business and discover you have a true passion for teaching!

#3. Digital Agency

This is a broad description covering the digital marketing and advertising needs of businesses in today's world. In the United States alone, there are approximately 30 million businesses, with almost a half a million new ones launching each month. Any reasonable business owner knows they need to spend money on marketing if they want to succeed, so there is an enormous opportunity to provide marketing services to businesses. Prior to founding ENTRE, this was the area I found my biggest success, generating over $30 million in revenue in under six years and providing services to thousands of businesses.

I'll give a basic overview of a digital agency and explain some of the most important things to be aware of when starting one, but by no means will this be an exhaustive set of instructions. My goal is not to teach you everything you need to know to start an agency, but rather to share some insights I've not heard in any other books or courses on the subject (outside of ENTRE, that is) and to answer two questions that can help you decide if an agency might be for you.

Question #1: What do digital agencies do?

A digital agency sells specialized services that generate attention, interest, and/or sales for businesses in the digital economy. This contrasts with a traditional (nondigital) marketing or advertising agency that focuses on old-school media like television, radio, print, and so on. Most large agencies now are hybrid and blend traditional media with in-house digital departments, but large agencies generally only serve large businesses with large (seven-figure per year or greater) marketing budgets. The main opportunity for independent entrepreneurs is in creating a smaller niche agency that serves smaller businesses that cannot afford the six-, seven-, eight-, or even nine-figure retainers of large full-service agencies.

When I say "niche agency," I mean either focusing on a specific subset of digital services to offer, a specific industry or type of business to target, or both. Examples of agency services you could offer are lead generation, social media management, reputation management, sales funnels, marketing automation, sales process consulting, information technology (IT), branding/design, public relations, web design, and so on. Examples of industries you could target are home services (or any subset thereof like plumbers, roofers, pest control, solar, etc.), medical (or any subset thereof like dental, chiropractic, hospitals, dermatologists, plastic surgeons, etc.), real estate (or any subset thereof like realtors, appraisers, inspectors, mortgage lenders, etc.), professional services (or any subset thereof like attorneys, insurance agents, CPAs, etc.), and many more.

The possibilities are endless for combining services and industries to create a specialty niche that has reduced competition and is relatively easy to dominate. Ideally, you will find a lucrative combination that puts you in a category of one within your market, for example, lead generation for dentists, reputation management for CPAs, IT for medical offices, social media management for real estate agents, marketing automation for coaches and consultants, and so on. Get creative and think about what you might be drawn to. The agency opportunity is so big that even when you narrow the competition by combining a specific digital service with a specific business category there is still a huge slice of pie to go after in any decent-sized market. Pick any one of those examples above—let's use IT for medical offices—and consider how big that market is in any medium to large city in the United States. There are literally thousands of markets in any city, each potentially worth millions of dollars if you dominate them. When I started my agency, I focused initially on lead generation for home services companies, and then later expanded into reputation management and website design services while adding a few professional services categories like insurance agents, attorneys, and real estate agents. And that was plenty for me to do over $30 million in less than six years.

What makes the agency model so attractive is how you typically get paid, because it's in the form of service retainers (meaning monthly subscriptions that pay for a set number of hours or services). Retainer agreements are defined in advance and usually contracted for at least six months to a year. The predictability of having contracted revenue that recurs monthly offers huge advantages.

Once you hit your Awesome Life Number and are personally taking out five times your cost of living as owner salary and/or profit distributions, it is easy to move into the growth and wealth phases with an agency. We'll talk in more detail about these two phases in the coming chapters, but remember from chapter 17 the goal of the growth phase is to make our cash flow "predictable, bankable, and sellable." With monthly retainers, that is already in place. Agency cash flow is predictable (it's contracted), bankable (once an agency has a year or two history of retainers, it can be borrowed against via factoring or revenue-based lending), and sellable (this I know because a software company bought my agency for its customer contracts).

Question #2: What type of clients should an agency look to serve?

In nearly six years, my agency sold services to over ten thousand businesses. I built a high-volume model that was efficient at attracting customers and converting them into a basic suite of services that I knew I could fulfill consistently and affordably. My experience, and the experience of the mentors I learned this business from, taught me this was the right approach—pick a few services and get great at fulfilling them for a few specific types of clients. Don't try to be all things to all possible clients.

This is different from how most agency owners do it. The majority of agencies use what I call a "skyscraper model," which means focusing on a few large clients and trying to win all their business by stacking whatever services those few clients are willing to pay for. These agencies have a "we can do whatever you need" philosophy toward their clients, which sounds like a good approach until you actually get into fulfilling it. *"Need a website? Sure, we can do that." "Oh, you need email marketing? Sure, we can do that too." "And you want someone to post weekly on Instagram? Got it, done." "And you need logos and business cards? Oh yeah, for sure we can do that."* And so on it goes, with every *"Sure, we can do that"* creating a need to hire or contract for another competency.

I did the total opposite, having found some very successful mentors in the business who taught me to be selective about the services I offered and up front with customers from the beginning about what services I wouldn't offer. I focused on being the best at just those few services I offered (initially just lead generation, later reputation management and web design) and limited the types of businesses I went after (initially home services, later some professional services too). This was the key to my success and my quality of life as an agency owner. If you ever hear horror stories from agency owners of being woken up in the middle of the night by demanding clients threatening to quit if they don't babysit them, you can be sure those are skyscraper agencies. When you have five clients, you live in fear of losing one and you'll do anything to keep them, including taking calls in the middle of the night. When you have fifty, or five hundred, or five thousand clients, and you stick to being the best at a core set of services, you sleep quite well, and they are scared to lose you.

To make all this work and not end up one of those horror stories, you have to get a couple things right. You have to choose the right businesses to go after, and you have to sell only services that you can fulfill efficiently and effectively at scale. As a small agency owner, you will have the best results targeting businesses that meet three criteria:

1. **$250,000—$10,000,000 per year in revenue:** If a business is smaller than $250,000 (approximately $20,000 a month), it is unlikely they will have the money and/or risk appetite to invest in a meaningful monthly marketing budget, while businesses larger than $10,000,000 require an approach that is less suitable for a small agency. The exception to this is if you provide very specialized services that are technical in nature, like IT or search engine optimization; then you may be able to target businesses larger than $10,000,000 in annual revenue.

2. **Four to fifty employees:** If a business has less than four employees, they likely have other operational challenges that are not marketing

related that can hamstring the results you can create for them. Imagine committing to building a website for a client in ninety days and then wasting sixty of those days waiting for them to review the initial design you sent them because the owner/operator is so busy every day on service calls that they never check their email. You can also run into sales or fulfillment capacity issues with tiny clients where the better you do your job of getting them more business the more likely you are to lose the account. Imagine tripling the volume of inbound sales leads for a client, then getting a call saying, "Thanks, but we're booked for the next six months and can't handle any more business so we need to cancel our contract." On the flip side, if a business is greater than fifty employees, you have the same issue as with them having over $10,000,000 yearly revenue—an impersonal relationship where you are treated merely as a vendor and can easily lose the relationship over factors you have no control over.

3. **Customer lifetime value (CLTV) greater than $2,000:** This is critical to understand. Regardless of what specialty you end up focusing on as an agency, ultimately your job is to help your client grow revenue in the only three ways that any business can: by getting new customers, by increasing average purchase amount, or by increasing purchase frequency. Since most small business owners do not want to be told how to run their business (however badly they need to be), you will likely not have a chance to help them with the latter two options, so you are left with basically the option to help your client get more customers. Your services will be valued based on how many new customers you acquire for the client *and* how many of those they are willing to give you credit for. That latter point is key. You can run an ad campaign that sends one hundred customers their way, but what if the business owner wants to attribute the new customers to the little league team he recently sponsored rather than attribute them to your hard work? There are lots of ways to make sure you get credit for the customers you generate that go deeper than the scope of this book, but the point of looking at CLTV is to avoid the problem altogether. You don't want to have to generate hundreds of customers in order for the client to value your services—that's hundreds of opportunities

to not give you proper credit. If your client sells pizza (and has an average customer value of, let's say, $20), and you are charging them $1,000 per month for marketing services (which would be low), you would need to generate enough customers to earn more than $1,000 in additional profit per month to justify the cost of your services. I don't know the profit margins of a pizza restaurant (I never had one as a client), but I imagine it's 20 percent or less, so you'd have to send them $5,000 or more in new total pizza business (Two hundred fifty customers at $20 each), get 100 percent credit for every new customer, and trust that the owner is good at math. Two hundred fifty customers is a lot of customers to generate for a $1,000 marketing fee and it's unlikely that even if you pulled it off there would be tracking in place to convince the owner that all those customers came from your efforts. Moral of the story? Don't be an agency for pizza parlors. It's so much easier to generate a few new customers a month (and get credit for them) for businesses that sell higher-end products and services, not pizzas. Try to find businesses where the average customer spends $2,000 or more either upfront (attorneys—not bankruptcy or defense attorneys, though, whose clients are often broke—plastic surgeons, roofers, solar systems, general contractors, realtors, etc.) or over time (dentists, chiropractors, pest control, pool cleaners, CPAs, etc.). Those are the clients who will love you for just sending them a few new customers per month who were easy to track and give you credit for.

As far as what services to offer, you need to focus on services that have a high perceived technical acumen, a high annoyance factor (meaning business owners really don't want to do it themselves), or an easy-to-prove correlation with new customer acquisition. Examples of services that fit these criteria are online reputation management/search engine optimization (high perceived technical acumen), social media management (high annoyance factor), pay-per-click ads (high perceived technical acumen and easy-to-prove correlation to new customer acquisition), inbound marketing (all three), and so on. Examples of services that do not fit these criteria are web design (nowadays, small business owners do not value this skill and will make your life crazy with endless change requests and nitpicking) and branding (small business owners generally don't properly value this skill even though it is highly complex, and they will resist paying what it's worth). Obviously, these are generalizations that may change by industry (a luxury home builder may value branding more than an RV park), but the key is understanding what small business owners value given that most of them don't know as much about marketing as they think they do. Bottom line: the more they think you make the phones ring or the customers walk in, the better off you are. And anything you can't prove in simple-to-read reports, you won't get credit for.

After all that you might think that I sound kind of jaded and that maybe I didn't make building an agency sound very enticing. It's actually quite the opposite. I spent six years and millions of dollars to learn exactly what works and why. Make no mistake, the agency model is fantastic if you do it right. It's one of my favorite digital business types and one of the types I see ENTRE students having the most success with. I just also know how tempting it is to break the rules we set for ourselves once a potential client is offering us money to do so. Discipline is paramount when running a successful agency. If a business doesn't fit your profile, don't take them on as a client, and if a client asks you to provide a service that doesn't fit your model, don't be afraid to say no. When the latter happens you should have on your Power List some other agencies that provide services you don't and be referring customers back and forth.

Even though I sold my agency a few years ago, I can report directly from the front lines that the opportunity is bigger than ever. In addition to all the ENTRE students I see building agencies, I have friends in the business too. One is a textbook example of what I described above. He picked one specialty (pay-per-click advertising) and one niche (digital knowledge businesses), and in a few years has grown an agency to over a half-million dollars a month at a (shockingly) healthy profit margin. He now lives in an exotic location, runs his agency part-time, and spends the rest of his time buying real estate, working out, and hanging with his wife and kids! This opportunity is out there for anyone to take; just make sure to stay disciplined and follow the formula I've laid out.

#4. E-Commerce

Technically, e-commerce ("e-com" for short) means any commerce transacted online, but generally, when digital marketers refer to e-com, they mean stores that sell and ship physical products via either standalone online stores or on aggregator platforms like Amazon or Etsy. E-com stores are one of the best ways to really understand the advantages of doing business digitally because they can easily be compared and contrasted with offline stores. The following table summarizes some of the differences between owning an online store versus an offline store.

Offline store	Online store (e-commerce)
Limited hours	Open all the time
Service usually in local area only	Service wherever you can ship your product to
Must pay someone to be on premises when open	No employees required
Inventory ties up money	Usually don't have to pay for goods until they are sold
Support, service, refunds handled in store	All support handled remotely
Rent, utilities, insurance, etc.	Minimal fixed expenses
One unhappy customer = bad Google reviews, hard to get reviews from happy customers	Easier to protect reputation, easier to get reviews from happy customers
Security concerns, physical liability	No such worries

Even with all these advantages, there is still a right way and a wrong way to do e-commerce. It is much like a digital agency in this regard, along with the fact that also, like a digital agency, there are thousands of books and courses to teach you how to do it. I'm not going to teach you everything there is to know about e-com, but rather give you some examples of the right way to do e-com, enough information to know if e-com interests you, and some valuable insights that I've learned through being in this business myself that you aren't likely to hear elsewhere.

There are right and wrong ways to do e-com. *The right way* is what I call a *specialty store* approach that involves being very niche focused with a relatively small number of products that serve a clearly defined audience *and* building a clearly identifiable brand that creates trust and value, so customers don't just go buy knockoff or equivalent products on Amazon. *The wrong way* is a *general store* approach, which involves having a multitude of products that appeal to a wide range of people and/or trying to be the cheapest or the generic version of your product. Whether you have your own standalone store or you are selling through a platform like Amazon, Etsy, eBay, or Poshmark, these principles apply. Full disclaimer: I have lots of experience running standalone stores (I have owned three of them, all built on Shopify), but I only know about selling through platforms like Amazon from the experience of friends.

Let's use one of my stores as an example of the specialty store approach. The first e-com business I own sells three simple marketing products, only three, that were developed to assist members of one particular direct sales company in promoting one specific product of that company. Read that sentence again—that's the level of specificity I'm talking about with the specialty store approach. Because my store is so unique and specific, I have no competition, I have total clarity on which customers to target and how to target them, and it is incredibly easy for me to attract them by explaining what my store sells. Since my store and my offer is so unique, I don't want to risk creating any competition for myself by disclosing it, but I will use a made-up example modeled off of my actual store to illustrate the level of specificity and clarity that makes a great specialty store e-com offer.

Imagine that you, my potential customer, are a distributor for a direct sales company called Rugula (which is a completely made-up company I just invented whose name rhymes with arugula). Now imagine that as part of Rugula you sell a product called Staino that can get any stain out of any rug with a single treatment. One day you're in a Facebook group of other Rugula distributors and you see an ad that says, "Attention Rugula Distributors: Sell More Staino Without Having To Explaino!" (Sorry, I couldn't help myself.) This incredible piece of advertising copy gets your attention and you click right away. The click brings you to a simple e-com store with a homepage featuring only three products, all obviously designed for people just like you who distribute the Staino product by Rugula. The first product is a sample kit that allows you to more easily give out Staino samples to your friends, the second is a DVD you can hand someone that explains the amazing Staino technology, and the third is a presentation binder that does the same as number two, only for people who don't have a DVD player. The offer is so simple . . . it's just three products that can help Rugula distributors sell more Staino in less time. You, the potential customer, either want them or you don't. For me, as the e-com store owner, I don't have to have some fancy, complicated site with a thousand shopping cart options and a big elaborate sales presentation. And I don't need to worry that you're going to go try to get a better deal on Amazon. It's a specialty product with little to no competition and a clear value to the right customer. My job is just to find the right customers, get them to the site, and make sure the products are always in stock.

Obviously, that was a fictional example, but it's pretty close to how my actual e-com business works and it illustrates the value of having a crystal clear offer that solves a defined problem for a specific audience. Now compare that with most of the e-com sites you see people try to start—sites that sell cheap, generic products like sunglasses or vitamin containers. If you try to build a store like that, you're only ever competing on price or customer service, both battles you'll likely lose to Amazon, who can always offer faster shipping, lower prices, and a more trusted brand.

Another store of mine, which I don't do much with anymore since I started ENTRE so I'm happy to tell you all about, sells headrest attachments for road trips. If you're going on a road trip and want more comfortable and supportive headrests in your back seats so people can take naps or just reduce neck strain, you can strap a simple piece of plastic with some padding and a cloth covering onto your car's existing headrests. Again, this is a very specific product that is easy to promote to a specific audience that is relatively easy to target on Facebook and in Google searches. How did I target them? I would target people searching for AAA memberships, for example, something people often do before long road trips, or people who follow National Parks online, or people searching for trailer hitches, or people who follow brands associated with travel and camping, and so on.

Both of these store examples, along with my third, which is accessories and apparel for entrepreneurs (store.entrenation.com—the online store of ENTRE) are good examples of the specialty store approach and have products that are easy to source or manufacture, simple to understand, have low to no competition, and are easy to find customers for in niches that are not saturated or overly competitive. Although one of my stores does involve a product that required some innovation and product development (the first example), this is not a requirement to be in e-com. I found a cheap source for those headrests where I could buy them in bulk and have them shipped directly to a fulfillment ware-house, and for the ENTRE store we use a combination of "print-on-demand" fulfillment (POD) which is easy to source, and a third-party fulfillment house (also easy to find online). There are numerous sites where you can either buy preexisting e-com stores, or get good ideas for them, as well as huge platforms and even live events that specialize in wholesale and/or white-label products for e-com stores. White label simply means a product that is ready to sell but without a label, so you can apply your own label to the product and mark it up before selling it.

Now let's return to my store that sells the marketing products for the direct sales company distributors and drill deeper down into the mechanics of running an e-com business. The entire business model is simple. I run Face-book ads that use Facebook's interest-based ad targeting to show ads only to people who follow the Facebook page of that direct sales company. My store is built on the Shopify platform and I use a plug-in that displays the individual products configured in Shopify into a "carousel" inside my Facebook ads. So the Facebook ad appears as what looks like a mini-brochure of the three products that the viewer can scroll through. For the three products I have two suppliers. One of the products involves manufacturing a small plastic device, and the other two involve mass replication of print or video materials. The plastic product supplier is in China and the video and print products supplier is in Chicago. I found them both online in less than thirty minutes of Google searches and a few back-and-forth emails. The ads are super cheap to run because they are so targeted to a specific group, the customers come back again and again because they use them over and over in promoting their direct sales products, the products sell for at least twice what they cost me, and the entire business is hands-off for me because I pay one person a percent of the profits to handle all fulfillment and customer support. My entire time commitment to the business involves placing reorders with my two suppliers two to three times a year, and even this responsibility I could offload, but I just happen to like the guy I place the orders from China with and enjoy talking to him when it's time to reorder.

Regarding the Facebook ads, I set them up one time and haven't looked at them again in years. The store does six figures a year in revenue at about 50 percent profit margin (30 percent of which goes to the one employee who runs everything). So, basically, I make high five to six figures a year for what takes about two hours a year to run. Obviously, this is a mature example and it took time and energy to set it up in the first place, but as long as you stick with a simple specialty store model, it's doable to get things running as smoothly as I'm describing. Also, I should mention I don't think the store has ever had a refund, chargeback, or customer support problem. By keeping the customer base very focused and the product set very small you eliminate 99 percent of problems (similar to what we discussed in the agency model).

Here's another example. Some good friends of mine sell equipment in the bowhunting space. They are a husband/wife pair who have one supplier (a company that also supplies a lot of hunting and outdoor stores), a single Shopify website, and a business they love because all their customers love bowhunting as much as they do and end up becoming their friends. As an added benefit, they get to film themselves trying out new gear and doing product reviews on hunting trips and post those videos to YouTube, which generates additional revenue and helps promote their store, all while doing what they love anyway. Stores like this proliferate all over the internet and many are far bigger than mine. E-commerce isn't my main business, and I literally sometimes forget that I even have these stores until I get the deposit notifications.

So much more could be said about e-com, but again, the point here is to whet your appetite and give you enough info to know if it interests you. There are so many directions you can go with e-com—creating your own products, building your own brand on top of white-label products, cross-promoting your store between a standalone version and the big platforms like Etsy and Poshmark, even creating your own platform where you focus on marketing and branding in a niche and allow other sellers to list their products.

The sky is truly the limit with e-com, but as with so many wonderful things, there are bad apples out there threatening to spoil the bunch. Make sure you don't get sucked into the world of hype and promises from people making it sound too easy or uncreative. Steer clear of "no skills required" or "guaranteed results" type marketing hype. There are those who will tell you that all you need to do to build an "e-com empire" is go on aliexpress.com, find cheap made-in-China products to list in a generic store with no branding, creativity, skills, or even time required. That is the "general store" approach and is a sure-fire way to waste time and money while getting no results.

#5. Digital Freelancer

Something I say often during our training at ENTRE is that "certainty in life is about skills, not a certain business or a job." I want to make sure that people understand there is no business, business model, or career choice on earth that guarantees success. Think of a business as a machine, and like any machine it is made of parts and those parts are built and maintained with tools. Similarly, a job is just a part in a larger machine that, like all machine parts, is built and maintained with tools. The tools that we use to build and maintain a job or a business are skills—*general skills* like communication, math, or people skills, and *specialized skills* involving whatever is needed to do the job or business. Ultimately, it is our skills that determine our success in any job or business, not the job or business itself. Just being an attorney doesn't mean you'll get rich, considering that roughly half of all US attorneys earn below six figures annually. But being a highly skilled attorney, you could end up like Richard Scruggs, who is worth $1.7 billion. Skills—not jobs, businesses, or industries—pay bills.

When it comes to business ownership, many people struggle because there are so many different skills involved in operating a successful business that people are bound to struggle with at least a few of them. Successful business owners are not those who become masters of every skill, but rather those who know what they're good at and become proficient at outsourcing or hiring for the skills and roles they are not strong in or do not have time to do themselves. But what about people who are not even skilled at managing and delegating? Or those who simply don't want to be responsible for managing the entire skills bundle it takes to successfully run a business?

Welcome to the wonderful world of being a digital freelancer! A digital freelancer is simply someone who has become proficient in one or more skills for which there is demand in the market and which can be marketed and delivered remotely via technology. That's it. A person can make a wonderful life for themselves and carve out highly valuable digital real estate without even needing a business if they have a single high-value skill. Just mastering one skill is enough for a digital freelancer to have many of the perks of owning a successful business with less responsibility and more flexibility. Heck, if I'm being honest, on my toughest days, I fantasize about simplifying my life by just picking one skill and becoming a digital freelancer.

And who do digital freelancers serve? Mostly business owners who themselves are trying to outsource and delegate the skills they don't have. Millions of businesses need help in literally hundreds of different specialties and subspecialties. Here's a (not so) short list:

In HR there is administration, recruiting and staffing, health and safety, training and development, compensation and benefits, labor and employee relations, disciplinary process management, onboarding, culture consulting, and process or policy development and documentation.

In finance, there is accounts payable, accounts receivable, accounting and reporting, budgeting and forecasting, financial planning and analysis (FP&A), expense management, auditing and compliance, tax, and data analysis.

In marketing, there is strategy, reputation management, public relations, branding, product marketing, design (with subcategories like graphic design, logo design, web design, interior design, industrial design, user experience, etc.), paid ads (with subcategories by platforms and types like Facebook, Google, YouTube, Snapchat, Instagram, display ads, print ads, radio ads, streaming TV ads, etc.), video marketing (with subcategories like animators, transcriptionists, digital asset managers, audio editors, platform specialists for Instagram, TikTok, YouTube, etc.), copywriting (with subcategories like ads copywriting, sales letters, videos scripts, etc.), social media management (with subcategories like strategy, community engagement, content writing, image design, multi-platform repurposing, scheduling, etc.).

In technology there is (just kidding, I'm not even going to break down technology because there are so many specialties).

You get the idea. I could spend page after page of this book breaking down all the categories and subcategories that businesses of various sizes sometimes fill with full-timers, part-timers, contractors/freelancers, consultants, and agencies. You can make a wonderful living and a wonderful life by becoming skilled in any one of the hundreds of areas related to business *that can be fulfilled virtually* (that part is the key) and then deciding how far you want to take your skills. Do you want to be a freelancer-for-hire on a per-project basis? Do you want to be a consultant for hire on a term basis? Do you want to be a full-time employee? A part-time employee? Do you want to build an agency around your skills? Or do you go all the way and found a company, focus on just your specialized skill (along with probably being the CEO for a while until it gets off the ground), and outsourcing the other roles that aren't your specialty?

It's a lifestyle question. That is the whole point of escaping the broken system—to be able to design and live the lifestyle you want. It's a simple analysis. What type of life do you want, what type of work would best support that life, and do you have skills that allow you to do that type of work? If you take nothing else from this entire book, please remember this: acquiring the right skills is the single most important component of designing the life you want. Choose the right skills and get really good at them and you can do anything, be anything, and go anywhere. But you must choose strategically. If your skills involve working on automobiles, it is unlikely you will find a work-from-home position, so if you want to work from home, don't focus on auto repair. If you don't like talking to people, maybe focus on IT rather than sales. If you're impatient, don't become a web designer where you'll have to deal with change requests. I meet so many people who are not happy with their lives and think it's because of the job they're in or the business they own, when really, it's about the skills they have chosen to focus on.

In the modern world, it is essential to constantly assess your skills in terms of the opportunities they qualify you for. This is hard for a lot of people who have invested in learning skills that they don't want to admit are not serving them anymore. I've encountered this emotional attachment to outdated skills many times. I would honestly rather coach someone who lacks any skills than someone who has great skills that aren't the right ones for what they want out of life. Bring me someone who is unskilled and happiness becomes a very simple process of figuring out what they want and focusing solely on those skills that will lead there. But bring me someone who is unhappy but highly skilled, and they will often resist going in a different direction, feeling that the time, energy, and money they have spent acquiring their current skills will be wasted if they make a change. I try to explain that the time, energy, and money is already wasted because that skill isn't creating the opportunities and joy they want for their life, and that continuing without focusing on new skills is an even bigger waste. I know this is a logically sound argument, but I also know how resistant people are to it—and the more skilled they are, the more they resist because their ego doesn't want them to go back to being a beginner. When I used to do personal coaching with entrepreneurs, I sometimes had to let clients go because even though they were telling me they wanted to make a change, they could not handle going from "successful but unhappy _____" (doctor, attorney, mechanic, plumber, etc.) to "starting from scratch _____" (copywriter, graphic designer, funnel architect, ads manager, network administrator, etc.). They would sit there for hours, unable to work on their new business because they hated not already being good at the thing. Every time I see this it takes me back to when I used to teach piano lessons to adults who would claim they had no time to practice when in reality they just didn't like being bad at stuff. There is a huge issue in our society related to ego and adult learning and it tragically limits the potential of so many people, which is why I get so worked up about it.

But assuming that's not you and that you are willing to do the work to learn the right skills, being a digital freelancer is an amazing option if you don't want to go as far as starting your own business. There are so many ways now for freelancers to find businesses who need their skills and a wide variety of ways to offer them (per project, per time interval, per hour, etc.). The freelance marketplace is huge and the various sites that comprise it have different focuses and level of quality control. At ENTRE, we often fill needs with contractors we find on various websites like upwork.com, toptal.com, freelancer.com, fiverr.com, and even LinkedIn. Which site we go to depends on the type of role and the level of vetting we want already done on the candidates. Some of our best people have initially been contracted as freelancers who eventually came on full time because they loved the company, and they still get the same perks they got as freelancers (ENTRE is a completely remote company with no office—everyone works from home). This is another perk of being a digital freelancer—if you do it well, you can often convert part-time or contract jobs into full-time positions that still offer huge flexibility and better opportunities than more traditional jobs your old skills might have kept you stuck in.

Socioeconomic mobility has increased in the modern world because you are no longer limited in what you choose to get good at. Whether it's through a digital business or just monetizing the right skills, pick something that can give you the life you want and become amazing at it. That is the key to creating your anomalous cash flow phase, increasing your income to create surplus, and pushing through the income phase of legacy.

22

Why Do So Many
People Fail?

When I started with affiliate marketing in 2008, it was a completely different landscape than the internet today, especially for entrepreneurs. There were no easy website builders or funnel builders like Entresoft, Leadpages, or ClickFunnels. Everything had to be done manually in code or by hiring developers, which I could not afford to do. As I write this, I still have my old copies of *HTML for Dummies*, *CSS for Dummies*, *JavaScript for Dummies*, and *PHP & MySQL for Dummies* sitting on my bookshelf, reminding me not to do myself what I can afford to delegate to someone better. But back in 2008, before "offshoring" brought down the cost of development for the average startup, developers were a lot more expensive to hire, even for basic projects. And I couldn't afford them, which meant my only other option was to give myself roughly the equivalent of a bachelor's degree in computer science just to be able to build my own online sales funnels.

If you've never been on the construction side of the internet it's easy to take for granted the enormity and complexity of the codebase that powers it, but I quickly learned not to be so blithe. Every little thing I tried required putting on my overalls and hard hat, so to speak. Say I wanted to put a countdown timer on a page for a discount that would expire at midnight. Today that would take a few seconds with a funnel builder, but in 2008 it required hours hunkered over *Javascript for Dummies*, piecing my own code together line by line.

Here's what a simple countdown timer looks like in Javascript:

```
<head>
<meta name="viewport" content="width=device-width,
initial-scale=1">
<style>
p {
    display: inline;
    font-size: 40px;
    margin-top: 0px;
}
</style>
</head>

<body>
    <p id="days"></p>
    <p id="hours"></p>
    <p id="mins"></p>
    <p id="secs"></p>
    <h2 id="end"></h2>
    <script>
    // The data/time we want to countdown to
    var countDownDate = new Date("Dec 31, 2009 23:59:59").
getTime();

    // Run myfunc every second
    var myfunc = setInterval(function() {

    var now = new Date().getTime();
    var timeleft = countDownDate - now;

    // Calculating the days, hours, minutes and seconds left
    var days = Math.floor(timeleft / (1000 * 60 * 60 * 24));
    var hours = Math.floor((timeleft % (1000 * 60 * 60 * 24)) /
(1000 * 60 * 60));
    var minutes = Math.floor((timeleft % (1000 * 60 * 60)) /
(1000 * 60));
```

```
var seconds = Math.floor((timeleft % (1000 * 60)) / 1000);

// Result is output to the specific element
document.getElementById("days").innerHTML = days + "d "
document.getElementById("hours").innerHTML = hours + "h "
document.getElementById("mins").innerHTML = minutes + "m "
document.getElementById("secs").innerHTML = seconds + "s "

// Display the message when countdown is over
if (timeleft < 0) {
   clearInterval(myfunc);
   document.getElementById("days").innerHTML = ""
   document.getElementById("hours").innerHTML = ""
   document.getElementById("mins").innerHTML = ""
   document.getElementById("secs").innerHTML = ""
   document.getElementById("end").innerHTML = "DISCOUNT
EXPIRED!!";
   }
}, 1000);
</script>
</body>
```

If you're a coder, that sample seems laughably simple to you. If not, you may have a headache now. I know I had an incessant one for months. Teaching myself to code by building an actual online business from scratch was like teaching myself a language by writing a novel. I had jumped into the deep end of the pool and was either going to learn to swim or die trying. I spent a week trying to get an opt-in form on a website to properly connect to an email list. I spent two days trying to reduce the file size of an image so a single page would load faster. I spent hours in online forums asking real developers how to do stuff and waiting for responses. Over and over I questioned what I was doing and if it was worth it. I hadn't signed up to become a computer programmer; I just wanted to sell stuff online and pay off my debt. Every day there was some cipher I had to crack that took hours and seemed so much harder than it should be. But eventually I accepted that "how things should be" was just a subjective and meaningless concept I had invented because I was in a hurry. Eventually, I accepted what Jim Rohn told us back in chapter 10; I stopped wanting things to be easier and just focused on getting better. It's funny how well that strategy always seems to work. When I stopped resisting and accepted what needed to happen, I became a passable self-taught coder in a few months. After all, I was a piano player. I was used to solving problems at keyboards. Only now my keyboard had 104 keys instead of 88.

The ability to take credit card payments almost did me in, though. In 2008, PayPal was pretty much the only plug-in option for collecting online payments, but their experience for the end user was terrible, so using PayPal on check out pages was consistently costing me sales. I knew this because I would compare my funnel data to fellow marketers running the same offers using identical sales pages but with different checkout options and, as it always does, the data told a compelling story. My checkout pages that used PayPal were consistently causing 10 percent or more of my potential customers to "abandon their cart" before completing their purchase when compared to identical pages that used a different checkout solution. The last straw was when PayPal deducted $200,000 from the bank account of one of my mentors without any warning before sending him an impersonal and unapologetic email notifying him they would be holding his funds for six months. That $200,000 was the entire amount he had processed through that PayPal account over the previous six months and they were exercising their right to "claw it back" simply because a single customer had disputed one $1,000 charge claiming it was fraud. This was my first introduction to what is known in merchant processing as "friendly fraud," wherein consumers dispute online transactions (known as CNP or Card-Not-Present transactions) claiming they are fraudulent when in fact they are not. In friendly fraud, the consumer is the one committing fraud by claiming they are a victim of fraud themselves in order to get out of paying for something they knowingly purchased, often while getting to keep what they bought.

The credit card and merchant processing industry, including PayPal, is well aware of friendly fraud but they generally turn a blind eye and side with consumers for a few reasons: (1) it's easier to let consumers win than to do any real fact-finding on small charges; (2) fraud protection and easy charge disputes are a big part of credit card companies' sales pitch to consumers, so they tend to resist creating processes or policies that might make it more difficult to claim fraud or dispute any charge for any reason; and (3) government regulators working for agencies like the Federal Trade Commission, state and federal attorneys general, and various consumer protection agencies get a lot more glory (and career advancement) when they "go to bat for the little guy" by investigating fraud *against* consumers rather than *by* consumers, so the credit card companies know they have little to worry about for tolerating and even encouraging friendly fraud.

Anyway, my mentor's experience was my first exposure to this shameful consumer behavior, and to the underbelly of the merchant processing world in general, so after confirming that my own processing agreement with PayPal allowed them to do the same thing to me at any time, I now had another battle I needed to fight, or "opportunity for learning" as I had learned to see such things. I now needed to find a merchant processor that was friendly to online businesses, then teach myself how to integrate it into my checkout pages.

So I went to an online forum where I knew a bunch of digital marketers hung out, and I asked for advice. "Find an ISO that's friendly to online merchants," is the advice I received. So after learning what an ISO was (an Independent Sales Organization, which, in the merchant processing industry, means a third-party intermediary that onboards small business merchant accounts for banks and other large financial institutions), I started making calls. Everyone who I spoke with took down my email address and emailed me a long and detailed application that I had to print out and fill out by hand (back then, they didn't just send you DocuSigns you could fill in and sign online). I would then have to drive to Kinko's (now known as FedEx Office), print them out, fill them out, scan them (I couldn't afford an all-in-one printer/scanner/fax either), and email them back. Between printing ($.08 per page) and scanning ($.20 per page), each application cost me about $10 and an hour of my life to complete. That's when I would then get rejected by the ISOs, one after the next, because apparently they ran credit checks when underwriting merchant accounts, and although I had started paying off my $495,000 debt, it was still showing on my credit report. Then, to add insult to injury, I realized that all the credit inquiries from the ISOs were making my credit even worse, even though I was paying down my debt. I ended up having to get a family member to cosign in order to get a merchant account, and then, once I did, I had to decipher how to integrate it into my sales funnels using the ISO's Developer API (Application Programming Interface) documentation, which assumed sophisticated technical knowledge. It was time to order *APIs for Dummies*. All told it was a month-long ordeal, but eventually I did get a new merchant account integrated and weaned off of PayPal. And my conversions did improve—hard battle fought, small victory won, bring on what's next. Compare that story to now. Today any adult with a pulse can create a Stripe account in five minutes and have it connected to a Shopify store in another two minutes with zero technical knowledge required. Times have definitely changed.

Another thing that weighed heavy on me at the time was my debt. Even though I was paying it off as fast as I could, the credit industry views past-due debt in very black and white terms. Either you're behind on debt or you aren't, and if you are, you don't get much clemency while you're paying it down. All the relief comes once it's paid off entirely. In the meantime you're persona non grata with banks and financial institutions. Not only had all my bank accounts been frozen, but I had been reported to a service called ChexSystems for having accounts closed with a negative balance, so I couldn't open new bank accounts anywhere. What little credit I did have I was cycling multiple times a month to run my ads and I was having to use my PayPal wallet to pay the cards off since I couldn't open a bank account. On top of all that, I had been sued by two landlords, one from each of my restaurants, and was being pursued by the State of Texas Comptroller's office for past due sales taxes, the Texas Workforce Commission for past due unemployment taxes, and the US Treasury for defaulting on a Small Business Administration loan. I had a plan for paying off my debt, but my creditors were not putting any stock in my good intentions and were aggressively trying to take whatever they could get from me through legal channels. I did not want to be found online growing a business, lest my creditors come after my new venture before it was solidly off the ground, so I went incognito and, for public purposes, I modified the spelling of my last name to Learner. I figured if I could just buy some time to work "in the dark," I could make the money to pay off my debt and get back on my feet. Obviously, as evidenced by the name on the front of this book, the plan worked, and a year and a half later, with my debt fully paid, I got to be Jeff Lerner again.

Looking back, it was a mess of stress. I was working fourteen hours a day learning new languages and skills to build a business that was taking months to show any signs of progress and for which I could afford no help from anyone. The business required constantly reinvesting money into ads on a credit card that was often on the verge of being maxed out and that I could only pay down as sales came in. I had worked out payment plans with some of my creditors so I now had monthly debt payments due, and I would first have to make those payments before I could use whatever was left to pay off the credit cards. I was robbing Peter to pay Paul, as they say, spending most of my time calling my online leads trying to sell products and earn commissions so I could get Peter some more money for me to rob and give to Paul. By April 2009, when I came back from that Lake Tahoe event, I had started to get momentum and could see light at the end of the tunnel, but during the several months prior I was barely staying afloat, maxing out my credit card over and over while having to close sales to get funds to pay it off so I could turn my ads back on. And remember, I couldn't open a bank account during any of this, which made everything twice as complicated. And hiding from creditors had required telling my in-laws, at whose house my then-wife and I were living, that if anyone called for me, I wasn't home, and then having to explain to them why I was getting mail at their address with my name misspelled. They were not impressed, and I would occasionally get to hear about how unimpressed they were. Meanwhile, my then-wife was barely speaking to me, which was actually a blessing compared to everyone else in my life, who was telling me to just go get a job. Never mind that the economy had just crashed and getting a job was easier said than done, but honestly, I wouldn't have anyway.

So why am I sharing all these woe-is-me stories? Do I want your sympathy? Do I want you to be impressed? No, that's not why. I'm sharing these stories to explain why veteran digital marketers, including myself, roll our eyes and smile when we hear people say that starting a business on the internet sounds hard. We are the proverbial grandpas talking about how we used to have to walk miles to school in the snow. Seriously, starting an internet business today is the easiest entrepreneurship has ever been in all of human history, by a factor of a hundred. On today's internet, funnel builders make websites easy. Platforms like Stripe, Shopify payments, Amazon payments, Google payments, Apple Pay, and any number of e-commerce-friendly merchant providers make collecting money easy. The cost of developers has plummeted. In 2008 I was quoted $5,000 to set up a basic WordPress site, while today I can find someone on Fiverr to do it for $100 or less. And the idea of printing out a large document at a Kinko's to sign and scan is now laughable. Regardless of Jim Rohn's advice, things have gotten so much easier.

If there's one thing I wish I could bottle a solution for that would change the world, it would simply be the willingness to do hard things until they pay off. That's it. As for the question posed in the chapter title, "Why do most people fail?," it's simple. Because they aren't willing to keep doing hard things until they pay off. That's why most people don't lose that weight. That's why most therapy doesn't save that broken marriage. And that's why most people never get through their income phase and earn five times their expenses. But why? Why don't we all just do better? Why don't we all just buck up and get gritty? For that, we need look no further than some tragic, but illuminating, rat torture.

In the 1950s, a professor at Johns Hopkins named Curt Richter did some experiments on rats. The experiments were cruel and thankfully would not be allowed today, but we should not dismiss their findings. They looked at how long a rat can swim before it drowns. The details of the study make for interesting, if a little gruesome, reading, but I'll just share the high-level summary. The first few rounds of studies established a baseline that a rat will swim in a beaker that it cannot escape from for about two minutes before drowning. In the final round, Richter would save the rats from drowning right at the two-minute mark when they were about to give up. He would pull them out of the water, giving them a brief reprieve and, this is the key, *a sensation of hope*, and then put them back in the water to swim for their lives again. And get this: even though they were fatigued from the previous swim, these rats that now had *hope* planted in their minds that, if they kept swimming, they might eventually be saved, swam for days before finally succumbing to exhaustion and drowning. There are 1,440 minutes in a day. This is a profound difference. Rats with no hope give up after two minutes, while rats with hope will swim a thousand times longer or more.

In my experience, we human beings are not much more evolved than rats in this regard, but there is an ironic distinction. Lab rats are right in most cases to have no hope—after all they're lab rats, their fate is pretty well sealed. But a human being, alive today in the modern world, in a developed country with internet access, a phone, and basic mental and physical faculties, should be the most hopeful species in the history of all species, regardless of their circumstances. In the historical scheme of things every person alive today in a developed country is a top 1 percenter. But that's not what we learn in school, is it? That's not what the broken system teaches us. We are taught that without that expensive college degree and the white-collar job, there is no place for us, no hope for us. And even for those who end up with that white-collar job, some quick midlife math usually reveals we're still going to outlive our retirement and die working, leaving a legacy from nothing to negative for our children. Cue the reverse mortgage.

I was recently on the phone with two people who work at the high school level of education, talking about piloting a training program ENTRE created for teens that helps students who are not college-bound find an alternate path in this world. We were discussing why the program might struggle to get support from the school districts because their metric for success, and the basis for their funding, is what percentage of students they get to go to college.

One of the educators told me that in his state, California, the high schools were fixated on matriculation rates into what they called "tier one universities." Tier one universities are the most expensive universities in the state, but have only 50 percent graduation rates, which means that half the students who attend them drop out with debt but no degree. On the other hand, the tier two universities, which the high schools are discouraged from recommending, are less expensive and offer more programs for students who cannot afford, or are unlikely to finish, a four-year degree. This smelled like a broken system smoking gun so I wanted to make sure I had the facts clear.

"Let me get this straight." I asked, *"California, already the most insolvent state economy in the United States, is incentivizing high school administrators to push students into attending more expensive schools that they are less likely to graduate from, and steering them away from less expensive schools they are more likely to graduate from?"* He confirmed that I did have the facts straight and it was further explained to me that the University of California and California State University systems have enrollment quotas to hit to maintain their budgets. So I did some quick research. It turns out that the UC school system is the second largest employer in California, employing over 227,000 faculty and staff. And guess who the largest employer in California is with over 270,000 employees? Wells Fargo Bank, which is also the largest servicer of student loans in the United States. Ah, now it all makes sense. So to put it bluntly, we are sacrificing our children's futures and burdening them with unnecessary debt so that today's adults can have job security. And people wonder why I am on a crusade to reinvent the educational system. The Nelson Mandela quote comes to mind, *"There can be no keener revelation of a society's soul than the way in which it treats its children."*

Suffice it to say, we concluded on that call that the idea of creating a curriculum that encourages students to consider not going to college, but rather to pursue an entrepreneurial path, would likely be difficult to get a school district onboard with. And then we decided to proceed with the project anyway because, well, all that is needed for evil to triumph is for good men to stand by and do nothing, right? The state of California might not want students to know that entrepreneurs, with or without college degrees, are a hundred times more likely to end up in the top 1 percent of net worth in the United States compared to employees, but we're going to do our best to make sure they find out. There is so much data that says we should be encouraging our children to think outside the box, take risks, consider different paths, and create their own future by focusing on entrepreneurial skills and learning self-reliance, but instead our schools, run by debt-burdened, pension-dependent, over-educated administrators who have never had to actually manage a profit-and-loss statement, are telling students to take on large student loans to pay for schooling they might not need, might not finish, and will need twenty-plus years to pay off.

The modern education system survives in its current form by perpetuating the idea that without it humans are incapable of thriving. Modern schooling is like a hot air balloon that to keep afloat we have to keep filling with hot air (what a perfect metaphor). The hot air that keeps the system afloat is the lie that without the balloon we'll crash, and the heat comes from keeping out of school curriculum any discussion of how students might succeed *without needing more school*. Remember how in chapter 21 we revealed that the Department of Education curriculum guide completely omits any mention of a career in sales? I can't help but think that's because employers have never cared about degrees when hiring for sales, so teaching kids to go into sales would be showing them a way to bypass college that's not only viable, but likely to pay better than most jobs. We might think that it would be a challenge to deceive so many people and perpetuate this grand delusion in the face of so many people (like me) who succeed wildly through self-reliance rather than school-reliance, but remember our rat friends and how little fight animals have when there is no hope. That is why talk of sales cannot be tolerated in schools. If the rambunctious kid with ADHD and bad grades was to realize while he was still in school that if he harnessed his energy and extroversion he could probably out-earn all his classmates with a career in sales, the balloon would deflate. The school systems must keep that kid hopeless so optimism around entrepreneurship doesn't turn into contagious skepticism over the necessity for more school.

I'll never forget the opening chapter of the great book *Think and Grow Rich* by Napoleon Hill. It tells the story of R. U. Darby who, after having struck gold with his uncle in the nineteenth-century gold rush, lost the vein and could not find it again. Disappointed, Darby abandoned his efforts and sold his digging equipment for scrap metal prices. It turned out he was three feet from the richest gold discovery in US history when he quit. What happens when a creature loses hope is tragic. Ever seen a cowboy break a horse? It's hard to watch, yet we're all watching it happen to our kids, just as our parents watched it happen to us. We live in a self-perpetuating system that deprives ordinary people of the hope that they can create better lives for themselves *without relying on the system*. That is the great tragedy of the modern world and what gets me jumping out of bed every day ready for a fight.

PART VI

Growth and Wealth

23

Get Rich or You're Screwed

As you've probably already detected from the title of this chapter, it's not going to be the most fun chapter to read. It will be technical and perhaps even a bit depressing, but once you get through it, you will be far better off than most and fully understand the urgency of doing what it takes to increase your income and build true wealth. In the modern world, ignorance is not bliss, and those who do not understand the forces at play in the present have a very bleak future.

This chapter is intended to accomplish three things:

1. Demonstrate that the ideas in this book, particularly those around "the broken system," are founded on real research and reflect a deep understanding of powerful forces that cannot responsibly be ignored
2. Ensure you have urgency around implementing what's in this book and don't waste any time in doing so
3. Show you how far gone the situation is so you take individual responsibility for creating solutions in your own life and don't make the mistake of thinking things will get better in time

Let's dive in.

SAVING WILL NOT SAVE YOU

One of the most telltale signs of a broken system mindset is when people get cash and hoard it. For generations, the prevailing thought around money was first and foremost to protect it. Warren Buffet famously says, "The first rule of investing is never lose money, and the second rule is to refer back to rule number one." On the surface that makes sense, and for the record I agree that not losing money is good advice. I sometimes refer to a "replenishment tax" that you pay when you have to replace money. Consider that if you lose 20 percent of a sum of money, you will have to make 25 percent return on what's left just to get back to even (100 percent – 20 percent = 80 percent, then 80 percent x 125 percent = 100 percent). That 5 percent difference between what was lost and what had to be re-earned is the replenishment tax. And it gets worse the more money you lose. If you lose 50 percent of your money, the replenishment tax jumps to plus-50 percent, meaning you will have to earn 100 percent of what's left to get back what you lost. This mathematical principle is the essence of why losing money is so costly, but we cannot let fear of the devil we know drive us into the arms of the devil we don't. There is a different tax we pay when we hoard money for fear of losing it—a tax paid daily by millions of people whose money is parked in savings accounts, CDs, money market accounts, treasury bonds, and the like. Call it "the tax of what might have been." It is the *opportunity cost* we pay when we forego opportunity because we are too scared to risk our money. Remember that 88 percent of millionaires and 70 percent of those with a net worth of $30 million or more are self-made. There are clearly things we can be doing with our money that can actually get us rich, and we need to be doing them because while prioritizing preservation over growth is a fine strategy once we are rich, it is a horrible strategy for getting there, and one that gets worse by the year. Let me explain why.

The twenty-first century has been defined by a very different approach to monetary policy across the developed world than previous generations. In a single span of sixteen months (from September 2019 to December 2020), the US Federal Reserve injected over $9 trillion into the US economy. This means that 25 percent of all the money in the United States was created out of thin air in an unprecedented sixteen-month span, more money than had previously been created in the entire 200-plus-year history of the United States. I'm not an economist, but I know that creating that much money in that short of a period is a dangerous setup for inflation. This is very bad for the average person, and it's even worse than it would be otherwise if the system were not so broken.

Inflation disproportionately harms people with less money who spend a greater percentage of their income on essential goods and services. Rich people, on the other hand, do very well in times of inflation as the value of their investments inflates. Think about it. If you buy real estate, stocks, and other investments that wealthy people tend to buy, you want prices to go up; the more the better. But when most of your income goes to living expenses like rent, transportation, and food, you do not want prices to go up. Inflation, especially the inflation that will likely characterize the first half of the twenty-first century based on the insane amounts of money the government keeps pumping into the economy, is the number one reason the 3 Phases of Legacy are so important for everyone to live by, and why people need to be so aggressive about creating their anomalous cash flow phase and increasing their income to their Awesome Life Number as fast as possible. Things are changing too fast, and time is not on the side of the average person. Even if it still existed as a practical reality, the "40/40 plan" of working forty hours a week for forty years is too slow now and given that the average employee changes jobs every twenty months, that plan doesn't exist anyway.

Here is the breakdown that explains why the average person needs to get so aggressive about boosting their income. Historically, inflation in the United States has averaged about 3 percent, which means prices doubling about every twenty-four years. At the time I'm writing this we're already seeing it at double that (the last number I saw was 6.8 percent), and it will likely go higher still. Remember 25 percent of the US money supply was created out of thin air over sixteen months with no new value produced. That is a lot of extra dollars that must get absorbed into the prices of existing goods and services, so 6.8 percent is just the beginning. Even at 6.8 percent inflation, though, prices will double every ten and a half years. At 10 percent inflation (which is not unprecedented at all; it was 14.5 percent in 1980 at the end of Jimmy Carter's presidency), prices will double every seven years. This has dramatic future impact. At 10 percent inflation, if you need $2 million to retire today (a conservative number promoted by most financial planners, which I think is already low), you'll need $4 million in seven years, or $8 million in fourteen years. Said another way, if you're currently spending $1,000 a month on groceries today, at 10 percent inflation in fourteen years you'll be spending $4,000 a month for an equivalent *basket of goods* (a term used to quantify consumer price increases).

I don't want to get too deep into the history of US monetary policy (though I'm a huge economics nerd and in a different book would love to), so I'll just say that since 2008 there has been a resurgence across the westernized world, led by the United States, of what is known as "Keynesian monetary policy." This started with the first round of "quantitative easing" initiated during George W. Bush's presidency and, sourcing from the ideas of early twentieth-century economist John Maynard Keynes, involves using "fiscal stimulus" (i.e., printing lots of money) to keep the economy growing and prevents "corrections," or contractions. The newly printed money flows to banks who are then incentivized to loan it to businesses. The businesses then do what businesses do, making investments into growth, which creates jobs, fills tax coffers, feeds the stock market, and makes politicians look good for the time being. We'll talk more about the mechanisms that the Federal Reserve Bank (which is neither a federal agency nor a bank, by the way) uses to create all this money, but for now let's just state the obvious. You can't add dollars into an economy faster than the economy is growing without reducing the value of each dollar. Slicing a pie into more and more slices doesn't equate to more pie for people to eat.

Since 2008, governments around the world have gone to unprecedented lengths to drive economic growth at all costs and distorted the money supply in a way that is politically expedient in the short term (which is how non-term-limited politicians think) and a ticking time bomb in the long term. Hear that term, *ticking time bomb.* Let it frighten you a bit, then channel that fear into a desire to do what it takes to get rich, if not for yourself, for your kids. Otherwise, you are playing with fire and hoping inflation doesn't do what it's done to every economic superpower in the history of the world. Basically, if you are not doing everything in your power to get rich, you are betting your family's future on the idea that slicing a pie and baking a bigger pie are the same thing. Please don't do that.

Keynesian economics doesn't just involve fiscal stimulus. Rampant money printing has a close cousin, another man-made force in the world that is silently eroding the future of the average person: suppression of interest rates. When allowed to fluctuate openly based on free-market supply and demand, interest rates have a natural checks-and-balances function in the economy. Historically, when the economy is booming, interest rates go up. Investments are viewed as more likely to produce a return, so borrowers are willing to pay more for the money to make them. This increasing cost of borrowing money naturally discourages exuberance and excess risk taking, which keeps the economy from overheating and forming a bubble. Eventually, higher rates cool growth, and when the economy starts to drag and investment returns decrease, investors become less willing to pay interest to borrow money so banks naturally lower rates to encourage them to keep borrowing. Low rates then stimulate the economy as more profit can be made when cost-of-borrowing is less. Profits then get reinvested so the economy heats back up, and the cycle continues. This is how it is supposed to work.

But this natural cycle has been disrupted because the Federal Reserve (and the World Bank and all the other power centers in the global economy) doesn't allow rates to rise anymore, at least not nearly as much as they would if borrowers and lenders were allowed to reach their own agreements. Since 1942, interest rates in the United States have been set by the Federal Reserve, which is really a council of private-sector bankers given expansive powers to regulate the US economy under the auspices of the Senate. The stated goal of the Federal Reserve, or "the Fed," is to keep rates as low as possible to stimulate economic growth and to allow the government to borrow money at low interest rates (more on that later). And this all works fine to a point, as we have admittedly seen great prosperity since 1942, but keeping interest rates suppressed only works until it doesn't and, as I'll explain, there is a reckoning coming.

The economy has been in a prolonged boom since quantitative easing (QE) began in 2008. Admittedly, QE did pull us out of "The Great Recession" and send the stock market soaring, but rates should subsequently have been raised to cool growth and they weren't, at least not enough, nor can they be for reasons I'll explain when we talk about the national debt. Fast forward to 2020 when the pandemic broke out and the economy should have contracted, and we saw the government once again do what it had to in order to keep the economy growing by printing money and lowering interest rates. But just like in sports, plays don't work as well when you run them again too soon. Back in 2008, the Fed had room to significantly lower interest rates and in a span of about eighteen months it dropped the Discount Rate from 6.25 percent to 0.5 percent. The Discount Rate is the rate that banks pay to borrow money from the Fed, so by making money dirt cheap banks can easily borrow it and turn around and loan it cheap to businesses. But in 2020, when the Fed tried to run the same play, the Discount Rate had only crept back up to barely 3 percent, still near its historic low. So lowering it again, this time to 0.25 percent, didn't have the same effect, and at 0.25 percent, it can't go any lower. Obviously, the entire system would collapse if money was being loaned with zero interest being charged, so the Fed basically lost one of its two plays and was reduced to profligately printing more and more money and shoving it into the banks to be loaned out at absurdly low rates. But the underlying economy was having major problems. There was a pandemic raging, millions of businesses were closing, and tens of millions of employees were quitting, which all sounds like a risky time for banks to be making large loans. But banks know they have nothing to worry about; the Fed has shown time and again it will be there to bail out their friends, America's "too-big-to-fail" banks, if they make bad loans. And it's easy to see why.

A quick glance at the Federal Reserve's Board of Governors and Open Market Committee rosters (the OMC is the committee that sets interest rates and controls the US money supply) reveals a fox guarding the henhouse. Every senior member of the Federal Reserve has clear ties to the investment banking and/or private equity world, and there is a long history of ethical concerns dating all the way back to the 1970s involving not only the Fed bailing out big banks, but even Fed committee members taking personal financial actions, such as trading individual stocks, that benefit from advance knowledge of the Fed's actions. And who picks up the tab in all of this? Taxpayers. We get the double whammy—loss of buying power through inflation as well as increased taxes to cover the banks' losses if necessary.

Bear in mind, I'm an avowed capitalist and an evangelist for entrepreneurship who believes that free market commerce, including the lending activities of banks, has done more to measurably improve the human condition than any force in human history. But the government's job is to protect the *free* in free markets, not use the economy to manipulate political outcomes. When that happens, short-term political expediency diverges from the long-term good of society, and that is what is what we're seeing happen. The political playbook is now to print more money, keep interest rates as low as possible, hijack natural economic ebbs and flows, and kick the can further down the road whenever necessary, pushing the reckoning off so it can be the next administration's problem. I hope this is landing with you. We hear often about the death of the middle class; I am explaining to you the mechanism of the slaughter.

HOW INTEREST RATES
ARE SUPPOSED TO WORK

I wish that was all there is to say about it. But sadly, there's more. Let's talk further about interest rates (come on, you know you want to). The regulation of economic growth through the rise and fall of interest rates is critical to the health of the free market. It's a symbiotic relationship that works when it is allowed to happen naturally, a relationship that forms a self-regulating system so natural and elegant we see parallels to it in biological systems.

In case all this money talk is hard to follow, let's look at the human digestive system for an analogy that might be easier for some to process (the puns just keep writing themselves). When we eat, our blood sugar increases and the pancreas releases insulin. Insulin then escorts blood sugar into our cells, where it gets used as energy, with excess being stored in the liver or as fat. As blood sugar falls, insulin levels correspondingly decrease, which signals our stomach to produce ghrelin, a hormone that makes us hungry, and if we don't have food available, our decreasing insulin level will also signal the liver to release stored blood sugar. Either way, we end up with sugar back in our blood, the pancreas producing more insulin, and the cycle continuing.

Now think of blood sugar as money, and the economy as the human body. When there's lots of money flowing (sugar in the blood), natural market forces (the pancreas) should produce higher interest rates (insulin). The higher interest rates will then slow down the flow of money by encouraging it to be invested (used as energy) or saved (stored in the liver or as fat). Then as money flow decreases, interest rates (insulin) lower and create an appetite (ghrelin) for more money flow. That money flow either gets supplied by private capital (more food) or will be provided by the government (the liver releasing stored sugar). In either case, interest rates (insulin) will rise again and the cycle repeats. This is how the economy is supposed to work, just like a finely tuned living organism, and just like with the body we can only get away with interfering with it for so long. At the risk of wearing out the metaphor I'll suggest that our government's addiction to quantitative easing is much like our society's addiction to high-fructose corn syrup and other processed foods—cheap substitutes for real nourishment that are easy to sell to the public and produce a quick high but are ultimately destroying us through overconsumption (think insulin resistance).

In both the body and the economy, the natural checks and balances of complementary systems like we've described are about managing risk. The body knows that if blood sugar gets too high or too low the body is at risk. Economies have a similar sort of risk-awareness, which Adam Smith, the Father of Economics, called "the Invisible Hand," a self-regulating mechanism intrinsic to large, mature economies. In principle, when money flow increases quickly and an economy starts to get riskier, interest rates go up because those who possess capital, like banks and private investors, demand a higher return on their money in exchange for making loans or investments in the riskier environment. But this principle has broken down. In the United States, at present, there are huge economic risks that *should* be causing interest rates to rise and would be if the Invisible Hand hadn't been amputated.

Here are a few of the risks that should be getting priced into interest rates but aren't due to Fed policy:

• Prices keep rising year after year (inflation, which we've discussed).
• Currency is devaluing (by all the money printing).
• The government operates at a huge annual deficit (old news by now).
• The United States is a massive net importer (we consume far more than we produce).
• The United States has unsustainable financial commitments related to social policy (everything from social security to benefits for illegal immigrants).
• The US government is way over its head in debt, owing far more debt to numerous parties than it can ever pay off.

This last item is the nail in the coffin. As of 2021, the US national debt is over $28 trillion and expected to rise to $40 trillion within just a few years. We hear about "the national debt" all the time, but to most people it's just an ugly number with lots of commas that doesn't seem to impact daily life. But it does impact daily life in numerous ways, some of which I'll explain, and the day will come when its impact is painfully felt by all. Hopefully, by then you have acted on what's in this book and insulated yourself.

And before we get into the mechanics of the national debt let me point out for international readers this is not just a US problem. I just know more about how it happens here than elsewhere, so I am using the United States as a proxy to explain the process. There are currently thirteen countries in the world with trillion or multi-trillion-dollar debts (United States, United Kingdom, France, Germany, Japan, Italy, Spain, China, Canada, Switzerland, Australia, Singapore, and Belgium), and the United States which is widely considered to be the worst of the debtor nations, is only the seventh worst when debt is calculated as a percentage of gross domestic product.

So, here's how we got here and why it matters. When the government operates with a "balanced budget" it means that it does not spend more than what it collects in taxes and other revenue. Unfortunately, it has not done this since 2001. When the government spends more than it collects, it uses the issuance of various instruments that others can invest in, such as savings bonds, treasury bonds, and treasury-backed securities, to cover the shortfall. These instruments pay investors interest while allowing the government to operate at a "budget deficit," meaning it spends more than it collects in taxes. Another way to think of the national debt is as the total amount of securities the government has sold to investors to pay for things that it couldn't afford. Unfortunately, the government has gotten lazy and mostly abandoned any idea of a balanced budget. In 2021, for example, its twentieth consecutive year running at a deficit, the federal government spent $6.82 trillion against revenues of $4.05 trillion, a deficit of $2.77 trillion. Wow, maybe I shouldn't be so hard on Americans for how we spend money; after all we do far better than our government by only spending 107 percent of our income when our government is spending 168 percent of its income.

THE LUCKY FOX

Now I know I've thrown a lot at you here, so let me make sure something is clear. There are two separate issues happening simultaneously—money printing by the Fed to stimulate the economy and deficit spending funded by government borrowing from investors. The Fed increasing the money supply by 25 percent over sixteen months did nothing at all to pay the government's $2 trillion-plus annual deficit. That was only to flood the banks with currency so they would make cheap loans and keep the economy humming. Of course, whenever the government engages in this type of money printing it argues to the public that it will stimulate tax revenue and help cover the budget deficit, but in practice the government always increases spending and squanders any tax revenue increase. In 2021, the budget deficit had to be covered through the sale of securities for the twentieth year in a row. So once again the taxpayer gets the famous double whammy—the government now owes investors an additional $2.77 trillion, plus interest, guaranteed by us, the taxpayers, but they also diluted the money supply by 25 percent and devalued every future dollar us taxpayers will earn. Thanks, guys.

So let's ask ourselves the critical question underneath all of this: What would happen if the Fed allowed interest rates to rise as they naturally should given the risk factors begging to be priced in? It would mean that the world's largest debtor, the US government—which currently owes 12 cents of every dollar of debt owed to anyone, anywhere in the entire world—would see its debt payments go up, just like any borrower does when their interest rate increases. But the government already can't pay its bills, so in that case it would have to borrow more money to pay more interest on the money it borrows. Plus, the amount it needs to borrow is increasing because the things it needs to pay for, like goods, services, and wages, are getting more expensive because of inflation from all the Fed's money printing. So the government has a double whammy of its own—paying interest on money it borrows to pay interest on money it borrows while all the money it's borrowing buys less and less as the value of all money decreases. It's a slippery slope that the government is already sliding down and keeping interest rates near zero is just a too-little-too-late gambit to buy time. And in the end, it will be the United States' creditors who get screwed, along with the taxpayers. So who are the United States' creditors? Well, that's where things get pretty scary.

The United States creditors are (as of 2021):

- **The US government, $11 trillion:** The United States owes *itself* $11 trillion (say what?) Yes, this means what it sounds like—the government loans money (our money, as you'll see) to itself to operate, a form of lending known as intragovernmental debt. The largest of the intragovernmental debt holders are the Social Security System (almost $3 trillion of US debt) and the Military Retirement Fund (over $1 trillion), followed by Medicare, other government retirement programs, and so on. All of this represents money paid into the government by US citizens that is supposed to be returned to us at a future time, with interest, as retirement, medical, and other types of benefits. But this money that we paid in was not kept in trusts like it was supposed to be (including the retirement contributions of our military). Instead, these trusts loaned the money they collected to other departments of the US government in exchange for "promises to pay" that are "backed by the full faith and credit of the United States." That all sounds sort of okay until you realize what the full faith and credit of the United States is— it's a pledge of future tax dollars that the government will collect from US workers—the same workers who are banking on getting their benefits someday. If you're thinking this sounds a little like a Ponzi scheme, you're right. The government convinced (forced) people to pay money into investments that will supposedly pay them back someday with a return (Social Security, Medicare, etc.), and then, instead of investing it soundly, they loaned the money to themselves to fund the growth of government. So now the government's future obligations to its own citizens (Social Security, Military Retirement Fund, health care, tax credits, etc.) are not backed by the cash that was paid in, but rather secured by debt that can only be repaid by the money the government plans to collect in the future from the same group of people who paid in in the first place (US workers). Only now, the government will have to collect far more taxes in the future than it currently collects to afford the increased cost of future benefits owed, which are increasing faster each year because of inflation, as well as the interest it owes from borrowing the money from itself in the first place. This piece of the overall boondoggle is the biggest factor in why interest rates can't go up—Social Security is already trending toward insolvency by 2033, and that date accelerates really quickly if interest rates go up even a little.

- **Foreign investors, $7 trillion:** The United States owes foreign governments and/or foreign investors $7 trillion, including over $2 trillion just between Japan and China. Try to imagine a scenario where the United States defaults on over $1 trillion to China, and you instantly understand the second main reason why interest rates cannot be raised.

- **The Fed, $7 trillion:** The United States owes another $7 trillion to the Fed. If alarm bells are going off in your mind, good; it means you're paying attention. So let's look more closely at exactly who and what is the Fed. The Fed is a privately organized central banking cartel that manages the US money supply, sets interest rates, and controls broader policy and strategy of the US economy. It is an organization that is *theoretically* accountable to, but not technically a part of, the US government. It is run by a board of governors who are nominated by the president and must be approved by the US Senate, but then operates independently and behind closed doors. (Fed meetings are private, and they are not required to disclose who they are making loans to or for how much. Seriously.) The Fed is allowed to participate in what it calls OMO (open market operations) to generate income, which it does through the Fed Open Market Committee (OMC), which we mentioned earlier is comprised of powerful and well-connected banking industry veterans. Through these operations, it has acquired $7 trillion of US Treasuries, and thus gets paid a large amount of interest by the federal government. So while, in theory, the Fed is supposed to be held accountable by Congress, they are also *the single largest creditor of the US government* and the ones who set the interest rates that dictate how much the government has to pay them (so the lucky fox gets a second henhouse to guard). While it might seem that the Fed would thus be inclined to raise interest rates (and their income in the process), at this point, they cannot do so without bankrupting the US government. If that happened the Fed would either have to do more quantitative easing to pump more money into the banks to drive more tax revenue, or it would have to buy more treasury securities through OMO, which would be throwing good money after bad once the government had defaulted. Of all the creditor situations, this one is probably the messiest. It gives me a migraine just writing about it. Finally . . .

- **US-based investors, over $10 trillion:** The United States owes the rest of its debt, over $10 trillion, to United States–based investors, including many state and local governments, private pension funds, mutual funds, insurance companies, and private individuals. Similar to the intragovernmental creditors (Social Security, Military Retirement

Fund, etc.), many of these entities represent large groups of current or future retirees, along with general public interests like state and local governments. In other words, it is not just Social Security that would be pushed toward insolvency if interest rates went up and the government couldn't pay its debts, it's private retirement plans too, along with thousands of state and local governments.

THE BROKEN SYSTEM ON FULL DISPLAY AND OTHER STUFF YOU CAN'T MAKE UP

Wowzers. What a mess, huh? Where do we even go from here? Well, what we don't do is hide our money under a mattress. Remember the first thing we said in this chapter—hoarding money is what the broken system wants you to do. Unless you are already in the top 1 percent (which, at the time of this writing, would be a net worth of $11 million or more), you need to be in the money-getting business, not the money-saving business. The average rate of interest on a savings account today is 0.06 percent. Remember when I said the system would fall apart if loans paid no interest? Well, banks are perfectly fine paying you no interest (or next to none) on your money, but they're never going to loan theirs to you (or someone else's to you, technically) at such a low rate.

For the average person, it's time to change our standards on what rate our money returns. Even a 5 percent return now is not preserving the value of our money, not in the era of 6 to 10 percent inflation, which, again, I see no way to avoid over the next decade or so based on how the money supply is being managed. For the foreseeable future, it's not unreasonable to say that if we aren't generating double-digit returns like 10 percent, 12 percent, 15 percent, or even 20 percent, we're getting poorer. Inflation is starting to rear its head in ways the average person can't miss, and the government can't deny (for example, from 2018 to 2021 the price of a gallon of milk rose 26 percent, and in 2021 alone energy prices rose 33 percent), so it's not surprising we see the public's appetite for risk increasing. People are sinking their life savings into speculative investments like cryptocurrency and NFTs, which is not the right asset class for most people in my opinion, but they do have the right idea going after bigger returns. Unfortunately, like we said, the market is not being allowed to price in the risk of such speculation, and not surprisingly there are bad decisions being made. I recently read about a trend of people taking out second mortgages to buy NFTs—something that would be a lot less enticing if interest rates were higher.

And the same principles apply to student loans, which should have higher interest rates too, but that would discourage students from borrowing and encourage more scrutiny of the economics of college education. As long as student money is cheap people will ask fewer questions about whether or not college is worth it at any price. Better to let us suspect how broken the system is than to choke off the cheap money that feeds it and remove all doubt, right? Given the poor outcomes of college educations in the labor force (the percent of degrees that go unused or the average twenty-five-year-old still living at home, changing jobs every twenty months, taking twenty-plus years to pay off what are supposed to be ten-year loans, etc.), there is obvious risk in making these six-figure loans to eighteen-year-olds that should be reflected in higher interest rates, but the government can't let that happen. Not only do they guarantee every student loan issued in the United States (backstopping them with our future tax dollars) but now the government actively purchases these loans from private lenders so banks don't have to deal with the fallout as students default. In a little-known provision of the Affordable Care Act of 2012, which I seem to remember was supposed to be about health care, the majority of student loans in this country were consolidated into the federal government as the creditor. Student loans now represent over a third of the assets owned by the US government. Let me write that again so you're sure to catch it: *student loans now represent over a third of the assets owned by the US government.* That is crazy to think about. The government has gone hard into the student debt business and can no more afford for the value of a college education to be questioned than it can afford to raise interest rates on the national debt. And so, the plot gets really thick. Students are taught the unquestionable value of a college degree, steered into expensive schools (remember the California example), and given large loans they can't afford and shouldn't qualify for at artificially low interest rates that do not reflect the borrower's or the bank's risk. Those loans are then purchased by the US government, who is essentially using the banks as an intermediary to originate the loans by feeding them the money to loan out and then buying the loans back, which feeds them more money to loan out again. And now we have an entire generation of children who come out of college with the same problem I had from my SBA loan default—owing the

US government hundreds of thousands of dollars. Take it from me, that's not a fun position nor one we should be conscripting our children into. By the way, did you know that student loans are one of the only types of debt you can't discharge through bankruptcy thanks to an act of Congress? The government really knows how to cover its bases.

Ultimately, who is responsible for collecting from these borrowers? We are, the US taxpayer who backstopped the loan in the first place. Ironically, as college graduates enter the workforce they become part of their own creditor constituency. We know these loans are a low-quality class of debt because even though they get issued at artificially low interest rates they still usually end up getting restructured (what starts as a ten-year loan product takes over twenty years to pay off on average). But the government doesn't care because it uses our money to cover the bad debt via its two favorite mechanisms for raising money. Either the Fed buys more US treasuries using money it creates out of thin air and devaluing all of our money in the process (making things like milk more expensive), or it borrows from our futures by raiding Social Security and other government trusts.

See how it's all connected? There are many more colluders in the broken system: banks that arbitrage their depositors' savings (at a cost of 0.06 percent) into credit card loans that pay 20 percent or better; employers who have a vested interest in keeping their employees from realizing what their futures actually look like; the government itself who wants to keep people in jobs because they're easier to tax; investment banks and insurance companies who create retirement products that only remain solvent as long as people keep pumping money into them; heck, even the military, which relies on an inflated sense of the value of college degrees (and the non-affordability of them for many students) to drive enlistment through the GI Bill.

I hope this is all hitting you hard and you're seeing the house of cards our government has built and how it is up to us to save ourselves. There is a cradle-to-grave broken system in the developed world, so complex it could rightly be thought of as a "system of systems." Its complexity and ubiquity is how it stays hidden and most people do not even know it's there. Much the way it is said that a fish only learns what water is when it is removed from it, once you escape from the broken system you will see it everywhere like I do. It ensnares us from birth to death, and for most of us our only chance to escape it is to start a business and build real wealth through the phases of legacy.

In light of everything I've shared, what other choice is there? The broken system claims to be built upon "full faith and credit" (in itself), but I believe I have demonstrated that it has abused your good faith and squandered your credit. Remember the third goal of this chapter: I wanted you to see how far gone the situation is so you wouldn't wait to be saved. The time has come to save ourselves because no one else is coming. I also hope you can appreciate the risk I take in saying all this; there will be those who respond by labeling me a kook. That is one of the reasons I was so detailed in explaining everything; I need my arguments to be beyond reproach so they are harder to discredit.

It is so tempting to whitewash this stuff and it is hard to just say it plainly because I don't like scaring or hurting anyone. But I'm just the messenger and the truth is what it is. In the world today, "the little guy" is taught from a young age there is only one game to play by institutions and complicit people who know it's a game they will not win. I've waited this far in this book to really say it this bluntly, to have our "red pill" moment. But everything I've written are easy-to-verify facts about how the world works. These are the forces that make it so essential that you power through your income phase, hit your Awesome Life Number, get into your growth and wealth phases, and escape from the broken system for you and future generations.

Hopefully, you've seen now that the age-old strategy of *saving* our way to wealth, or even *investing* our way to wealth if we haven't first dramatically increased our income, is not going to get us where we need to be in the modern world. The rate of return the average person would need to achieve through investing to get wealthy is not achievable without undue risk. And risk is difficult to assess in a world where it is being systemically downplayed to avoid alarming the public, contracting the economy, and even bankrupting the government. So given that we can't save our way to wealth, and that it's too risky for most people to invest their way to wealth on the minimal surplus they have to work with, and that the average pay raise is 4 percent less than the current rate of inflation, that only leaves one option for the average person— dramatically increasing income through some sort of entrepreneurial income vehicle. This is why I consider myself an entrepreneurial evangelist. I realize that not everyone in the world is a natural entrepreneur, and many probably decided a long time ago they are not interested in owning a business. I just don't see what other option people have now. I'm sympathetic. Owning a business is tough, and even though I have a great business teaching entrepreneurship, part of me wishes there was still a nice cushy option for those who don't want "tough" and would prefer to just work the 40/40 plan and sail into the sunset. But the system is broken, and whether we like it or not, it's time to get gritty and uncomfortable if we want to even be okay, never mind get rich. For those who aren't ready to start a full-fledged business, there is the digital freelancer option we talked about, but one way or another, we've got to get our incomes up, and learning new skills and monetizing them through either a business or contract work is the best way for most people to do it.

I'll assume from here I have you convinced and you are ready to get entrepreneurial, learn some skills, and boost your income. So let's talk about your future.

24

The Growth Phase

Tactically, this book is mostly focused on the income phase since that's
the phase that 98 to 99 percent of people are in or need to be in,
but we still want to dig into what comes after the income phase. The
growth and wealth phases are as unique as each person who goes through
them, and it would be irresponsible and impractical for this book to give
specific, one-size-fits-all advice on complex activities like scaling a business
or investing, but I will give recommendations on resources you can use to go
deeper inside each phase.

First, let's review and summarize the 3 Phases of Legacy.

- **Phase 1: Income.** This phase is about increasing income to create surplus, or money that is not needed for daily living. The goal is to get to
  where your income is five times what you need to live (your Awesome
  Life Number). Once you achieve your Awesome Life Number, you are
  now living on 20 percent of your income, with the remaining 80 percent split between taxes and investing. Assuming a tax rate of 40 percent, you are now investing the other 40 percent of your income, which
  is twice what you're spending to live. This is the key to graduating
  to the growth and wealth phases—investing twice as much money as

you're spending. Until you hit that threshold, your focus needs to stay on generating revenue and creating surplus.

- **Phase 2: Growth.** This phase involves expanding and/or converting your surplus from the income phase into income-generating assets that produce predictable, bankable, and sellable cash flows. For most, this means expanding whatever business or other income vehicle was used in Phase 1 by increasing and/or diversifying revenue streams. The goal of this phase is making your income predictable and futureproof. The best way to think about it is to ask, *Would a bank or investor lend on or invest in this cash flow?* For that answer to be yes, that cash flow has to be highly stable and secure.

- **Phase 3: Wealth.** This phase involves diversifying into (usually income-producing) assets that are outside your primary business or income vehicle, and which are stable, low risk, tax advantaged, and heritable. Ideally, during this phase, the majority of your income shifts to passive sources, so you are no longer having to work for money.

Now let's explore these phases further. In the income phase, we do whatever we have to in order to get income up. We might be working a second (or third) job, taking classes to increase the value of our skills and time, building a side hustle, running a business full-time, selling bodily fluids, or all of the above. The only "rules" as we aim for the five-to-one income to cost-of-living ratio are that we should try to increase our income by increasing the value of our time (rather than simply working more hours) and we should trim our expenses wherever we can (a dollar trimmed is five dollars we don't have to earn in this equation). This is why starting a business is the recommended income vehicle for most—it's much easier to dramatically increase the value of your time through growing a business than through growing in a job, and the tax advantages of running a business effectively lower your cost of living right out of the gate (your cell phone, internet connection, and a portion of your rent if you have a home office are now no longer considered living expenses, but rather business expenses, which you can remove from the denominator of the income-over-expenses equation and on which you no longer pay taxes).

The growth phase is where we try to reign in the chaos and craziness that often characterizes the income phase. One could say the growth phase is the *growing up phase.* For most people, the income phase has a sort of "white-knuckle" feeling about it, with a lot of hit-and-miss results and a sensation that we were chasing after something the whole time. Frankly, by the time most people hit their Awesome Life Number, they're run pretty ragged and ready to normalize and stabilize. After interviewing hundreds of highly successful people on my podcast, *Unlock Your Potential*, I can report to you that hitting your Awesome Life Number is probably not going to be easy. Every person I have interviewed went through a crazy period of time when they were shedding the baggage, expectations, and identity of their past, learning to operate at a new frequency, and getting used to the frenetic intensity that it takes to make a lot of money. This is why I call this the anomalous cash flow phase—it's meant to feel unnatural while you're in it, like an anomaly, or even full-on lunacy. To hit your Awesome Life Number is going to require a level of exertion that might feel unsustainable if you had to maintain it for your entire life. But you won't have to sustain it forever, and anyway I've observed that once people acclimate to what they're capable of, they often enjoy it and prefer not to go back to their old level of output. So don't resist the challenge and don't psych yourself out before you start. The income phase is just that, a phase, and you only have to do it once to change the course of your life.

In the growth phase it's time to make sure that our life is stable, set up for long-term success, and that there is a point at which we can slow down. The three adjectives we use to describe the growth phase are *predictable*, *bankable*, and *sellable*. Let's look at each of those concepts.

Predictable

In the income phase, *we* were what needed to be predictable. We needed to know that every day *we* would wake up at the appointed time and *we would do the work.* For me, my conscious income phase, meaning the period when I was in the income phase and aware of a specific level of income surplus I needed to hit in order to complete the phase, lasted fifteen years, from sixteen to thirty years old. I knew from my very first business idea at sixteen that I needed to escape the broken system and figure out my own path to making good money and designing my own life. During every major decision I made from sixteen on, I was conscious and aware that I was designing my life and navigating a phase on the path to freedom. I didn't have the language yet of "the 3 Phases of Legacy" but I had the feeling. And I knew it was something I only had to achieve once, and then I'd be able to move to the next phase, whatever that was.

Every decision I made in my income phase had the same theme: rejecting life in the broken system that for whatever reason revealed itself to me when I was a teenager. Fifteen years it took, and eleven business failures. I am a good example of how messy the income phase can look when someone lacks guidance, but I'm also a good example of how relentless and consistent someone needs to be in that phase. During that period my friends sometimes referred to me as the Energizer Bunny because every day I woke up and went hard at whatever I was doing (and it wasn't always meant as a compliment). All the motivation that I needed was the awareness that without surplus of both income and time I would be relegated to life inside a system I knew was broken. We get what we tolerate in this life, and I had decided that what most would tolerate, I would not, so I never ended up with it. The tradeoff was that I had to be ruthlessly predictable during this phase, even when everything around me was chaotic. Most people in life want external predictability as an offset to internal inconsistency, but when you know you are a rock of consistency and execution, your need for external predictability (aka, a comfort zone) goes away. I did a lot of things wrong in my twenties, but getting this one thing right, being internally consistent and predictable while never expecting the world around me to be, is how I eventually made it through my income phase, which officially concluded for me in 2010 when, using my digital business, I had cleared my $495,000 debt and was consistently exceeding my Awesome Life Number.

Once we hit the growth phase, then it becomes reasonable to want *external* consistency and predictability. This is the benefit of having surplus income: we can start to force our will on the world around us, shape our environment, and create predictability. Now that we've built an income vehicle that is producing our Awesome Life Number, we have a lot to lose if the boat gets rocked. The transition from the income phase to the growth phase is primarily marked by this single concept, that in the income phase *we were what had to be predictable,* while in the growth phase *we start shaping our external environment to be predictable like we are.*

Bankable

When something is "bankable," you can "take it to the bank" as the saying goes. In the growth phase, we want our income, or our cash flow as it may be called, to be so solid and steady we can literally borrow money against it or use it as the basis for underwriting credit with a conventional bank (not just some rich uncle).

To evaluate the bankability of our cash flow, we have to learn to look at it the way banks do. Generally, banks have specific criteria for considering a stream of cash flow credit-worthy. Banks look at the consistency of the cash flow, the history of the cash flow, the source of the cash flow, and the terms of the cash flow. We should look at our cash flow the same way. Is it a "feast-or-famine" cash flow, or does it hold steady month after month? Is it seasonal or evergreen? Is it the same customers paying month after month, or new customers that have to be acquired each month? If it's the same customers, are they on month-to-month agreements or under contracts? How long are the contracts? How do the customers pay: cash, checks, or credit cards? Hint: if it's credit cards, a bank might not consider it to be "your" money until six months after the sale due to merchant processing agreements (remember the "friendly fraud" conversation?). Do the products or services have a long fulfillment window, meaning a full or partial refund could be requested long after the original purchase? How long has the cash flow remained steady? These factors dramatically change the bankability of cash flow. ENTRE grew over 4,000 percent in one year, which actually made it harder the next year to get credit from banks because the majority of our cash flow was so new and hadn't "seasoned" with more than a year of history. What industry are you in? Does the industry have history, or is it a relatively new product or service category? Does your business have a strong brand and reputation? What comes up when a bank Google searches you or your business? These types of questions are what a bank uses to determine the "bankability" of cash flow, and we should ask them too.

Banks are among the most conservative entities on the planet. Their model is about making a large volume of loans relative to the deposits they have on hand, and they typically operate on a lot of leverage. They aren't trying to get rich off of any one loan, and though we have discussed their tendency to make questionable loans when they have a government guarantee backing them, they are extremely conservative in underwriting small businesses. As an entrepreneur trying to get working capital for our business, this conservatism can be annoying, but it does give us an extremely useful filter to look at our business and investments through. Business owners and investors are often like parents who don't see "their babies" objectively. So, trying to see them the way the bank does and asking, "If I were a bank, would I invest in me?" is an often-humbling reality check.

Sellable

This one's pretty simple and comes down to one question: Would anyone buy this cash flow?

Here's a fact: if a stream of cash flow is healthy enough, there is always someone willing to buy it. If you can't sell your cash flow, it's because your cash flow isn't healthy enough and you aren't through your growth phase yet. There's a nuance to this because there are two kinds of buyers for any business or stream of cash flow: transactional and strategic. A strategic buyer might be interested for any number of reasons, such as the customer list, employees, products, services, and how those elements might be a strategic fit with the buyer's business or other interests. Every day, businesses get sold for strategic reasons that involve qualitative factors beyond just cash flow, but this is not the "sellability" we're talking about here. To graduate from your growth phase, your cash flow has to be so stable that a *transactional* buyer would buy it purely as an exchange of present value (meaning today's dollars) for the projected value of future cash flows based on size, timing, and risk. That is a cold and clinical description of how to evaluate a cash flow, and that's the point—it forces you to be objective about your baby.

Once we get to the growth phase, we cannot be emotional. For many of us, the income phase was characterized by passion, and that's exactly why the growth phase is the *growing up* phase. In the growth phase we lead with our head and even tell our heart to step back if necessary. The inability to make this heart-to-head transition is why many entrepreneurs hit a ceiling or get stuck in a phase. We have to learn to be as coldly objective as a bank. I made this mistake when I sold my agency. I declared my intention to sell, and the buyer knew I was making other commitments on the assumption the deal would go through at a certain amount. But I had not been ruthless enough in my own analysis of what the business was worth, so when the buyer started to ask tough questions, I didn't have tight and polished answers. I had a good business that had pushed through its income phase nicely and created surplus, much of which was flowing down to me, but I had some growth phase loose ends I had not tied down before I tried to exit the business and move to the wealth phase. For example, over half my customers were on month-to-month contracts instead of retainer agreements. This alone cost me at least a million dollars in what the gross sale price could have been, and more than that, it forced me to accept the buyer's terms of a two-year payout because, as they rightly pointed out, they had "no contractual assurance that my customers would keep paying."

This is a perfect example of how a lack of thinking like a bank can bite you in the butt. When the deal closed and the customers all got transferred over to the buyer, there were hiccups in the handoff. The buyer fumbled and did not properly reach out to the customers to facilitate the transition. As such, many of the customers did cancel, since they had no contracts, and a year later, halfway through the payout, the buyer ran into financial problems and stopped paying me altogether, which cost me another million dollars on top of the million that got trimmed off the sale price, plus I got to waste a bunch of time with lawyers deciding if it was even worth suing or not (it wasn't). If I had just made sure my customers were all contracted, I would have pocketed another $2 million and been done with the deal a year sooner. This is the kind of price we can pay by not looking at our business the way a bank does, thinking our baby is cuter than it is, and being in a rush to get through the phases.

———

So what then do we do to make our cash flow predictable, bankable, and sellable? It varies from case to case, but there are some principles we can use to steer our actions once we get through the income phase and it's time to make things bulletproof. This table shows the different mindsets in how we approach business between the income and growth phases.

Income Phase	Growth Phase
Main priority: Generate revenue	Main priority: Create consistency
Do the main things yourself (learn how everything works)	Get help and find people who are better than you at the most important things
Keep expenses low	Invest in responsible growth
Focus on fewer products	Deepen the product stack (ask what else can you sell your customers)
Market to create new customers	Market to create both new and repeat customers
"Wow" by overdelivering to your customer	"Wow" by growing a great brand
Fewer people wearing many hats	Dedicated specialists in critical roles
Avoid debt or dilution of equity	Could consider debt or investment capital

A good exercise is to actually speak to a bank about your business or income vehicle. Nothing forces you to get your act together and level up like being underwritten for credit. Go to three banks and tell them you want an X line of credit for working capital where X is, say, two months' revenues. Depending on your type of business, they will provide you a list of documents you have to submit ranging from the mundane—business certificate, articles of organization, operating agreement—to the challenging—multiple years of audited financials, detailed financial statements for you and the business, your operations manual, your revenue recognition policy, your owner distributions policy, and so on. This humbling experience is the single best way to figure out where you really are and how close you are to having something stable you can use as a basis for the next evolution—the wealth phase.

25

The Wealth Phase

Wealth Phase definition review: Diversifying into (usually income-producing) assets that are outside your primary business or income vehicle, and which are stable, low risk, tax advantaged, and heritable. Ideally, during this phase, the majority of your income shifts to passive sources so you are no longer having to work for money.

The wealth phase is where we get to reap the rewards of all our hard work and actually build the *legacy* that sent us on this crazy odyssey in the first place. When you reach this point, you should be very proud of yourself. It means you first did what most never do, achieving your Awesome Life Number and pushing through the income phase. Then, you kept up the hard work to create predictable, bankable, and sellable cash flow and push through the growth phase. And now, you're ready to create the future you were dreaming of when you started this whole journey. Welcome to the 1 percent! So, what now?

The wealth phase doesn't look the same for everyone, but it does tend to have some commonalities between all of us. Generally, this is when we evolve into the next phase of our life. In business, this might be when we exit, or

IPO, or hire a better CEO than ourselves and sit on the board, or even retire into other work altogether. In ENTRE, we have an entrepreneurial-life-cycle framework we teach called Launch > Grow > Shift. The wealth phase is about shifting—shifting your business, potentially shifting your assets and income sources, and most of all shifting your entire life into your true purpose and whatever gives you the most fulfillment. Obviously, in the wealth phase, we have very different concerns than we did when money was tight or uncertain. In the wealth phase, we think about how to make sure that our assets outlive us and become fuel for the impact we want to have in the world, even after we're gone. In short, we start actively thinking about and planning our legacy.

Legacy. That word gets tossed around a lot, and its definition seems to change with each generation. According to the dictionary, legacy is a fairly boring word that simply means:

1. An amount of money or property left to someone in a will
2. A thing handed down by a predecessor

Nowadays, legacy means more than just money or property we leave to our beneficiaries. I recently saw an Instagram post from Gary Vaynerchuk with the headline, "Legacy is still greater than Currency," so clearly legacy is not just a monetary measure. Obviously, there's more to life than just accumulating assets, but I'm actually glad the dictionary definition is so cut and dry because it reminds us that even if monetary assets aren't all there is to legacy, they're a big part of it. I think sometimes in the modern world it's considered impolite to suggest that money is still the biggest part of legacy. Parents today rightly think about intangibles they are going to leave their children, things like memories, traditions, values, and experiences, not just their estate. And don't get me wrong, I'm not trying to downplay those things or roll back the clock to a more rigid time. I love being an emotionally awake, twenty-first-century man who goes to therapy and cries and handles conflict with words not fists or duels. But I loathe political correctness and do not think coddling feelings is a good reason to be imprecise in language. Legacy involves money. It just does. To say otherwise is postmodern softness that serves no one.

There is good reason that for most of human history, you were expected as a parent to leave assets to your children, and this expectation had a very absolute quality about it, a judgment, even. Until recent times, being a pauper who left no tangible legacy was viewed as a moral failure, not just a financial one. Nowadays, people pass away all the time having spent whatever money they made in their life and leaving their children no hard assets, or worse even, a reverse mortgage to pay off. I don't think that's right. I think we need to bring a little bit of intolerance back to the idea of dying broke and leaving nothing to our kids. Hear me out on this. As parents and human beings, we have both a biological imperative to provide for future generations and a moral imperative to leave a lasting and positive mark on the world, and as comforting as it is to think that having been a nice person or having made people smile constitutes a great legacy, it doesn't. In multigenerational terms, the person who doesn't leave real assets behind when they die doesn't leave any legacy at all. Sure, the small number of people who knew us will be sad for a bit when we pass and hopefully remember us fondly if asked, but if we don't build up, preserve, and operationalize wealth that will outlive us during our life, then our "legacy" is just a wisp of collective memories that quickly fades.

I believe we were meant for more than that, and that although scarcity has always existed and probably always will, it is far more achievable today for *anyone* to build wealth than at any other point in human history. To a large degree (and this is the central premise of this book), building a tangible legacy in the modern world is mostly about making the decision to do so, becoming educated on how, and then being willing to do the intensely hard work that most people aren't to follow through. It is undeniably hard, but also imminently doable, to get and stay uncomfortable, even in a world that constantly tempts us to trade our potential for comfort.

For me, this book is part of my wealth phase. I'm forty-two, I've run the race to get free, and against what most people saw as great odds, I've won. Now, it's time to drive roots so far into the ground they can never be ripped up— roots of wealth, roots of knowledge, roots of opportunity paid forward, and roots of love. I know my story inspires a lot of people (I hear about it on social media every day), but this isn't a story of heroism or overcoming long odds. Nelson Mandela, Dr. Martin Luther King Jr., Gandhi, Mother Theresa, they did *great things* against *great odds*. Me? I didn't defy the odds. I proved how wrong the oddsmakers were. The takeaway from my story isn't that I did the impossible; it's to realize that what I did was always possible, even reasonable. Since my epiphany at sixteen, I've had better odds than most people to create an extraordinary life because I never wasted my time or energy betting on the broken system to deliver me to the promised land. I saw the system early on for what it is, called its bluff, and improved my odds by opting out of it. If I've done anything well, it's been to resist temptation—that's it. I went to a "good school" and came from a "good family." I had the yellow brick road all laid out for me. I could have finished high school, borrowed the money to go to college, majored in something I didn't love, gotten a "good job" that drained my soul, and lived what most people think of as the American Dream, right up to the point where it unravels for most people when they can't retire because the math doesn't hold up anymore.

I had that option the whole time. And honestly, I can't say why I saw the world the way I did; I really don't know. Maybe it's because my dad was an investor. I grew up taking things for granted that I thought everyone knew. I minored in finance in college and it wasn't until my financial accounting class when I saw how confused many people were that I realized financial literacy was not so common. I grew up listening to conversations about net present value of cash flows, internal rates of return, price-to-earnings ratios, leverage, book value, and so on. I remember as a kid looking over the *Forbes* 400 billionaires list and my dad telling me that there were only three kinds of people on that list: people who built companies, people who developed real estate, and people who inherited fortunes. I just always had a sense that the way the world was headed, the "successful" person working a "good job" wasn't really on the right track the way they thought they were. Hopefully this book gets that same message to millions of people; better late than never.

Speaking of this book—this is designed to be a mass market book, written with a goal of reaching large numbers of people and inspiring in them a different set of possibilities for their life. This book is not designed for the person who is already wealthy, so I'm not going to spend much time on specialized advice about what to do in the wealth phase. Instead, I'll give an overview of the types of things you can look forward to in the wealth phase, along with exploring what financial vehicles exist in the market that people can start using now to plant seeds that will blossom when the wealth phase arrives.

Note that these three phases are not equal. Life and business are fluid, and the transition points between these phases usually only become visible in hindsight. Someone in the income phase might have a business that still needs to be managed with a growth phase mindset. Someone in the wealth phase might also be working on a new business that has an income phase of its own. I am currently in the wealth phase of my life but with a business in the growth phase. It's rarely perfectly cut and dry. So, the rest of this book will touch on various financial strategies that I have used or explored in my own journey—particularly the last few years, since I've had enough money and high enough stakes that I really had to become financially savvy. I'll also share books and resources along the way you can learn more from—many of the same books and resources I have used.

26

Investing 101

First order of business: the mandatory disclaimer. I am not a financial advisor and this book does not contain investing advice appropriate for any one person's situation. Everything I say is for education or entertainment purposes only. There, now that's out of the way.

I will start by contradicting most of the investment advice I see out there. I don't think most people need to worry so much about investing. *"Say what, Jeff? Did you really just say not to worry about investing?"* Yes, I did, at least not so much. I believe the average person spends way too much time worrying about which stock or mutual fund to buy, or which 401(k) program to opt into at work. The time and stress we give these decisions reflects an out-of-date mindset that we're going to get wealthy by investing small bits of money into just the right things. I'm not saying don't invest your money, and I'm not saying don't learn about investing your money; I'm saying don't fall prey to the delusion that you're going to build real wealth in today's world by learning to invest small bits of money in just the right way. In my opinion, the average person should be spending the bare minimum of time to feel secure in how their savings is invested, and as much time as possible working on earning a whole lot more to invest. The average American has between $1,000 and $5,000 in savings. There is no investment on earth that can turn $5,000 into real wealth in a normal

301

human lifetime without taking extraordinary risk (like buying Bitcoin in 2010 or some other "time machine" play that only seems sane in hindsight). Until you have at least six figures, preferably multiple six or seven figures, to invest, a simple index fund will do you just fine. The idea that we are going to invest our way to wealth using little accumulated bits of money we save here and there is anachronistic, however common it may be.

So where did this idea of investing small amounts over time to become wealthy come from (other than our Depression-era progenitors)? In 1998, a book was published called *The Millionaire Next Door* by Thomas Stanley. It broke society into two types of people: Under Accumulators of Wealth (UAWs) and Prodigious Accumulators of Wealth (PAWs), and identified seven traits of the PAWs. In general, I like the book, agree with its conclusions, and think a lot of it is relevant today. Of particular interest is that the first trait of PAWs is "high income." Thomas Stanley and I agree that high income is the best predictor of wealth. The other thing I really like that he points out is that there are more millionaires clustered in blue-collar neighborhoods than in white-collar ones. The author was surprised at that finding, while it doesn't surprise me at all. Why? Because blue-collar workers are much more likely to own businesses. If I were trying to get wealthy back in 1998 when that book was written, I'd definitely start a plumbing or electrical company before I'd become a CPA or an attorney. Just look at the deductions—a work truck I can write off versus a BMW I bought just to impress my coworkers? I could start a plumbing business at eighteen with no debt versus starting a law career at twenty-five with six figures in debt. I could use my sales skills to grow rapidly in my area and soon be leveraging the time and effort of other junior plumbers. As an attorney? I'm waiting years, if not decades, to make partner and start earning off the time of other people. *The Millionaire Next Door* wasn't written as a book about business ownership, but that's what it was. Unfortunately, though, that's not how it was understood. The book's title, along with the fact that 75 percent of people who buy books only read the jackets, meant the point was lost, and people took the book to mean that the way to become a millionaire is to be a "guy next door"— just an average guy—who lives frugally and saves his pennies. I've read a lot of articles about how to get rich and this book is probably quoted more than any other, even though it is usually misunderstood.

In 2004, another book was published called *The Automatic Millionaire* by David Bach. It spent thirty-one consecutive weeks on the *New York Times* bestseller list and picked up where the misunderstanding of *The Millionaire Next Door* left off. It told the story of an "average American couple"—him, a store manager, and her, a beautician, whose joint income never exceeded $55,000 a year, yet the couple retired at age fifty-five with $1 million in savings, two homes paid for, and two kids who went through college without borrowing money. David Bach was a fixture on national TV shows like *Oprah* and *The Today Show* for years, telling Americans that if they would skip their $4 Starbucks lattes and put that money in a savings account instead, they would "finish rich." I'm not anti-frugality and I think Starbucks has mediocre coffee at best, but that's bringing a knife to a gunfight if you think it's going to make you rich, or even comfortable, or even able to stop working someday. Maybe at the end of the twentieth century these strategies had a few years of viability left, but now, in my opinion, they do more harm than good because they give the average person a false sense of security.

Let me put it really bluntly: being sixty-five years old with $100,000 and being sixty-five years old with $0 are functionally not that different. Either way, you're broke. Even with $250,000, you're broke, assuming that ever stopping working is part of your plan. Honestly, even at $1 million, you better move to a tiny house somewhere like rural Kansas so you can afford to live out your days. Nobody wants to hear this stuff, but remember when I said that $10 million is the new $1 million (that bit where half my beta-readers said they didn't like this book)? It's true. In a world where short-sighted politicians and greedy bankers are destroying the middle class, and even the professional class's raises lag inflation by 3 percent a year or more, you are either getting rich or going broke; there isn't a middle ground in any future that I'm seeing play out. And getting rich means pushing to hit your Awesome Life Number and get through your income phase, not investing your latte money. You'd better be obsessively working on increasing your income and cutting expenses to create that five-to-one ratio. That's the only plan that's going to work. Any other use of time is a distraction. If investing small amounts of savings is taking time away from increasing your income, don't take the time to do it. If investing small amounts of savings is lulling you into complacency about increasing your income, don't take the energy do it. You get rich through dramatically increasing your income via one of a few income vehicles—probably either sales, a handful of freelance skills, or building a business. Once you've got surplus, and lots of it, then you can have a field day playing real-world monopoly.

Now don't overreact to what I'm saying. I'm not throwing the financial responsibility baby out with the harsh reality bathwater. Of course you should live below your means, save what you can, and set money aside to invest. That's all part of cutting expenses to get to the five-to-one ratio. Just don't confuse a good start with a complete strategy. If I had to put a number on it, I'd say frugality is 10 percent of getting wealthy, while earning a crapload of money is the other 90 percent. Yes, you should have a safety net. I recommend people have at least six months of living expenses set aside that can be accessed at any time. You just have to discipline yourself to work like you have no safety net even if you do. Fires burn nets, so assume a fire is going to break out at any time and your safety net will go up in smoke. Or better yet, pretend you don't have one at all.

If you do nothing else from reading this book, just do some real math on what your financial future looks like if I'm right about inflation and it stays at 6 percent or higher for decades. Use the rule of seventy-two: divide the projected rate of inflation into the number seventy-two, and that tells you how many years until your buying power is cut in half. So, for example, at 8 percent inflation, you would need twice as much money to retire in nine years as you would today (seventy-two divided by eight percent equals nine years).

Consider all the factors. Based on your age, how much will you need to retire well, and by what date? How much are you likely to earn through your job? How much of your income is going to get eroded by inflation? What is the impact of a large unplanned expense or disruption along the way? What are the prospects for your industry as technological progress continues to accelerate? Did you know that according to the Bureau of Labor Statistics the following industries will be largely automated and nonreliant on human labor by 2029?

Aircraft manufacturing and maintenance	Postal service
Milling	Electrical
Nuclear	Textiles and garments
Publishing	Drilling and machine tools
Refractory materials	Photography process

Grinding and polishing	Door-to-door sales and street vendors
Floristry	Executive secretaries and assistants
Printing press operators	Plastic and metal forging
Legal secretaries and assistants	Manufactured housing and mobile home manufacture and installation
Switchboard operators and answering services	Electronics installation and repair
Data entry	Travel
Cutting and trimming	Watches, clocks, knives, small tool repair
Parking and minor law enforcement	Typing and stenography

And did you know these other jobs are also predicted to disappear in the next ten to twenty years based on other sources?

Taxi and rideshare drivers	Pilots
Billing and collections	Land surveyors
Bus drivers	Truck drivers
Automotive and machine repair	Mining
Computer tech support	Most food service jobs
Wrangling, herding, ranching, farming	Referees
Telemarketing	Dispatchers
Air traffic controllers	Insurance underwriters
Sonographers and other medical technicians	Casino workers
Railroad workers	Translators

Purchasing agents	Bank tellers
Cashiers	Disc jockeys
Financial advisors	Jewelers
Semiconductor and microprocessor technicians	Tax preparers
Loan officers at banks and mortgage companies	Lumberjacks
Tollbooth workers	Librarians
Software developers and computer programmers	Flight attendants

On top of all that, did you know that according to a report by Dell Technologies, 85 percent of jobs that will replace these jobs by 2030 don't exist today? That means that when the time comes, if you try to get one of the new jobs to replace your old job, you'll be competing with new college grads who got trained in the new job (unlike you) who also likely still live at home, have no dependents, and are willing to work longer hours for less money than you are.

Does this all have your attention? Like I said, what needs to happen now for the average person is to make more money, and fast. The clock is ticking. Becoming a "millionaire next door" or an "automatic millionaire" through sound financial management sounds laughable if you can't earn even a basic a living. Sales, digital freelance skills (like copywriting, sales scripting, user experience design, conversion optimization, and other skills, mostly marketing related), or owning a business—these are the sure bets. There are others too; I don't know them all, and I certainly don't have a crystal ball. I can't say if your job will exist in ten years or not. But I know that, according to the World Economic Forum, in 2020 and 2021 Fortune 500 companies invested over 5 percent of all combined revenue into automation technologies, with 43 percent of those companies announcing their intentions to scale back their workforce on the backs of those investments. We're talking about a lot of money—Fortune 500 companies represent two-thirds of US GDP so that means roughly 3 percent of all dollars generated in America over those two years was invested into replacing the people who generated those dollars. And considering the bad optics of a company admitting to cutback plans during a pandemic, they probably invested more than they're saying and it's going to be a lot worse than anyone is forecasting. Is there any conceivable way your job could be replaced by a machine or a piece of software? If so, it's probably safe to assume it will be.

I realize all this may be scary and overwhelming, and frankly part of me wonders if I should even be writing it. Then again, I've already impugned the US government, the Federal Reserve, the school system, and every other institution of the broken system, so I probably can't make it much worse at this point. Will this book get *Fahrenheit 451*'d? Am I costing myself a spot on the bestseller list? Time will tell, but I knew on September 27, 2018, when I uploaded my "Let's Get Extreme" video, that I was having my "red pill" moment and there was no going back, so I accept whatever comes from sounding the alarm.

I know this: we have a huge problem on our hands, and solving it is the most important issue of our time. The broken system can only keep all the plates spinning for so much longer. Up to 30 percent of all current global "worked hours" are projected to be replaced by automation by 2030, and while there will be millions of new jobs created in their place, it is unlikely the new jobs will be filled by the older, less-skilled workers who lost their old jobs. Couple this with the looming insolvency of our retirement programs, which we dissected in chapter 23, and there is a very real possibility that tens of millions of people in the United States will be unemployed and unable to support themselves as they age and become infirm in the next ten to twenty years. And tens of millions becomes hundreds of millions or even a billion plus if we talk globally, not just the United States. I don't want to divert into dystopian, sci-fi speculation here, but the scenarios for all of this are not good. We have to solve this problem, for all of us collectively and for each of us individually. And like any big problem, the way we solve this is one step at a time, one person at a time, one decision at a time. So let's start with *you* and do everything in our power to make sure that *you* are not a casualty of the broken system.

For now, I'm going to move on from imploring you that you need to make more money and assume that you've gotten that memo loud and clear at this point. I trust that if you've read this far you are committed to having your own "Let's Get Extreme" moment and making a radical directional change in how you spend your time and how much income you earn. Maybe you've had your moment already? Incidentally, I highly recommend shooting a video when you do. It's totally cathartic and fun to go back and watch the moment you crossed the point of no return. If you post it, tag me, please. Anyway,

I think I've established that absent a major directional change, the average person doesn't have a bright future ahead of them. So rather than beat that horse further to death we'll spend the rest of this chapter on more prosaic investment discussions.

To start, let's talk budgeting and how to allocate our expenses. Are you familiar with the 50/30/20 Rule? It's a nice starting point because it gets you thinking in terms of ratios and is a stepping-stone toward the Awesome Life Number ratio of living on one-fifth of your income. 50/30/20 refers to your ratio of spending on needs/wants/savings. In 50/30/20, you start with your after-tax income and spend no more than 50 percent on things you need, 30 percent on things you want (but don't need), and 20 percent toward savings (which by now you know means investments, not just mattress money). Note this approach uses a different baseline than the Awesome Life Number calculation, which is based on pre-tax dollars and assumes that you're hitting the max tax bracket wherever you live. The 50/30/20 approach, which was popularized by Elizabeth Warren in her book *All Your Worth: The Ultimate Lifetime Money Plan*, is akin to the advice of David Bach, Suze Orman, and Dave Ramsey types, and though it won't allow you to comfortably retire, it is, as I said, a good way to start budgeting expenses in terms of ratios rather than fixed amounts. This way, as you drive your income up, the amounts can adjust proportionately. And again, keep in mind this is after taxes, so you might want to redo the math to account for taxes (one of the major shifts from employee-thinking to entrepreneur-thinking is to start thinking in pre-tax dollars since you pay your own taxes as a business owner). Let's say you are in a 30 percent tax bracket, you could then call this the 30/35/21/14 Plan (30 percent taxes, 35 percent needs, 21 percent wants, 14 percent savings/investing). With the numbers broken out that way, you can see how it's a stepping stone on the way to the Awesome Life Number approach: 40 percent taxes, 20 percent needs and wants, 40 percent savings.

Let's break out a real-world example. Say you earn $60,000 per year, or $5,000 per month before taxes. (Note: if your employer will allow it, please change your tax withholding designation at work so they stop taking your taxes out—that's your money, and you should be allowed to earn the interest on it until the taxes are due!) At $60,000, you can probably get by setting aside only 30 percent for taxes, so that would be $1,500 per month, which you will want to invest in whatever you can find that pays interest but is still liquid, secure, and accessible so you can earn a few extra bucks on that money before you need it to pay your taxes. That leaves $3,500 per month, so that's $1,750 or 50 percent of the remainder to cover *needs* (rent, food, utilities, clothes, transportation, and other essentials), $1,050 or 30 percent of the remainder to cover *wants* (eating out, travel, recreation, entertainment), and $700 or 20 percent of the remainder to cover savings and investments.

Assuming you live this lean, you are now saving $8,400 per year. If you're thirty-five years old, that rate of savings compounded at 6 percent annually would equal $664,000 in savings by the age of sixty-five. That's more than most people, but not even close to where you need to be, which I'm sure is not a surprise. Even in today's dollars, you are already over a million dollars short of a comfortable retirement using even the conservative estimate of most financial planners, which is $2 million to retire in today's dollars. But what if inflation was 5 percent during the same thirty years? In that case, instead of needing $2 million in thirty years, you'd need $8 million, so now you're over $7 million short. Yes, I oversimplified the math and statistically your savings would increase about 2 percent each year, proportional to your raises, but that's still 3 percent short of the rate of inflation *and* assumes you never went a single month without being unemployed, which is highly unlikely considering the average employee changes jobs every twenty months, or about eighteen times in the thirty years of our example.

Now, let's run the example using someone who is obsessed with hitting their Awesome Life Number, had their "Let's Get Extreme" moment, went a little crazy, and is doing *whatever it takes* to get through their income phase. Say you continue to earn $60,000 per year, but you also start an online business you devote your nights and weekends to and are able to earn another $60,000 from a digital side hustle, totaling $120,000 per year. Using the Awesome Life Number plan (40/20/40), this is how you would allocate your $10,000 per month: $4,000/month to taxes, $2,000/month to living expenses (which includes both needs and wants so you start to realize the level of sacrifice I'm talking about making $120,000 a year and living on $2,000 per month), and investing $4,000 per month. Assuming the same thirty-five-year-old starting point, with a thirty-year retirement horizon and investments compounding at 6 percent annually, you would have $3.8 million at sixty-five. And the fact that you started a business means your contributions would have likely increased considerably along the way and you would have realized numerous tax savings, had opportunities for tax-deferred growth, and at some point, could probably sell the business you've built or use business revenues to secure additional capital for investment in further growth. Adjusting for all of that, you could be at $10 million or more by age sixty-five in this second scenario.

These two examples illustrate side by side how no amount of frugal living and smart budgeting is going to help the average person finish life well on an average income. Starting a business or finding some other significant income vehicle to create an anomalous cash flow phase and jumpstart real wealth creation is the only option for the average person to create wealth and build a legacy in this world. Starting a business allows you to do the following:

1. Use a business to increase your income faster than inflation can erode it
2. Live much leaner than most people are willing to do, something that is made easier when you pour yourself into building a business because then you have less idle time to blow money and less fear of missing out (FOMO) to medicate with wasteful spending
3. Reinvest surplus into growing the business, which increases income further and keeps productive dollars away from being taxed
4. Leverage your business to get access to capital and credit you can use for additional investing
5. Build a network of other business owners and investors, which opens up far more attractive opportunities than you'll hear about through your bank, financial planner, or company benefits department

Whatever formula you use to calculate your rate of savings and investment, make sure to be dogmatic and consistent about it. Other things in your life can be flexible, but not this. Think of it as another tax you have to pay; it's nonnegotiable. Learn to live as if that money isn't even there. I recommend using a forced savings method where the money gets pulled out before you see it or have a chance to spend it (*The Automatic Millionaire* got that part right). Use an app like Digit, which we mentioned earlier, or just a recurring auto-transfer from your checking account to savings account. The key is to not stop there but have a plan where that money gets periodically invested into something that produces a meaningful rate of return. Every dollar in that account above what is needed for your six-month security cushion (your monthly needs times six, which equals $12,000 in the $120,000 per year Awesome Life Number example) gets transferred monthly into an investment.

As for what to invest in? Here are some of the options out there today that provide a mix of greater-than-inflation upside potential and liquidity, so that you're nimble if better opportunities come along. Feel free to check out jefflernerofficial.com/resources for an updated list of books, guidance, and other resources.

Investing in Stocks

Warren Buffet is possibly the most successful investor of all time, and he only invests in well-established, financially stable companies. If you're dead-set on investing in individual stocks, you want to invest in a few established companies that you believe in and want to be a part of. If you try to spread your money out across too many companies, you can end up paying a lot in fees based on a large number of smaller orders. I recommend never buying less than $1,000 of stock at one time since trades on non-broker-assisted platforms like E*TRADE or Ameritrade average a $9 fee per trade, so if you are always placing at least $1,000 orders, it means you won't lose more than 1 percent of each trade to fees. I personally like investing in stocks because studying individual companies is also a great way to learn about business and management, and I'm always more apt to do the research on great companies if I'm putting my money into them. But, not all investors want to go that deep, and in my opinion, unless you have six figures to invest, buying individual stocks is a low bang-for-your-buck use of your time.

Index Funds or Exchange Traded Funds (ETFs)

Index funds and ETFs are an efficient way of diversifying your investments while earning historically significant rates of return and avoiding some of the fees you pay with mutual funds. Some of the most popular index funds are issued by the most recognizable names in investing: Fidelity, Schwab, and Vanguard. Index funds are similar to mutual funds in that they represent a pool of holdings into which you can invest with a single purchase, but unlike mutual funds, which consist of stocks individually chosen by the fund manager, an index fund has a predetermined list of stocks they own based on the particular index they track, like the S&P 500, the Dow Jones Index, or the Russell 2000. ETFs are very similar to index funds, but vary in a few small ways that many investors prefer. ETFs trade freely whenever the market is open and can be bought and sold as actively as you want, whereas index funds only change price once per day when at the end of the day, the index fund manager sets the price for the next day. Also, sometimes index funds have a minimum investment of a few thousand dollars, whereas ETFs are available to anyone who can afford a single share. Both index funds and ETFs can be pegged to investments of varying criteria, such as the size of company, industry/sector, type of investment (stocks, bonds, commodities), social causes (sustainability or green energy), currencies, and international exposure (companies doing business in certain other countries). Pretty much anything you can imagine can be invested in via these vehicles without the responsibility of having to track specific stocks. For the average person, just buying an S&P 500 ETF is probably the most efficient way to get upside to the growth of the US economy while minimizing distraction, mitigating risk, and maximizing time available for increasing your income.

Roth IRA

Most entrepreneurs I know shy away from 401(k)s, pensions, and Social Security because we like to be in control of our money, but I am a big fan of Roth IRAs. This is a special type of retirement account that offers tax-free growth. If you put $2,000 into a typical investment account, and it goes up to $3,000, you would have to pay tax on that $1,000 at the end of the year if you "realize the gain" by selling the asset. But with a Roth IRA, you don't. Instead of paying the capital gains tax (which is currently as high as 20 percent, and I suspect will go higher as politicians get desperate to pay for their shenanigans), you are allowed to keep that money and reinvest it inside the same account. That may not sound like much but remember Warren Buffet's first rule of investing—not to lose money—and realize every time you pay taxes, even on gains, you're losing money. If you can keep that extra 20 percent and reinvest it for more growth, it will continue to compound over years and decades. Even small amounts reinvested over time can create a six- or even seven-figure difference after a few decades. And an IRA forces discipline because you get penalized if you take any of that money out before you are fifty-nine years old. That part I especially like because, in general, anything that makes you feel poor, like not being able to access your own money, is a good thing because it gets you focused on increasing your income.

Peer-to-Peer (P2P) Lending

Now we're into what I call "ADHD territory," meaning stuff for people to get involved in because they're bored. Personally, I say just buy index funds or ETFs or trade stocks if you really need some stimulation, but I include this here because I do often get questions about it and I know some people who just love the idea of being the bank, which I can appreciate. With P2P lending you get to make loans, like a bank, only you pool your money with other people and collectively earn interest together. Think of it as crowdfunding for loans. Each investor who contributes to the loan gets paid back their prorated percentage of the loan with interest. LendingClub is a company that has helped P2P lending become a major player in the personal loan marketplace. You have the ability to diversify and invest in multiple loans because you aren't the only person lending the money to the borrower. What makes this so appealing is that there is a predictable rate of return that is consistent with what banks get paid for making loans, but you don't have to have as much money to get started as a bank (obviously).

Real Estate Investment Trust (REITs)

I've seen good results investing in REITs and if you have the bug to do real estate but not enough capital yet to do your own deals, this can be a good place to start. REITs act like a stock, but are basically trusts that own multiple investment properties. This allows you to put your money into a single diversified investment where you own a share of multiple properties. There are multiple ways to get started—one site is fundrise.com—where you can get started with an investment of $500 and the fees are minimal.

Invest in Yourself

This is the number one investment you should make until you reach a state of consistent savable surplus. If you're using 50/30/20, this is an acceptable use of the 20, and if you're using 40/20/40, this is an acceptable use of the latter 40. As you make *the shift* you will start to appreciate how valuable of an asset you are and recognize that investing a dollar in your own growth and education is probably going to yield higher ROI than any dollar of equity you could buy in any business or asset. Whether you're hiring a coach, investing in your business, paying for training, or learning a skill that can help you generate income, investing in yourself can pay you capital gains for life. As an extreme example of this principle, before I started ENTRE, I hired a consultant for $10,000 a month to advise me on a proper launch strategy. I worked with him for six months, and that $60,000 investment easily recouped itself a hundred times over within eighteen months by accelerating company growth and reducing costly mistakes.

Now, let's switch gears to one of my favorite concepts in all of finance. I love talking about this strategy, I love doing this strategy personally, and I particularly love posting videos about it online because it gets people who don't understand it so riled up.

INFINITE BANKING

This is a super powerful concept that I've been doing for over ten years now. It allows you to become the banker in your own life, so instead of borrowing money from a bank, you're borrowing money from yourself. It's all done through a specially constructed whole life insurance policy put together by an insurance broker who understands this model (see jefflernerofficial.com/resources for a referral if interested).

Unlike term life insurance, a whole life insurance policy accumulates a cash value over time. Term life insurance has no cash value and simply pays out a guaranteed cash amount when the insured party passes away. But with a whole life insurance policy, the cash value, which is essentially excess premiums paid into the policy, can be borrowed out of the policy at an interest rate much lower than you would typically pay for a loan without collateral. The reason the insurance company will make this loan is because the collateral is the death benefit on the life insurance. This isn't free money, and you still have to pay back the loan, but if you can't pay it back, the insurance company can't take anything from you; they simply no longer owe the policy beneficiary the loaned amount when the insured party dies. As long as you've continued to make the minimum monthly premium payments, the insurance company simply repays the loan and any outstanding interest out of the death benefit before paying out the remaining balance to the beneficiary.

There are some cons, which are why the mainstream financial media tends to downplay whole life policies, and I don't recommend this policy if all you're after is the life insurance—this is a "self-banking" strategy, not just a way to buy life insurance. That distinction is where most people misunderstand it and criticize it. Whole life policies provide less insurance dollar for dollar than term policies, and the dividend you earn on the cash value is lower than you might earn with other investments, but once you start using your policy as a borrowing vehicle to make purchases you would otherwise borrow money from a bank to make, the whole equation changes in some beautiful ways. You are now able to borrow your own money back from the insurance company at a low interest rate and with no collateral, *while the cash value continues to earn a dividend that is usually pretty close to the interest rate you're paying on the borrowed money.* Really think about that. The money you borrowed is covering most, if not all, of its own interest cost via the dividend, so when you pay yourself back with interest (just like you would a bank), you're actually putting more money into the policy to compound over time and borrow out later if you need it.

These policies are a nifty way to have your cake and eat it too. You can invest your money at a decent rate of return (decent considering the return is guaranteed and virtually risk free), and still have access to the money when you need it by borrowing it back without losing the rate of return it is producing. This can stretch the imagination at first, so I recommend a book called *The 5th Option* by a good friend of mine, Walter Young, to better understand it.

I personally have six of these whole life policies, and I am presently earning a 5 to 6 percent dividend on the cash value of them with absolutely zero risk. Every one of the companies my policies are with haven't missed a dividend payment in over a hundred years. And since there is no risk, I am comfortable funneling a much greater percentage of my personal cash flow through them than I would be otherwise for a single investment. I currently run about 20 percent of my personal income through these policies, knowing I can always borrow the savings back if I need to. I recently bought my wife a new car, which I admit goes against my own advice on not buying new cars, and the reason I was comfortable doing it (other than the obvious "happy wife, happy life" reasoning) is because I knew I could borrow the money from myself and offset the depreciation by paying myself back with interest that would create additional compounded dividends over time. This is honestly a pretty big hack in the financial system. There aren't many investments where you can earn 5 or 6 percent with virtually no risk, especially in the interest rate–suppressed world we live in today. And all of these policies are tax deferred, so you don't have to pay the tax on that income as long as it builds up inside the policy.

Now let me arm you with what you're going to hear if you talk to traditional financial planners and other experts (who usually earn commissions selling alternative products) about this strategy. The first thing you'll probably hear about is "annual rate of return" (ARR). Financial planners and investment advisors love to talk about ARR and will use it as an argument against the whole life policies that are the core of the infinite banking strategy. ARR is for sure an important metric, but it can also be deceptive. Let's say that you have a hundred dollars invested, and it goes down 10 percent the first year, so you're left with ninety dollars. Then, the next year, it goes up 10 percent (from ninety dollars to ninety-nine dollars, a gain of nine dollars, or 10 percent). Well, it sounds like you should be back to even. Down 10 then up 10 equals an average of 0 percent ARR over two years, right? But you actually lost a dollar. Even though the ARR was breakeven, there was really a 1 percent loss. Plus, you probably paid some fees to your money manager. This is a small example of how an advisor could tout breakeven returns over a two-year period, even though his or her clients actually lost money. Manipulating the way they present ARR is one of the most common strategies investment advisors use in their salesmanship. Especially as the time horizon extends, ARR calculations can be very misleading because they don't account for year-to-year fluctuations and they aren't discounted for time or risk. I've seen financial advisors publish ARR numbers over a ten-year period where the real rate of return (IRR, or internal rate of return) was only half the ARR number. However, insurance policies have a "smooth compounding curve" where it's the same year after year with no volatility and no need to discount for risk. There is no fuzzy math in whole life returns, and (this is the key) because they are zero risk, you can afford to put much more of your investment dollars into them than would be wise with other more volatile investments.

Let's look closer at that last statement. As of 2021, the bottom 90 percent of income earners in the United States (those earning roughly $150,000 or less per year) save only 4 percent of their income. Given such a low rate of savings, it is no wonder that people are so obsessed with rate of return. If you're trying to get 4 percent of all the money you ever earn to equal 100 percent of the money you're going to need saved someday, you need it to grow a lot, and fast. Imagine only having 4 percent of your time (roughly six hours per week) to earn all the money you need to live. You'd likely end up making some reckless decisions. But what if the bottom 90 percent of Americans saved 20 percent of their income instead of just 4 percent? If they were saving five times as much, they could be less aggressive in chasing rate of return and still create far more wealth over time. Most people would say the reason they don't save more is because they need the money to live. But what do we spend our money on? The two largest single expenses for most people are a house payment and a car payment, right? So what if we weren't sending those payments to the bank, but we were sending them back to ourselves? In other words, what if the money we saved or invested had been there waiting for us to borrow from ourselves when we needed it to buy a car or a house, and then the income we earn went to paying ourselves back, with interest, instead of making bankers richer? *That's* infinite banking. It's obviously a nuanced strategy to be worked out with an insurance professional, but hopefully you're getting a sense of how powerful it can be.

If you're thinking it all sounds strange and risky (we do often connect those two things), you should know that financially savvy people and institutions do this stuff all the time. In fact, banks and financial institutions have something called *tier one capital*, which means money they have to keep on hand and cannot risk because if they lost it they would jeopardize their ability to operate. Tier one capital is money these institutions cannot afford to lose but still want to generate a return on. Guess what they do with it. Twenty-five percent of all tier one capital among US financial institutions is held in these types of policies, the single largest category of tier one capital investments. And it gets even better. These policies are extremely useful in estate planning and are how many of the wealthiest families in America pass money down generationally. They also protect your money from lawsuits and other types of liability; even the IRS has trouble getting to them if you don't pay your taxes.

One person who illustrated the unique attributes of these policies, albeit distastefully, was O. J. Simpson. After he lost his civil suit for the Nicole Brown murder and was ordered to pay $33.5 million in restitution, many people wondered how he continued to live a comfortable lifestyle. You guessed it. He had several of these policies, and those funds were off-limits to a civil judgment. It's definitely worth talking to an expert about these policies. There are not many financial instruments that are widely used by the largest banks and wealthiest families in the world that are also available and advisable for the average person.

―――――――

Now that we've covered "intangible" investments, or assets you put your money into electronically that you can't touch or see, let's look at the oldest and most wealth-creating asset class in the history of civilization, one that has the added appeal that we can actually touch it and it isn't dependent on computer algorithms to track.

27

Real Talk About
Real Estate

Translated from Latin, "real estate" basically means "real status." For most of human history, your status was a function of your land, so much so that they became synonymous. I believe real estate is the single best way for most people to transition into their wealth phase. As you save your money and use various instruments to grow it, you should be thinking about converting at least a portion of it into real estate once you hit certain junctures. We'll talk about what those junctures are, and while they may vary for different people, I cannot think of a single financial scenario in which someone shouldn't have real estate as a significant portion of their wealth strategy. Of all the asset classes, it's the only one I can say emphatically that I believe everyone should own.

Real estate has so many fundamentals that make it unique and special. More wealth has been created through real estate than all other assets combined in human history. It's the only asset class that is physically impossible to create more of. It's an asset that's relatively insulated from government interference because housing the citizenry is not a role that the government wants to take on itself (that's my theory, anyway). There is also a certain peace that comes from owning something that is attached to the earth, and every real estate investor I know talks about the feeling of standing on their own asset. Providing people a place to live, work, shop, or play is as elemental as business gets, which is why real estate is also the most predictable and consistent investment in the world.

Remember how I said to look at your finances the way a bank does? Well, what's the only asset class a bank is willing to lend many dollars on for every single dollar the borrower puts in? It's real estate, because it's the safest thing to lend on, which means it's also the safest thing to invest in. I've been investing in real estate since my twenties, and other than investing in myself or my own businesses, it has consistently been the best investments I've made.

Here's a quick example of the types of small real estate investments that can make a huge difference in your life. Last year, I got a phone call from a property manager in Houston who manages my rental portfolio down there. He had a deal for me, but I had to move fast. An older couple had passed away and left their townhouse to their three children. The kids started bickering about what to do with it and eventually decided to sell it and split the cash. The house was worth $160,000, and they were looking for a quick cash offer, so it was suggested I offer $120,000. Instead, I offered $95,000 in cash, which was sitting in my savings account thanks to forced savings transfers, and I offered to close in three days. They accepted, and I even closed a day early. That property is now leased for $1,300 a month ($15,600 per year), which even after taxes, insurance, and maintenance, represents about a 10 percent cash-on-cash return on money that was just sitting in a savings account earning half a percent. The property is also appreciating on average probably another $10,000 a year, rents will go up probably 5 percent per year, and because I was able to move quickly, I got the property for $65,000 less than it was worth on day one. In five years it will be worth probably $210,000 and have paid me about $85,000 in cash for a $95,000 investment. That's a $200,000 gain realized on a $95,000 investment in five years, an average rate of return of 25.4 percent, and that's not counting depreciation and other tax incentives. And if/when I sell it? As long as I roll the proceeds into another single-family rental property via a 1031 exchange I won't even have to pay long-term capital gains tax.

Now if you're thinking that it would take you forever to save up $100,000, consider that I could have gotten a loan instead and only needed $20,000. This is what I mean about migrating your invested capital into real estate at certain junctures. This deal happened to fall in my lap, and the unique circumstances called for an all-cash quick close, but I could have just as easily decided that every time that account got to $20,000, I would call my property manager, and say, "Hey, I've got twenty grand, what have you got for me?" Do this a few times, and people will see that you are serious and not just a tire kicker, and they'll start calling you.

As far as how much you need to get started, that changes by market, individual appetite, and timing because real estate prices go up too with inflation. My general rule of thumb is that until someone has $100,000 to invest, they should not consider real estate as something that is going to generate meaningful income for them. That doesn't mean you can't get your hands on a decent rental property with less than that out of pocket, but the income is going to be nominal, and it will take time to generate significant returns through appreciation alone. Fortunately, there are experts who specialize in helping people with different amounts of money get into real estate. I've bought properties through several of them, and as I continue to find qualified professionals and responsible options, I'll add them to jefflernerofficial.com/resources.

A lot of people ask me if they should invest in residential or commercial real estate. This is a question that generates much debate in REI (real estate investing) circles, and there is no right answer; however, I think beginners should start with residential. I personally only dealt with residential properties for my first decade in real estate investing for a few reasons. For the average person, getting financing is much easier on a residential property. The required down payments are lower, and there are more options for people with less-than-perfect credit. Also, residential properties typically rent faster. In almost twenty years now of REI, I have never had a residential property sit vacant for more than two months. My experience has taught me that the name of the game in real estate is to make sure you always have sufficient cushion to weather the speed bumps that come along the way. Reducing the likelihood of a prolonged vacancy ensures you are not stuck paying the taxes and insurance on a vacant property for too long.

Another thing that I've learned is that if something adverse happens to a property (water heater leaks, roof caves in, etc.) it is likely going to be easier to deal with the insurance company on a residential property than a commercial one because there are laws protecting how insurance companies treat residential property owners that force them to be on better behavior than they might be with a commercial claim.

Residential properties are also cheaper to lease. Typical commercial property leasing negotiations involve tenant improvement (TI) allowances, which means the landlord putting their own money up to build out the property for the tenant and then being paid back through a higher lease rate. If you are a cash-strapped new owner who just put all your money into a down payment, you might lose prospective tenants who elect to lease other properties where the owner is offering to advance more TI money up front to build the space out for them. Now that I have built an actual real estate business that generates its own cash flow and provides its own cushion, these concerns are lessened and commercial is an attractive option (and typically produces higher ratios of income to equity), but until your real estate is self-sustaining and you aren't using personal cash flow to fund it, I recommend sticking with residential.

Here are some general principles you can build on as you consider getting involved in real estate.

#1. Knowledge Is Power

You should not be spending money on real estate investment properties if you haven't taken the time to be an expert. Much like everything else, it all starts on the internet. Today, you can go online and figure out everything you need to know. You can learn the cost to acquire the property, estimated rents, and how much money you will have to put down. You can do credit analysis to learn what interest rates you qualify for and get a pretty accurate appraisal. You can almost vet an entire deal sitting at your computer. If you're serious, I recommend that you start crunching the numbers on a deal a day to become proficient. Check out jefflernerofficial.com/resources for some helpful REI spreadsheets.

#2. You Need Solid Credit and Consistent Income

There are videos and programs that try to sell you on the idea that you can start buying real estate with no money, no job, and poor credit. That's not true. Real estate is a leverage-dependent business model where you want/need to be able to borrow money. This is a great thing—using other people's money to (OPM) acquire assets far more valuable than you could afford on your own. But on the other side of the transaction, whoever is putting up the OPM is taking a chance, and no institution is going to take a chance on someone with no money and no credit. There was a time when banks and mortgage lenders actually did that, back in the early 2000s when they were loaning money to people based on "stated income," meaning non-verified income, or even "no doc" loans, meaning zero documentation. They built a giant real estate bubble on making funny money loans to insolvent borrowers, and when the bubble burst millions of people lost their life savings and the entire global economy melted down. Trust me, however badly you want to be able to borrow money with inconsistent income and/or bad credit, it's a better world because you can't. Think of it as one more reason to increase your income. If you want to get into real estate, you have to prove that you can consistently generate income. You will also need to put money down to acquire a property (possibly up to 20 percent), and that money must have been sitting in an account for a reasonable period (usually at least three months, sometimes longer), and it can't have been borrowed or pledged for any other loans.

#3. Invest Only in Markets You Know

There is a level of understanding about a neighborhood that can only come from living there, or from people who do. You learn about the traffic in the area, what neighborhoods are good and bad, what the people are like, what the local job market is like, what the good schools are, whether a neighborhood is mostly renters or owners, and more. You can't learn those things from a flier, and most realtors won't know or won't tell you if they do, unless they are representing you. Investing in properties outside of your market comes with a whole new set of challenges that can be difficult to navigate, so when just starting out, I recommend targeting property in areas you're already familiar with or where you know and trust someone who is.

#4. Understanding Property Classes

You need to be ruthlessly unemotional about real estate. I'd go so far as to say that you should never invest in a property you've got any emotions around, even if it's a good deal, because your emotions make your judgment untrustworthy. When I started buying residential rental properties, I had a buddy who was already an active investor who taught me that instead of looking first at properties, I should start by looking at neighborhoods. The best properties for a beginner to invest in will be found in neighborhoods that have specific qualities. His ranking system for neighborhoods was as follows.

Class A: I call these aspirational neighborhoods. Picture the place where a young couple dreams of living, where there are gorgeous homes with well-maintained yards and great schools. These are great neighborhoods to live in, but not the best to invest in because there is a built-in premium on pricing due to the desirability of the homes. The people who live in these neighborhoods are willing to pay the premium, which drives up prices, lowers cap rates (I'll explain cap rates in a moment), and makes cash flowing on a rental next to impossible. These are the neighborhoods you want to live in, and likely will someday if you do what this book teaches, but they are not the areas to invest in.

Class B: These are lower-middle- to middle-class neighborhoods. The people who live in these areas are often blue-collar business owners and/or low- to mid-level corporate employees. You can spot these neighborhoods by the number of vans and trucks in the driveways with company names stenciled on the side. These neighborhoods are home to good, stable families, including more millionaires than you might expect (remember what *The Millionaire Next Door* concluded about these neighborhoods), and typically have less crime than either A or C neighborhoods (criminals often live in C neighborhoods and either commit crimes close to home or target A neighborhoods). B neighborhoods are what you want to target for an investment property, because they are a good mix of owners to renters—typically 60/40. Since the majority of residents are owners, the properties tend to be well cared for, local codes get enforced, property owner associations are active, and renters are more likely to be long term and even potentially offer to buy the house at some point from the landlord.

Class C: The vast majority of residents in these neighborhoods are renters, and the quality of the neighborhood is typically lower. As a real estate investor, you can't afford to be politically correct; you should simply not invest in these neighborhoods. I've been ranking neighborhoods this way for almost twenty years now, and I still exclusively target Class B neighborhoods for both residential and commercial properties. If it ain't broke, don't fix it!

#5. Get Good People to Check It Out

I once purchased a small apartment complex only to learn after the fact that there was rot in the staircase that ended up costing me $15,000 to repair. Had

I known that before I signed the contract, I could have incorporated the repairs into the deal or at least made it part of the loan so I wouldn't have to pay out of pocket. It was a quick-close deal, and I was competing with another buyer, so if I'd insisted on ordering an inspection, I would have likely lost the property. That was the last time I closed on a property without an inspection, and I usually order an appraisal too. It's also a good idea to develop a working relationship with an accredited contractor who can help you spec out issues and learn how much they will cost to fix. Even if you have home repairs experience, it's unlikely you'll catch everything an inspector would. And even if you do, you won't have the same negotiating leverage you will if the concerns are documented in an inspector's report. Spending $300 to $500 on an inspector's report almost always pays for itself and then some because you can use what they find to negotiate a better deal or get the seller to make the repairs before closing. Take the time and spend the money to pay people who know more to inform you.

#6. Your Financial Metric

There are a lot of money formulas and alphabet soup acronyms in real estate. Some of the courses offered in this area can get so complex that they're intimidating and make people hesitant about even starting, but for new investors, I feel that a lot of that is unnecessary. In my opinion, there are two terms you want to focus on: *cash-on-cash return* and *cap rate*.

- **Cash-on-cash return:** How much money does it take to acquire property and get it to a point where it produces income? And what is your return on that cash? This is unique to every deal and completely dependent on the circumstances. The first property I bought cost me $10,000 out of pocket (5 percent down on a $140,000 house plus $3,000 closing costs). All the other money in a real estate deal is "Monopoly money." It's not yours, so it doesn't count when calculating your cash-on-cash return. I did all the math beforehand and projected that I could rent it out for $1,200 a month. After servicing the debt; paying insurance, taxes and home warranty; budgeting for an assumed 10 percent vacancy (which is high at more than one month per year vacant); and paying for maintenance and property management, I ended up netting around $100 a month or $1,200 per year. On the $10,000 cash I had to come up with to acquire the property, that comes out to a 12 percent cash-on-cash return. That was my first property, and now my target is to average a 15 percent cash-on-cash return.

- **Cap rate:** This isn't based on money in and money out; it's tied to the value of the property, the money coming in from operating the property, and the long-term value. The cap rate formula is the net operating income (NOI) of the property, which is (income – operating expenses*) ÷ (purchase price of the property).

*Note that operating expenses do not include debt service or repayment of any money borrowed against the property. Hypothetically, if a property was bringing in $1,200 a month and, exclusive of debt, it cost $500 to operate (taxes, insurance, repairs, maintenance), that gives me a NOI of $700 a month or $8,400 a year. Let's say I paid $90,000, but the property was actually worth $110,000 (meaning I bought it with $20,000 in equity). I would divide my $8,400 a year by my purchase price of $90,000 and come up with a 9.3 percent cap rate. That's a good cap rate as long as the property is in a B neighborhood, not a C. You can often get higher cap rates on lower quality properties, but investing in a C neighborhood is still not worth the long-term headache and potential problems in my opinion. The one time I did it, I learned the lesson the hard way—a story for another book, but take my word for it.

I recommend shooting for at least an 8 percent cap rate in a B-class neighborhood. Your cap rate is based on your purchase price of the property, but when you go to sell a property, you should quote them a cap rate based on what you want their purchase price to be. So, on that 9.3 percent cap rate example, if you wanted to sell the property for $120,000, your potential buyers would be evaluating the deal as a 7 percent cap rate from their point of view ($8,400 dived by $120,000).

These are two very important numbers to know about any property before you consider purchasing it. If you can find properties that have close to 15 percent cash-on-cash returns, an 8 percent cap rate, and are in a B neighborhood or better, you've probably got yourself a solid deal. Just make sure to confirm that with an inspection and an appraisal. The "15-8-B" rule is a KISS approach to real estate investing (keep it simple, stupid). You can always get into more sophisticated transactions and metrics, but this is a good place to start. It's also important to keep in mind that your standards for each of these items may be different than someone else's. Some investors don't need to turn a profit as quickly. They might be looking to double their money in ten years, so they can invest in properties in better neighborhoods with a lower cap rate. My advice is based on people who are accumulating cash for one deal at a time, like I was when I started.

THE MAGIC FORMULA

The only way to get experience in real estate is to dive in, and that means doing it for the first time without the benefit of experience. There is a saying in real estate that you make your money when you buy. That means that you build in your cushion and your margin of error when you buy a property. When it comes time to pull the trigger, this formula is the closest I can give you to a security blanket so that your first deal is a success.

A. Never buy a property for more than 90 percent of market value. Yes, this makes it harder to find the right property, and it will take longer, but it gives you added protection. There is no certainty in real estate, and bad things can happen. If you have to sell quickly, that means you have to price it below market value and pay a realtor full commission, but if you paid only 90 percent of the original market value, you could still come out ahead. If they don't accept your offer, so what? Move on. You won't run out of properties to make an offer on. I'd rather have twenty lowball offers get denied than ever overpay out of eagerness. You can't get emotional or be impatient. You have to wait for the right opportunity.

B. Negotiate around the numbers you need to hit. If a seller has a property listed at a price that puts your cash-on-cash return or cap rate too low, just submit a low offer and tell them why your offer is what it is. That way, the seller knows they're dealing with a serious investor, and although they may not like your low offer at first, if they don't get the offer they want from someone else, eventually, they might take yours because they know you're a professional and are likely to close smoothly. A lot of sellers will list a property for more than they are willing to sell it for, hoping to get a quick hit or an unsophisticated buyer. Be the sophisticated buyer waiting in the wings in case they don't find a sucker.

C. As a general rule, rent should not be less than 1 percent of the purchase price of the property. For the property I purchased for $90,000, I wouldn't rent it for anything under $900. The rent for that property was closer to $1,200, so it checked that box. Before you buy, you want to do an analysis of rents in the area on sites like Zillow and Trulia so you know what you can expect to get. The 1 percent rule is an unscientific measure, but it's a shortcut to not wasting time evaluating deals that won't work once you take the time to crunch the numbers.

D. At a bare minimum, the cap rate must always be equal to or greater than your cost of capital. Your cost of capital is the average interest rate on all of the money you had to borrow. To calculate that, you multiply the percentage of the purchase price times the interest rate for each loan used to acquire a property, add those numbers together, then divide by the total percentage of the property you financed. So, let's say you borrow 80 percent of your purchase price at 6 percent then get a second mortgage for 10 percent of the purchase price at 8 percent. In that case, you financed a total of 90 percent of the purchase price with two loans. The calculation would be ((80% x 6%) + (10% x 8%)) ÷ 90% = 6.22%. In that case, you would never want your cap rate to be lower than 6.22 percent or else you are paying the bank more for the financed portion of the property than you are earning on it.

E. Don't get in over your head. Life may be unpredictable, but to offset any emergencies or problems, I recommend that you have a reserve fund equal to the cost of owning the property for six months if it were vacant. After the down payment, closing costs, and repairs, assume that you won't be able to rent it out for six months and make sure you have enough money to ride that out.

Why do you need to think this way? I bought a nine-unit apartment complex (the same one with the wood rot in the staircase), and after a few years of owning it, there was a massive hailstorm that put holes in the roof. Pretty soon, all nine of the apartments were leaking water from the ceilings, and I was contractually obligated as landlord to fix it. The repairs were going to be $20,000, so I filed an insurance claim. That was all fine, except for one problem: the insurance company insisted on using its approved contractors, but because the entire city had been hit by a hailstorm, their contractors were busy and it would be months before they could get to the property. My options were to either hire my own non-approved contractors, pay for the repairs out of pocket, and hope the insurance company didn't try to deny the reimbursement, or to wait months for their people to be available.

If I had waited months, the tenants would have understandably moved out, and possibly sued me for breach of my covenant as a landlord to provide them with a habitable dwelling. So, of course, I paid for the repairs myself and waited months for what ended up being only a partial reimbursement. It was frustrating, but much better than the alternative. If I hadn't had a reserve fund, I would have been stuck, the tenants would have moved out or sued, and I would have lost the property. A nine-unit property is considered commercial, so the insurance company could pretty much do what they wanted, and my only recourse would have been to sue them, spend far more than the $20,000 they owed me on attorneys, and still lose the property to the bank while waiting a year or more for the lawsuit to resolve. You get the point: to be successful in real estate investing, you need to have a reserve fund so you can weather the inevitable storms (pun intended).

AIRBNB HAS CHANGED THE GAME

This is something I've recently started doing after a friend of mine created one of the most successful courses online on how to do vacation rental investing. There's an art to it, and not every property makes a great short-term rental (nor are many properties zoned to allow for it), but for the right property, you can make an absolute killing renting it on Airbnb, Vrbo, or other short-term rental sites. If you're wondering about a property's viability for this approach, you can get a fairly accurate prediction of its short-term rental rates on a site called airdna.co. There are other sites, but that's the one I prefer because it pulls data from Airbnb, HomeAway, and Vrbo.

Short-term rentals operate from a completely different set of economics than long-term rentals because you're competing with hotel pricing, so you can charge much more per week and night than you would charge the average renter. One of my short-term rentals is in Atlanta. It's about a $400,000 value property that would fetch maybe $2,500 per month as a long-term rental (far short of the 1% rule). Instead, I consistently rent it out on Airbnb for $350 per night, and it's rented at least 20 days a month. That's $7,000 a month in income, so even after I pay the full-service 30 percent management fee (so I don't have to lift a finger to manage it), I still bring home about $5,000 per month, or double what it would bring in as a long-term rental. And the best part is that if I ever have to go to Atlanta, I have a place to stay for free. Personally, I know people who own short-term rentals in locations all over the world so they can travel using the income the properties generate and never have to pay for hotels by staying in their own properties.

One little known strategy involving short-term rentals is to use properties you don't even own. That's right, in many areas, you can sign a long-term lease on a property, and then sublease it on Airbnb or any of the rental sites, which means you don't have to put any money down and can keep the difference between the long-term rental cost and the short-term rental income. This is a great way to get started with short-term rentals for people who do not yet have the funds to acquire properties themselves.

Why would a property owner agree to let you sublease the property rather than just leasing it out themselves on Airbnb? You never know the situation of a property owner. They may not need that much income. Maybe they inherited the property or own it outright and just want to keep things simple. They may be intimidated by technology and think it sounds complicated. They may only want to deal with one person. They may have a loan on the property with a covenant that they will only do long-term rentals, or myriad other reasons. I know multiple people who tie up properties with long-term leases then turn around and list them on Airbnb and do very well. Just make sure you research the market so you aren't violating any local ordinances or laws.

No matter what approach you take, the important thing is to get started. You don't want to be in over your head, but I firmly believe that you don't wait to buy real estate, you buy real estate and wait. It may start slow at first. It took me a decade to acquire my first few properties while barely making ends meet as a jazz musician, but eventually, it starts to snowball. Real estate allows you to tap into leverage and growth potential unlike any other investment on earth. Just heed my comment about keeping adequate funds in reserve, using conservative estimates, and following the ground rules I've laid out on cash-on-cash returns, cap rates, and neighborhood classes (say to yourself, *"15-8-B will set me free!"*). Be smart. Leverage works both ways, and if you get in over your head, you can find yourself with a way bigger mess than you have the resources to clean up.

That covers the basic real estate primer and wraps up our section on investing. Now in the final chapter, I want to dive into the single most important concept that has to underlie any effort to escape the broken system. This single adjustment to the old-world paradigm is not only the key to long-term success in the modern world but also to unlocking previously untapped stores of joy available to any of us that choose this way of living day to day. A quick perusal of the jobs that are being replaced in the coming decades shows that the utility of man's body is decreasing. The economy isn't going to need us for our hands and backs much longer. Cars will drive themselves, freight will move itself, ultrasounds will administer themselves, toilets will plunge themselves. We will no longer be valued or needed for our availability to do physical things because machines can do them faster, longer, and with more precision. In the not-too-far-off future we will be measured and compensated entirely for the capabilities of our minds, our personalities, and our character. Pushing buttons won't be part of the job anymore. Our ability to think creatively, our ability to inspire others to action, our ability to make non-intuitive connections that can't be programmed into or predicted by a machine, our ability to sift through solvable problems to find the right problems to solve (and then assign them to machines to solve them), our ability to make art and make people feel things—these are the skills of the future. And in this paradigm shift the one variable most affected is time. We used to be needed for our time. The world needed us to sit for hours in a textile mill or behind the wheel of a taxicab. Soon we will only be needed for whatever time it takes to think and create. The doing will be out of our hands. And this is happening already. As the world shifts toward remote work, we're already seeing less and less of a "clocking in" mindset among employers. Sure, some are still resisting (even going full "big brother" installing monitoring services on home-based workers' computers), but the die is cast and the change is happening. We are heading toward a world where we will be entirely measured by the quality and efficacy of our work. There will no longer be credit or compensation given just for spending time on things. This is a terrifying proposition for a lot of people who think of work primarily as a trade of time for money. How it all shakes out will be interesting to watch but there is one group that will not be affected in the slightest—the entrepreneurial among us.

If I were to say simply "the entrepreneurs among us," I would only be referring to people who start businesses, but I say "the entrepreneurial among us" to include everyone who is compensated *only* on the quality of their work and the value they create, with no value placed on the time they spend. This is the single biggest distinction between the entrepreneurial and everyone else—the desire, even the insistence, that compensation should only correlate to value created, not time spent. For business owners, this is our only option, but I would apply this description to other categories too. Commission-based salespeople are highly entrepreneurial in this way. Consultants, good ones anyway, are highly entrepreneurial in this way. Athletes, artists, and most performers are entrepreneurial in this way. And I'll promise you, if you don't already think this way, learning to will get you paid a lot more than trying to sell your time.

As founder of ENTRE I never got paid for the year I worked for free laying the groundwork. Nor should I have been (and if I'd wanted to be I could have sold something sooner). LeBron James spends most of his work time practicing and training, but the value he brings in games gets him paid plenty. Can you imagine him trying to bill his team for his practice time? I have salespeople I pay seven figures a year with zero clue how many hours they work. I'm paying for their results, not their time. All the highest-paid people in the world get paid for results. This is why even though this book isn't saying you absolutely have to start a business, it is absolutely saying you have to learn to think entrepreneurially.

This one concept must be understood and embraced. It's also the concept I see people struggle with the most as they transition from employee thinking to entrepreneurial thinking. *"I've been working on this business every night for six months and haven't earned a dime. It's not fair!"* This is a common type of lament from someone who hasn't completely made *the shift*. Among entrepreneurs there is a saying, "No one cares; work harder." For a lot of people, making that shift and accepting that no one cares about your time anymore is the first piece of hard work to be done. It's time to stop thinking about time and become completely obsessed with value. In the world we're heading into, what's always been true for the entrepreneur will be true for everyone—that until and unless the market feels your value, and agrees with it, you won't be paid a dime. Personally, I'm excited for that world and am doing everything I can to usher it in. One of the things I picked up early on being outside the broken system was how often people settle for less than they're capable of because we live in a world that will pay them for less than their best. When you can get paid just to show up, you'll show up just to get paid. Ick. Wouldn't we take more pride in what we did if we had to be our best selves and provide huge amounts of value to others just to survive? Well, that's the world I believe we're heading toward and I'm glad for it.

28

Doing Work vs. Creating Value

S
o, who actually gets to achieve their full potential and live their best life? A quick glance at history shows that it's not everyone. Scarcity is a disease we have not yet eradicated and to which any person is susceptible under the right circumstances. But in a world where four thousand new millionaires are created every day with 88 percent of them being self-made, where compensation is shifting to favor value creation over trading of time, and where all the information a person could ever want about health, wealth, relationships, and all other determinants of quality of life are just an internet search away, the idea that success is primarily dependent on external factors, things like "being born with a silver spoon" or even just "catching a lucky break," is not only disempowering, it's dead wrong. Especially when we use a holistic definition of success that includes all 4 Ps—*physical, personal, professional,* and living a life of *purpose*—we find very little footing for our familiar excuses. More than any world that has existed previously, the modern world gives us every chance to create our dream life and thus forces us to constantly ask of ourselves, *"Do my habits and my schedule reflect my indisputable and unwavering commitment to the attainment of my best possible life?"*

Let's revisit this passage from chapter 15:

When your schedule is a masterpiece of organized 4 Ps living where you know every box of life is getting checked and every stressor is one you chose with intention, you stop looking for escapes and start trying to avoid them. Even sleep gets annoying when the life you wake up to every day is this on track. On that note, if you take nothing else from this chapter, please let this quote reverberate in your mind. *"Show me your schedule; I'll show you your future."*

At ENTRE, we have a very specific way we describe the person we are looking to enroll as a student. It's similar to the person this book is written for, a person who is three things that are not commonly found together: an insatiable dreamer, a lifelong learner, and a hard worker. Most humans were born dreamers and learners, but not so much hard workers. As kids, we lacked discipline, grit, and other hard worker traits. As we grew older, we (hopefully) learned about hard work, but unfortunately, all that "keep your feet on the ground" talk we heard from the adults in our lives beat the dreamer out of most of us. Meanwhile, school was busy robbing us of our love of learning by converting it from being something fun into being a measuring stick we used to compare ourselves to each other. By the time most of us are eighteen, or twenty-two, or whenever we finish going to school, learning has become unpleasantly synonymous with "passing or failing" or some other form of being rated or judged. I am forever indebted to Theodore Roosevelt for one of my favorite quotes that crystallized exactly how school ruins learning for children, or at least how it ruined it for me, when he said, "Comparison is the thief of joy." Very few of us make it out of childhood as hard workers who also have our ability to dream and love of learning fully intact, which is why so many people are struggling as the old American Dream fades and the New Dream emerges around the world. Speaking of Theodore Roosevelt, here's a quick tip. I strongly recommend you keep a copy of his *Man in the Arena* speech excerpt on your phone to refer to whenever anyone else in your life gets you down. We cannot be reminded often enough that *"It is not the critic who counts . . .",* nor can we be excessively warned not to end up one of the *"cold and timid souls who neither know victory nor defeat."*

The future belongs to those in the arena, those of us who dream and learn like children, while also working like "those possessed." It's the way it is now and if we lean into it, we'll be better for it. Critics, naysayers, skeptics, middle-management ladder climbers, our own family members, and, dare I say, many of the teachers in the broken system, are clinging to a time when they mattered more and the social norm was to let them tell us what to think. I remember when Gene Siskel and Roger Ebert told my parents what movies to watch, and *Consumer Reports* magazine was the go-to for electronics reviews. I remember when the piano faculty told me I'd never be a professional pianist, and my ex-father-in-law told me I was arrogant for wanting to be an entrepreneur instead of an employee like him. I remember the teachers who told my parents about the limits of my potential and tried to lower their expectations. I remember in 2008, when I told one of my best friends I was going to start "marketing products on the internet," and he replied, "I wouldn't say that to too many people. Sounds like a scam." For years I wished for a world where the opinions of others meant less, then one day I realized that was always my world to choose. It's yours to choose too, and thankfully that choice is getting easier.

One of the often-missed benefits about all the haters and trolls now having social media platforms to paint with their vitriol is that it's gotten easier to dismiss wholesale the opinions of others, since now the vast majority of those expressed are so unqualified and unconstructive. Embrace this new reality and tighten your circle of advisors to only include people who have the kind of life you want. There are almost eight billion people in this world, and technology is making most of us unnecessary in terms of keeping the world turning, and the recoil for many is to sound off about it. All such noise should be ignored. Let automation, machine learning, artificial intelligence, robotics, web 3.0, the internet of things, and other technological progress continue to marginalize those whose primary contribution to the world has been visionless "hard work" and/or or the wanton expression of mostly negative opinions. Their troubles are imminent; you just do you. And for goodness sakes, if you've lost it even a small bit, start rekindling your love of learning and your willingness to dream big dreams.

If you want to succeed in the world we're heading into, that's what must be done. All three of those legs must be in place—dreaming, learning, and working hard—if the stool of your life is to stand. I know that recalibrating our work ethic to also include dreaming and learning in equal parts presents a challenge for a lot of people, and understandably so. In the old world, dreaming, and even learning to some degree, could hold you back; I've interviewed enough people transitioning from corporate jobs to entrepreneurship to know that most corporate cultures are not designed to reward the people who dream the biggest and learn the most. For this, as much as much as any financial reason, I am an evangelist for entrepreneurship and any form of life outside of most corporate jobs. Life is just so much more fun when you can be childlike in these two ways.

I became an educator mostly because I love to learn, and teaching is one of the best ways to reinforce learning. I want to continue to grow my own knowledge base around how to be successful in this world and to keep showing people that there is a much different way to do things than the way we've been taught. This crusade of breaking people out of the broken system has become my life's purpose, and being the first guinea pig of what's in this book, and subsequently seeing thousands of others thrive with these principles too, has validated not just how to do it, but the fact that anyone can. My hope for this book is that it brings a million or more people to a similar reality of getting to dream and learn not just as part of making a living, but as the foundation of building an amazing life. So let's talk about how to stimulate our dreaming and learning muscles.

There are so many avenues available now to learn from and model brilliant and successful people. Twenty years ago, I had to be invited into the home of a billionaire to learn from him. But now, I can turn on any one of a dozen TV shows like *Shark Tank* or *Undercover Billionaire* and learn from them any day of the week. The hardest thing now isn't finding people to learn from or be inspired by, it's deciding which ones to give our attention to. Which teachers will you choose to grant the authority to lead you? That is one of the biggest questions you must answer to determine the course of your life. Now that we aren't letting the broken system tell us who our teachers are, it's time to choose our teachers for ourselves.

And you must choose wisely. You are most influenced by those to whom you grant authority in any form, and agreeing to learn from someone is to grant them authority. Over time, you evolve into a hybrid of whoever you have been in the past and who you are influenced by in the present. The best way to change your life is to take absolute dictatorial control over who you let into your mind. If you want success, find people who have succeeded and learn only from them while unforgivingly blocking out those influences who have not had the success you want.

But there's a twist to this principle. Just finding successful people is not enough. You will go much further if you find successful people whose origin and outcome you can relate to. Consider two examples of people whose accomplishments are obviously mighty: Jeff Bezos (founder/CEO of Amazon) and Jamie Dimon (CEO of Chase Bank). Both are fantastically wealthy and no doubt have many good habits and success traits to teach us, but how much do you have in common with them, and how directly will their playbooks for their lives apply to yours? I'm not sure there's much opportunity left to create an online mega-retailer, as Amazon has that pretty well sewn up. And the odds of becoming the CEO of a major US bank are equally slim, no matter how closely we mirror Jamie Dimon's modus operandi. I remember when I was young and looking for guidance, I would dig into the stories of all these wealthy and famous people, and although they were often inspiring, I rarely came across stories that could directly inform my own. It took that Lake Tahoe event full of misfits *like me* for me to realize that a misfit like me could succeed and to show me roughly what it could look like. You remember that event, the one with the muffler salesman, nightclub bouncer, personal trainer, mortgage officer, and amateur bodybuilder who had all become digital marketing multimillionaires? Those were the people I needed to meet and learn from. I'm pretty sure meeting Jamie Dimon at that time would not have had the same effect. What kind of people do you need to find and learn from to get information that is actionable and relevant to your own life?

This is why I think my story has gotten the traction it has and why I ultimately got asked to write this book. I didn't leave a cushy Wall Street job and raise millions from friends and family to start a dot com like Jeff Bezos. I didn't graduate from an Ivy League school and get hired at my dad's company like Jamie Dimon. I didn't get hired to be president of one of the largest real estate companies in New York City by my daddy to kickstart my real estate career like Donald Trump. I dropped out of high school to play the piano and got my butt kicked for over a decade by the school of hard knocks, all while being ridiculed not only by the straight-and-narrow types for my refusal to participate in the broken system but also by fellow musicians for my refusal to accept being poor as part of escaping it. I spent most of my life as a true misfit, a literal "miss fit," who didn't fit in inside the system or out of it. The concepts in this book are what saved me. I've been able to build a life outside the broken system far better than anything it ever dangled in front of me. Of course I realize there is no one single path to success, and my intention here is not to didactically tell you what your exact path should be, but I do steadfastly believe that the principles and facts laid out in this book suggest a general path that is the best chance for millions of people to live their New Dream in the modern world. For purposes of reinforcement let me briefly summarize what that general path looks like.

THE PATH

First and foremost, we must be highly disciplined to succeed in the modern world. I suggest striving to live a life so unyieldingly consistent it seems rigid to the people around you who are less committed to their goals than you are to yours. Every day make your 3 Ps deposits (at least one meaningful action of physical, personal, and professional growth) and pursue your fourth P (purpose) with determination and clarity. For many that starts with doing the work to figure out why you're on this earth in the first place. I don't just mean to survive or even to feed your family, I mean *what is the mission of impact you were born for that makes a difference to others, not just you?* From there, take great pains to engineer the 3 Legs of Successful Action into every nook and cranny of your life—the right knowledge, environment, and resources should be omnipresent. And, at all times, be consciously considering the phases of legacy. Know where you are in them and thus what your focus should be. At ENTRE we call this trio of ideas the 3x3 Success Matrix (the 3 Ps of Success, the 3 Legs of Successful Action, and the 3 Phases of Legacy) and more than any business tactic or strategy we teach it gets credited with changing people's lives positively and permanently.

I know this formula is not going to be for everyone, and certainly creating an entrepreneurial income vehicle will feel like far too big a shift for many. There are still doctors, lawyers, and MBAs having great lives and for the foreseeable future many more will want to go in those types of directions, but the numbers in those camps are dwindling and we know for certain new graduates entering historically high-paying, white-collar fields have a drastically different experience in front of them than their predecessors. According to the 2018 Future of Healthcare report, 70 percent of physicians would not recommend a career in medicine to a child today. And that was before the pandemic. As for MBAs, Elon Musk has this to say: *"They don't teach people to think in MBA schools. In fact, if you are in business and want to work for SpaceX, you will have a better chance getting hired if you do not have one. I hire people in spite of an MBA."* Times are definitely a-changin'.

But until the broken system changes, school-age children are going to continue to be railroaded down these paths and deprived of learning about the others that exist, just like you likely were. So, for now, discovering alternative paths will continue to require concerted, individual effort just like you have expended in reading this book. Congratulations on that, by the way. Let me just say I hope you didn't come all this way just to come all this way. Now it's time to find someone to emulate and learn from, someone who is blazing a trail of success in the modern world through outlier effort, willingness to dream, obsession with learning, and rejecting the outdated principles of a world that's fading like the old dream it was. If I end up being that person, thank you, I'm humbled. If not, no offense taken; just please find someone you resonate with who's legitimate and inspires you to believe in what's possible for your life. Just be wary of Instagram influencers posting from fake private jets.

And why should we do all this? To get rich? Sure, that's cool, but ultimately it's to get what we all really want even more than money. Happiness. A 2010 study by Daniel Kahneman at Princeton analyzed the relationship between money and happiness, and this is what he found. There is a direct and not surprising correlation between income and happiness up to about $100,000 per year (in 2021 dollars), the level up to which merely having more money creates convenience and reduces stress. But beyond $100,000 per year, it's not how much money we make but rather how much we are able to spend *in the right ways*. Obviously, to spend more we have to earn more, and using the 40/20/40 rule we know we actually need to earn five times more than whatever we want to spend, but for now we'll just keep the conclusion simple. According to Kahneman's study, above that "convenience threshold" the correlation between money and happiness comes from spending money on three things. The first is spending money to create memorable experiences, like vacations or time with family. The second is spending money to free up time, like hiring someone to do the lawn or laundry. And the third is spending money to help others. I have found all three of these to be true, especially the last one. One of my favorite quotes that I think about whenever old conditioning or some spiteful internet troll tempts me to feel guilty for preaching capitalism and the profit-motive is, *"Whoever says money can't buy happiness just hasn't given enough away."* On that note, let's dig into how we do get paid in the modern world, specifically how what we do gets valued and compensated.

THE MODERN-WORLD VALUE FORMULA

The problem with so many online courses and modern business training is they feed into the modern zeitgeist of deemphasizing the individual and putting our faith in the collective. Marketers know that people tend to be insecure and not believe in themselves so they are incessantly selling us on the idea that someone or something else is what will make us successful.

Think about the types of ads you see for how to make money in the digital economy: "Start an Amazon store and all your dreams will come true!" or "This simple Instagram cheat code unlocks the vault of influencer riches." These ads all use passive language that downplays what you'll have to do and overhypes what will be done for you or given to you. These promises pander to our insecurities as humans and keep us stuck thinking success is about finding the right external thing to plug into our lives. Of course, some income vehicles have better odds or more potential than others, but whichever vehicle you choose, *you* will be the driver, and if you haven't done the work on yourself to make success your foregone destiny, all roads lead to the same scrapyard.

Simply put, success is not about a business model, an industry, a career choice, or a guru. Success is about the value you create in the world. And there is a simple formula for determining the value you create in the world. It may look confusing at first, but I promise it's quite simple. The modern-world value formula is:

$$(S + I + C) \times P$$

The variables in the formula are:

S: Skills
I: Industry
C: Character
P: How you get paid

Let's break that down.

Skills

There are all kinds of skills that pay well, and we discussed many of them already. Copywriting, sales funnels, offer creation, behavioral psychology, and financial analysis are all skills that have a lot of value. There are three criteria for valuing a skill: How urgent is the need for it? How many people can do it? How good are you at it?

It can be a tough pill for people to swallow that the first criteria (urgency of need) is not enough to justify high pay in the free market. We constantly hear bemoaning of low pay for critical categories like teachers and first responders, but when we combine these criteria, we quickly see why these careers don't pay better. There is no scarcity in those careers. A lot of people can learn to do those things and many people in the world will accept a trade of low pay now for perceived long-term security (pension, benefits, etc.), so the market compensates accordingly. These are also professions in which results and processes are standardized (a fire is either out or it isn't, a student either graduates or doesn't) so it's hard to quantify who's good, better, and best at it. And finally, they are careers that de-emphasize individual achievement and focus more on team or community outcomes. For these reasons and more, these jobs are unlikely to pay a high income anytime soon, no matter how unjust we insist that is. Obviously, I am thankful for the work many of these people do and grateful they choose to do it, but no one made that choice blindly and we interfere with how the market values skills at great peril to our economy and overall well-being. Every failed economy in the history of the world has involved, at least in part, an attempt to force people to pay for and/or be paid for things differently than how the free market otherwise would.

Be really honest with yourself. What are the skills you have to offer others and how valuable are they based on the three criteria above? Are you waiting for the market to pay you more than it deems you to be worth based on your skills? Or are you working on acquiring more valuable skills so the market will reconsider your worth?

Industry

Whether we have a job, do freelance work, or run a full-fledged business, this fundamental stays the same: we are taking whatever skills we have and applying them to an industry. And the value of those skills is a function of both what the skills are and which industry we apply them to. Accounting skills are more valuable in the oil and gas industry than the floral industry. Design skills are more valuable in high fashion than mobile-home manufacturing. And industry value is calculated similarly to skills—how much people need the industry, how many people work in the industry, and how good you have to be to work in the industry. If you're a cardiologist, then people really need your services, you are in a relatively uncommon field, and you better be pretty good when people's lives are on the line. Thus, cardiology tends to pay really well. If you do car detailing, you're a "nice-to-have," not a "must-have," and your industry has a low barrier to entry. Your only shot at making a lot of money is to be the best because there is a market of high-end car owners who will pay a premium for that. But only to a point. I have some really nice cars but would never pay my car detailer what I'd pay my cardiologist. Again, be honest with yourself. How essential is your industry to those who want or need it? How competitive is it? And how good do you have to be to be good enough?

Character

If I could sum up the problem with our educational system in one sentence, it would be simply that we don't teach young people personal development. Stephen Covey nailed this in *The 7 Habits of Highly Effective People* when he observed that in the past, especially prior to World War I, success was associated with what he called *character ethic*, which is traits like integrity, humility, hard work, loyalty, self-control, courage, justice, patience, modesty, and morality. He contrasts this with how modern society (after World War I) focuses on *personality ethic*, which he defines as personality traits, skills, techniques, and "maintaining a positive attitude." I agree with him that we need to get back to "universal and timeless principles," and I also applaud his foresight for where the world was headed (he died in 2012).

In his follow-up book, *The 8th Habit*, he defined the need to "find your voice and inspire others to find theirs." This habit captures a lot of what this book has been about and what I agree is now a nonnegotiable element of success in the modern world. Covey is right that your highest level of success will be personalized and cannot possibly look like anyone else's. Each person's success is as unique as their voice or fingerprint, and when you find it, it inspires others to seek their own.

But I want to take this a step further. In the future I see, both ethics converge. To succeed now, Covey is absolutely right—we need to bring back character ethic—but in the noise and clutter of the new world it also takes personality ethic to be seen and heard. The old-world success formula was to have high character and apply it to the right fields (banker, lawyer, doctor, engineer, CPA, etc.). Now we become successful by having high character and doing what it takes to carve our own path. The reason most people today are not successful is usually because they're too much of one or the other. We have old-school professionals wondering why they still aren't on track to retire well, even though they have high character and did everything they were supposed to, and we have a new generation of creators and self-promoters that have big personality ethics but never got the memo about character. The right balance of both is how you create your dream life in the modern world.

How You Get Paid

Finally, we add those three areas up (Skill + Industry + Character) and multiply it by how you get paid for your work. There are three values for this variable, with the potential upside increasing as you go down the list:

- **Employee:** You're trading time for money on a fixed arrangement.
- **Freelance or self-employed:** You're still trading time for money but can set your own prices and schedule your own time.
- **Business owner:** You've created an organization, hired multiple people, and are utilizing leverage from multiple resources.

So let's state the formula again: (Skills + Industry + Character) x How You Get Paid. Pretty simple, right? To be more valuable, just work your way through the chain of variables. Start by looking at the value of your skills, then look at the value of the industry in which you're applying those skills, then look at your character (in particular how it's perceived by others), and finally take the cumulative value of those first three elements and look at the multiplier of how you're choosing to get paid for your work.

Employees take the least risk, so they get the least reward, and their value to their employer is a simple calculation of how much value they produce minus whatever they're willing to work for. Freelancers take personal risk but not risk on behalf of others, so they get the median amount of reward. And business owners take the most risk, putting up their own money, contributing indeterminate amounts of uncompensated time, and carrying the weight of other people's futures on their shoulders every day, so they get the most upside. It makes perfect sense and has a beautiful logic to it. People who have highly refined skills, provide highly valuable services in highly valued industries, operate with high character, and multiply all of that by founding, funding, and taking the risk in their own businesses are rightfully going to be the wealthiest people in the world. And we shouldn't want it any other way.

This simple formula is not only why capitalism is the most prosperous economic model the world has ever tried (since compensation correlates to value and we get a say in determining our own value), but also why I believe it is the most ethical. Obviously, it can get hijacked or distorted, and in current times it certainly has (mostly by the government), but at its core, the modern-world value formula is about as fair as it gets. A free market is a big democracy that is constantly casting its vote on the value of each of its participants. If you don't like the outcome of the vote, change your skills, and/or your industry, and/or your character, and/or how you get paid, and demand a recount! It's as fair as it can get and hating capitalism is just proxy for misanthropy because capitalism is nothing more than human desires aggregated into supply and demand equations priced in some agreed-upon currency standard. Promoting ethical capitalism as the vehicle to improve our lives and teaching people how to adjust their value within it so they can have the life they want is why I started ENTRE and why I wrote this book. But I can only take people so far. It's up to each of us to let go of the idea that any one person, business model, training program, investment opportunity, or anything else outside of ourselves is going to save us and ultimately bet all our chips on ourselves.

There are no guarantees, and there is always risk, but the greatest risk is that when confronted with an inconvenient truth, we will choose not to take action to avoid the inconvenience. It's one thing to take a road because we were told it was the only way to get where we wanted to go; it's an entirely different thing to willfully stay on that road even when we know it's headed the wrong way and there are other roads to explore. If you made it this far in this book, you've now been shown where the traditional road is headed and also alternate roads to explore, so there are no excuses. Fortunately, though, the road metaphor is not a perfect one. A traveler can only walk one literal road at a time, but in this case we can hop between roads, continuing for the time being to spend our nine-to-five hours on the old road while creating space in our life to sample others. Maybe starting a side hustle? Maybe taking some classes? Maybe going to an event? Maybe joining an entrepreneurial networking or social media group? Maybe enrolling in ENTRE? Whatever you're going to decide, my encouragement is to just do it now. Don't wait. Decisions are powerful. The word *decide* derives from two Latin words: *de* ("from") and *caedere* ("cut"). To decide literally means "to cut from." Decisions are about cutting alternatives from our lives and leaving ourselves no outs. The status quo of the world, the broken system, is simply one alternative that is ours to cut away from whenever we're ready.

Bill Gates once remarked that if you're born poor, it's not your mistake, but if you die poor, it is. Obviously, there are some people who have unbelievably difficult circumstances to overcome, but if you have access to the internet, drive, and desire, and have read this far into this book, then that statement probably does apply to you. If you die poor, it's your mistake because the tools exist to change your circumstances and having read this book you can no longer plead ignorance. It's now up to you to utilize the tools. That's all there is to it. Time to get moving. It's not impossible to create your dream life in the modern world, it's just hard. People break free from the rat race every day but never without first making the decision to do so. What's it going to be?

"What Do I Do Now?"

Steps You Can Take Today to Start Creating Your Dream Life

I want you to flip back to the introduction. Have a look at the date you wrote down, perhaps in the margin, or on a sheet of paper. Remember: this was the date you began your exploration of the opportunities all around you.

Now, I'm asking you to write down the date and time yet again, either right here on this page, or on a piece of paper. And, underneath this date, write the following: *This is the date I decided to break free!*

Life is full of disgruntled spectators. Monday morning quarterbacks. Deathbed regret stories. Cautionary tales. I'm asking you to step out of the stands and into the arena and take positive action toward your best life. It's a big ask, because most people have grown comfortable not with what makes them happy or wealthy, but with what minimizes the judgment of others.

But since you have read this far, I am betting that you are not such a person. This book was, in fact, designed to repel those people. So, after you write down the date and time and the note underneath, you have one of three actions to take. Feel free to take all three—you're encouraged to do so. I'll list them in order of ease, leaving the most impactful step for last.

Step 1: Subscribe

This one is easy. Head over to jefflernerofficial.com and use the links on the site to subscribe to my social media channels. I have hundreds of free training videos on all the major platforms and am constantly posting more on success, entrepreneurship, finance, psychology, business, health, relationships, communication, and anything I can find to improve our qualities of life. I teach to help myself learn and I'd love the chance to share with you along the way. Thanks in advance. Now it's time to . . .

Step 2: Commit

Grab a notebook or a sheet of paper. Then commit to doing something drastic and meaningful in each of the 3 Ps—physical, personal, and professional.

And this next part is important. I want you to post about your progress on whichever social platform you use and *tag me*. Please make sure to use the hashtags *#3Ps* and *#unlockyourpotentialbook* in your posts. I love sharing stories of people making big changes in their life, and I know from seeing it happen thousands of times that *your* post about *your* progress could be the inspiration that someone else needs to finally make the changes they've been wanting to make. I started this movement just a few years ago with posts about my own changes and you've heard how that story is going. Never underestimate what you can inspire in others!

And you can leave it at that, using the strategies in this book, making forward progress on your own journey, and inspiring others. But if you'd like to take it even further I'm honored to invite you to . . .

Step 3: Join the Movement

Come learn more about ENTRE. We are one of the largest and fastest-growing education platforms in the world and at the time I'm writing this one of the fastest-growing companies on Earth. If you like the ideas presented in this book but either are not crystal clear on what your success path looks like, or simply want to be part of a supportive community to help you get there, we can help. Visit jefflernerofficial.com/entre for more information and to schedule a free consultation with one of our advisors. We offer not only education about various paths and skills you can use to build your dream life but also the full suite of what people need to thrive today—community, networking, software, live events, coaching, an app, and more.

———

And finally, whether you enroll in ENTRE or not, let me say thank you. Thank you for your time, your attention, your trust, and most of all your willingness to think as highly of yourself as I do of you—as someone who is capable of incredible things and has an awesome life waiting to be claimed. I hope you will keep me posted as it unfolds (remember to tag me!).

Be yourself; everyone else is taken.
—OSCAR WILDE

About the Author

From broke jazz musician to building eight-and nine-figure companies from his kitchen table, Jeff Lerner's story and message are now inspiring millions. After a decade as a successful entrepreneur, including twice landing on the Inc. 5000, Jeff turned his focus to building the world's first all-in-one physical, personal, and professional growth platform. In 2019, he founded ENTRE, which enrolled more than 200,000 users in its first three years. He is now regarded as one of the most inspirational voices online in business and personal development.